Black, Brown, and White

STORIES STRAIGHT OUTTA COMPTON

Lynne A. Isbell, Rebecca Pantaleon, and Bonita Bradshaw

Bobely Books

ISBN: 979-8-9851540-0-9
Printed in the United States of America

To life as it could be — LAI

I dedicate this story of will, sacrifice, and betterment to those seeking a way out. You have the power to change your reality with each obstacle you overcome. Yes, you can! — RP

I dedicate this book to Mama (Maxine) Kemp, the Queen of Compton High School. She was my mentor, my other mother, and most importantly, my friend. When I told her we were writing this book, she said she couldn't wait to read it. Unfortunately, she lost her battle with cancer on September 6, 2021.
Mama, this is for you — BB

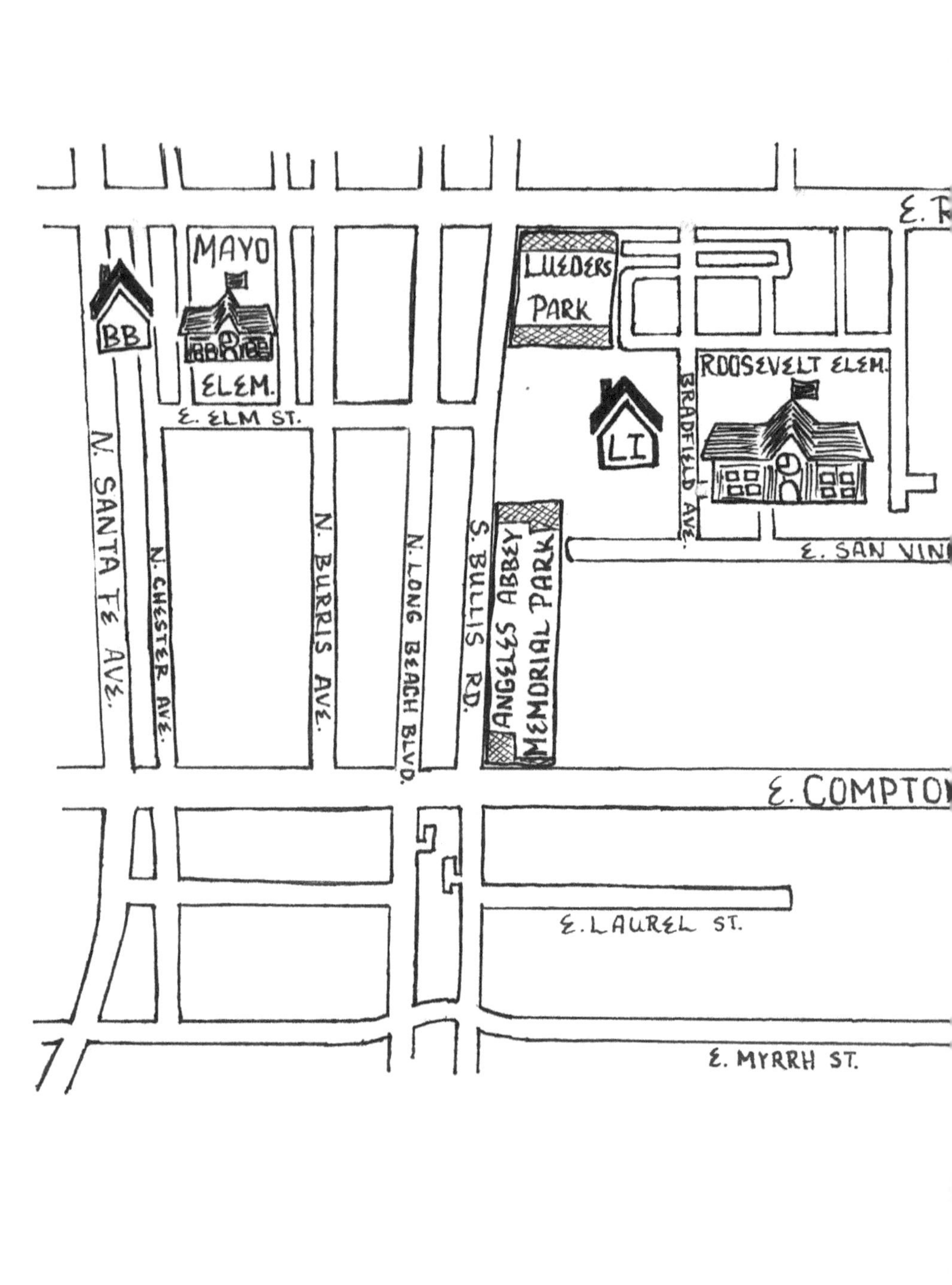

BB
MAYO ELEM.
E. ELM ST.
LUEDERS PARK
ROOSEVELT ELEM.
LI
N. SANTA FE AVE.
N. CHESTER AVE.
N. BURRIS AVE.
N. LONG BEACH BLVD.
S. BULLIS RD.
ANGELES ABBEY MEMORIAL PARK
BRADFIELD AVE.
E. SAN VIN
E. R
E. COMPTO
E. LAUREL ST.
E. MYRRH ST.

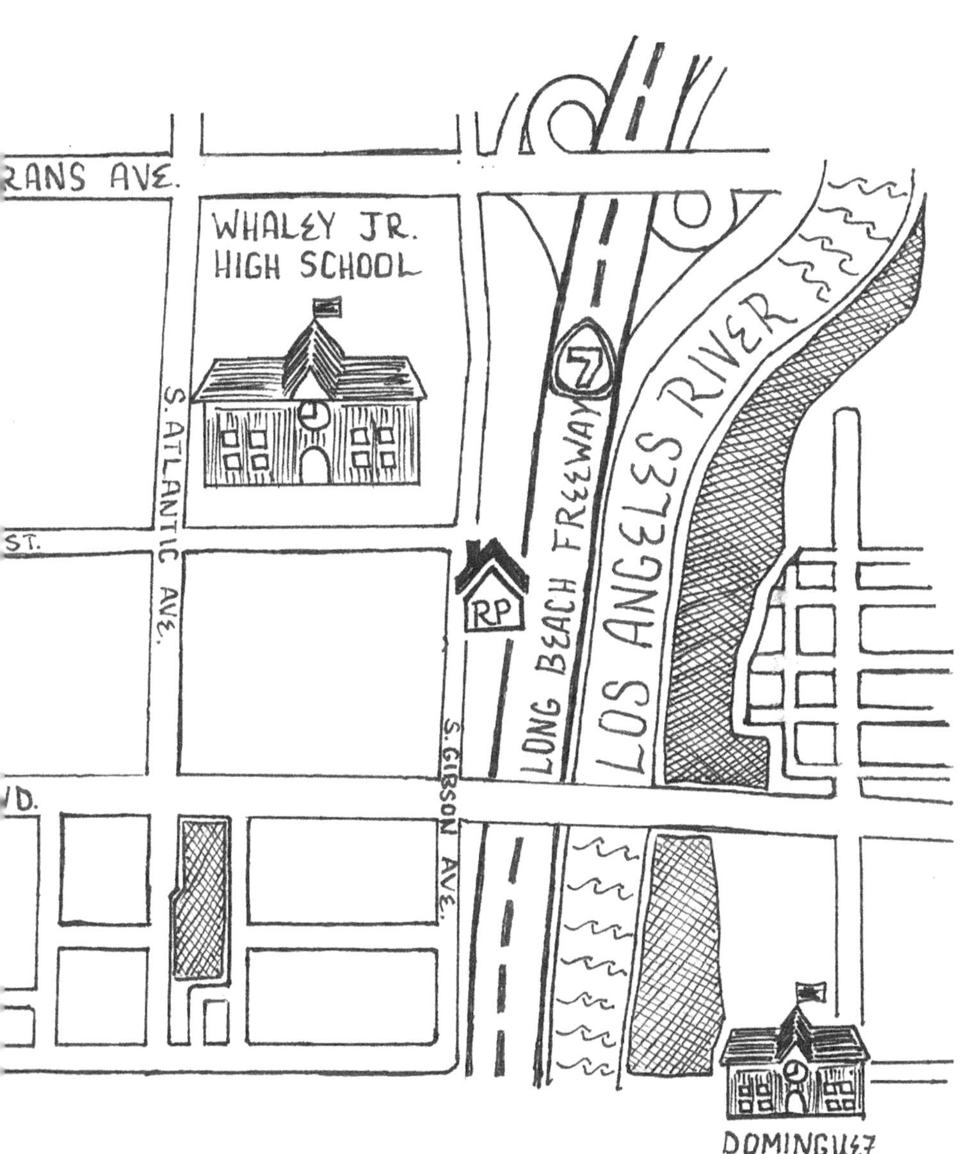

RANS AVE.
WHALEY JR. HIGH SCHOOL
S. ATLANTIC AVE.
ST.
VD.
S. GIBSON AVE.
RP
LONG BEACH FREEWAY
7
LOS ANGELES RIVER
DOMINGUEZ HIGH SCHOOL

Contents

Preface

Compton, California.

What do you think of when you hear those words?

Crips and Bloods? Gang warfare? Drive-by shootings? Murder? N.W.A.? Other rappers? Number one murder capital of the U.S.A? A place where you don't want your car to break down, especially at night? That's where we grew up… a white girl, a brown girl, and a black girl, during the 1960s and early '70s, an incredibly unstable time in the city's and country's history. But it wasn't always like that.

The Compton we started out in was populated by everyday people in their values, people not directly involved with gangs, crime, drugs, or violence. Their expectations were that their lives would be as normal as those in any other suburb in America. In our earlier school years, we all had access to a good educational system.

During the '60s and early '70s, change often occurred violently across the country as the Vietnam anti-war, Civil Rights, and Black Power movements took hold and grew more strident. In the middle of all that, Compton changed rapidly from a community that was largely White and working-class when we entered elementary school to one that was largely Black and desperately struggling when we graduated from high school just 12 years later. By the end of our high school days, gangs and crime grew to be very real. For some of us it was almost as if our education had stopped in junior high (middle school) as changes in Compton's social climate overtook our schools.

The precipitous decline in the quality of a once very livable town will be better understood, and the history of Compton will be made richer, by hearing from people of different ethnic backgrounds who came of age there during this time. We experienced the city's rapidly changing demography, and all that it entailed, firsthand.

We three were, at the time, also reflective of Compton's changing demography. We couldn't put that into meaningful context at the time — we were only kids, oblivious to race and politics. We just wanted to have friends and fun. We didn't think about the agitation around us, and we didn't feel it, at least not right away. It was against this background of growing turmoil that we became friends. Although the shades of our skin mattered to others, they didn't matter to us.

In Compton, one girl grows up struggling with racism and other forms of trauma that affect her into adulthood. Her story reveals that racism is not as simple and straightforward as popular perception suggests. It isn't inevitable or always lurking when people with different skin colors interact, and it doesn't always go in one direction. Racism can happen in America whenever someone is in the local minority, regardless of the color of their skin. The causes may be different, but the result is the same.

In Compton, a second girl grows up facing violence from her own kind, both within and outside her family, and yet she still manages to find deep and enduring love. Her story gives hope to struggling kids with no real power yet to control their lives, especially in a quickly changing world. Even for young people growing up in a stable environment, the conflict between needing and not being given control creates the potential for struggle, whether overt or internal. This girl's story offers encouragement for people to persevere, because things often do get better.

In Compton, a third girl grows up happy and insulated from racism. Her story affirms the benefits of strong guidance and emotional support from parents to their children, and of friendships that can develop and persist regardless of the color of one's skin, even in a society that has been long torn up over such differences. Our society needs to heal, and her story inspires us to make things a little better for others, starting with kindness.

We are just three of billions of people currently living right now. You might pass us on the street and not think twice about us. But look deeper. Friendship and racism, familial love and violence, connection and longing, achievement and loss…these deeply felt experiences "straight outta Compton" helped develop our own stories. How they were expressed and how they affected us during a tumultuous time helped create individuals who will never exist again after we die. Our stories exemplify the importance of celebrating the individual and all that goes into making every single one of us unique. Everyone has a story.

*****

A note about labels: throughout the book, when describing ourselves, we use the terms that we each prefer, regardless of what is currently the norm in America, but we have tried to use current norms when referring broadly to people of various ethnic backgrounds.

PART 1: THE WHITE GIRL'S STORY

1

What Do I Know About Race?

I was never taught how to deal properly with conflict by my father, who was a Methodist minister, or my mother, who was a quiet, unassuming nursing instructor, whose own parents, she claimed, never ever argued. My father, strangely enough, seemed to thrive on conflict. He chose to raise his family of six kids in Compton, one of the more notorious cities in southern California, to improve "race relations." During the time we lived in Compton, I watched the rippled exodus of White families, slow at first, but more rapid and inexorable once the color line jumped across the railroad tracks, violence increased, and property values plummeted. My father dealt daily with the conflicts caused by racial misunderstanding, economic disparity, and educational inequity. He spent so many long hours trying to resolve the problems of the community that he had almost no time for his own family. I suppose it was just as well. When he did come home, he invariably released his frustrations on us kids. Although he never beat us, it seemed he yelled at us nearly every day and, as was common back then, spanked us when we committed minor offenses.

I wonder what my mother thought about my father's heavy-handedness and whether she preferred his absence to his presence. My mother had a different way of dealing with conflict. She didn't have the luxury of staying away from home so she would shut herself up in her bedroom whenever possible, ostensibly to study for her classes or, later on, evaluate her own students' work, and we six siblings were left to our own devices to solve our problems. My older brothers solved the problems created by their younger siblings with both mental manipulation and simple threat of force. My oldest brother Scott devised a rule that anyone who left a desirable spot in front of the TV in the evenings without saying, "This place is occupied and reserved" could no longer lay claim to it upon returning. When we learned from our failures to remember to say that phrase, he made it progressively more convoluted over time so that we would err and therefore lose our spots. The final version went something like this: "This place is occupied and reserved for two minutes during which time no one is allowed to sit in it unless I don't return in the allotted amount of time, in which case anyone who pays attention may feel free to take it." What a mouthful for a six-year-old! My second oldest brother Rand created and enforced the rule that we girls were not allowed to sing on the "boys' side" of the house, the half of the house where the boys' bedroom was located. The punishment when we were caught was a punch in the arm. Of course, we girls took it as a challenge, and in defiance, sang on the boys' side of the house whenever we thought we could get away with it. In my early years, I learned one clear rule in conflict resolution: the older one always wins. In my later years, I was surprised to learn that others didn't abide by this rule, so it wasn't a rule at all.

We arrived in Compton by way of Gardena, another southern California city, with a population of about 36,000 people at the time. Although I had just turned five years old when my family moved to Compton, my memories of living in Gardena are still strong. We lived on a block full of kids who had the run of the neighborhood. When I was very young and restricted to the playpen outside, I was not content to simply watch the older kids play ball in the street — I desperately wanted to be with them. When I got a bit older, I followed my three older brothers and my older sister as much as they and our mother would let me. Among our explorations were crawls through drainage culverts near our house to look for bullfrogs, walks to the "Little Store" several blocks away to get candy, and runs across a cement footbridge over an intimidating drainage channel to watch Little League baseball games, with brief stops to pick pomegranates from a neighbor's tree along the way.

Our next-door neighbors were close companions. Louise Morrow was my oldest brother Scott's age, Lee was the same age as and best friend of next oldest brother Rand, and Ricky was just a year older than I. Ricky and I had a lot of fun together. One day he asked me to climb into a baby carriage so that he could push me in it down the gently sloping driveway of my family's house and into the street. He helped me get nestled in and then away I went. "Wheeee!" It was fun going fast. I felt how thrill-seekers feel on roller coaster rides. Only after I was much older did I realize that I could have easily been hit by a passing car.

A car didn't put an end to my fun on Cerise Avenue, but the Methodist Church did. In 1960, my father, the Rev. Earl W. Isbell, was transferred from Alondra Park Methodist Church where he'd spent nine years, to the First Methodist Church in Compton, just down the road from Gardena. The Methodist Church had a policy then of relocating its ministers regularly and my dad really wanted to go to Compton where he thought he could do some good. Compton was a "changing city" as he put it, and his academic training in the ministry was geared toward "human relations." With Compton growing and more Black families moving there, he wanted to minimize the tensions between Whites and Blacks that might come with those changes. The Methodist Church held their annual conferences at the University of Redlands during the summers, and this was when ministers found out where they were to be assigned next. Families also attended the conferences, the kids playing in a hot, non-air-conditioned basement in one of the dormitories while the adults discussed their issues elsewhere. It was there in the University chapel during the annual conference that I was baptized as a one-year-old. Three years later, I sat on my mother's lap in the chapel and watched my father and two other ministers walk onto the stage in their long black robes. They were to receive an award but I had no understanding of that. What I did understand was that there were three men on stage, the same number of men who were on one of my favorite TV shows, *The Three Stooges*. Making that connection, I suddenly pointed my little child's finger at them and loudly blurted out, "Look! *The Three Stooges!*" My mom shushed me and smiled sheepishly at those sitting near us who had heard my outburst, but many years later she told me she was thinking, "Out of the mouths of babes …"

The Isbells in front of the chapel at the University of Redlands, where Lynne, third from right, was baptized, 1956

That summer of 1960, we moved to the church's parsonage on Compton's west side, adding eight more people to the 71,804 others already living in Compton. Nicknamed the "Hub City" because it is at the geographical center of Los Angeles County, Compton was divided informally then into West and East Compton, with Blacks mainly living on the west side and Whites, mainly on the east side. My brothers were thrilled to be living near Charlie Neal, second baseman for the Los Angeles Dodgers, and an All Star that year. One day we walked right up to him to ask for his autograph as he was working on his car in his driveway. He didn't mind that we pestered him, or if he did, we were too young to notice. Compton was not as restrictive as other southern California cities to Black home ownership, and it was a nice place to live. Johnny Roseboro, another Dodger, also lived in Compton. As European-Americans, we were in the minority in our neighborhood, but I never noticed that, either. I quickly found a friend in Perdita, a young Black girl who lived down the street. We met as kids did back then, just from wandering around the neighborhood. We had fun climbing trees and getting sticky hands from attempting at the same time to hold onto peanut butter and jelly sandwiches.

The Methodist church in Compton to which my father was assigned had a long and illustrious history. Located downtown, the church was directly associated with the founding of the town because Compton was developed by Methodists. It was a beautiful old church inside, with a tall ceiling and a long central aisle between rows and rows of pews leading to steps that opened up to the chancel and the pulpit from which my father gave his sermons. The choir sat on benches behind and to his right, rising whenever they sang a hymn, and he often joined them. Large and beautiful stained-glass windows embellished its high walls, unobscured by parishioners' heads, in full view wherever one sat.

When I was young, I spent most of my Sunday mornings in an adjacent building to attend Sunday School, but each Christmas Eve I saw the full glory of that sanctuary. On that night, tall candles lit the

First Methodist Church, Compton, where Lynne's father was the minister from 1961 until it was demolished to make way for a courthouse in 1969

ends of every row of pews and their soft glow contrasted with the otherwise darkened sanctuary. My father told the story of the birth of Jesus in a way that in my mind no one else has ever come close to replicating, if only for the very practical reason that his style was simply what I grew up with. In between his readings of the relevant passages in the Bible, we would sing some of my favorite Christmas carols. Then our incomparably poised church member, Juanita Locker Ivie, standing so straight and tall with her hands clasped in front at her waist, sang "Oh Holy Night" in her classically trained operatic voice. When Juanita Ivie sang that carol, I felt a buildup of emotion in my body, and as she reached the chorus and crescendo, my stomach tightened and my breath stopped. I was swept up in it, listening with all my body. Much later in life I bought a t-shirt that said, "Music is what feelings sound like." Hers was the first music I truly felt.

The service always ended after my dad finished reading the passages in the Bible that described the birth of Jesus. His congregation helped close it by all of us singing a subdued "Silent Night" as we ceremoniously lit the candle of the person sitting next to us. When all the candles were glowing with light, we walked out together, pew by pew. We continued singing in a procession down the long aisle and out the door where my father waited to thank each of his parishioners before they left. I loved the beauty of that ritual, how holy it felt, and I always tried to hold onto the song and the candlelight for as long as I possibly could.

I began afternoon kindergarten in the fall. The first two words I learned to spell were "dip" and "stop" because they were on road signs that we passed every day as one of my parents drove me to General Rosecrans Elementary School. After school every day I walked back home with my older siblings, Rand, Dann, and Jeanne (Scott took the bus to and from Walton Junior High), crossing busy Rosecrans Avenue and walking the 0.7 miles down residential streets back to our house on School Street. West Compton wasn't entirely safe for us white Isbells. Scott was jumped after school several times, hit in the face once, and saved in the nick of time another day by my parents who fortuitously happened to be driving by when the altercation happened. We younger kids were also not immune. One day my sister Jeanne, then in second grade, was accosted by a tall fifth-grade girl who pulled her hair and threatened her for her milk money, which at that time was 5¢. Jeanne made it to safety by running to a friend's house. And nobody was safe from the half-lady/half-dog who was rumored to live in the area.

In my kindergarten class I was one of two White kids, along with 13 Hispanic and 16 Black kids. Compared to my earlier life, I only vaguely remember my kindergarten year, probably because it was not a particularly happy time. While I did learn apparently important life skills such as how to draw within the lines and use scissors to cut paper carefully, I was also required to lie down every day on a hard mat for a nap when I wasn't tired, and I always felt exposed then because I worried that my dress wouldn't always cover up my slip or underwear in that position, especially if I fell asleep. I must have been a highly sensitive little girl. I don't recall making any friends in kindergarten, but I clearly remember being teased. My most painful memory of kindergarten was the day I went to school with big wavy curls in my blond hair. Normally my hair is iron-straight, but my mom found the time and a willing child to set it with curlers overnight. She was usually very busy but every now and then she would spend hours doing something special for us, such as when she made me a special birthday cake hand-frosted with Little Bo Peep and her sheep on top. That she found the time for me, that she was willing to dedicate so much of her time making me look pretty, made me feel special. It showed me how important I was to her. I felt so proud and glamorous the next day, unaware that my new look just made me stand out even more than I already did. Unfortunately, my classmates saw my new look as an opportunity to laugh at me, drawing attention to my curls and making fun of me. I went from a puffed-up peacock to a deflated, plucked chicken. In retrospect, it was a hugely meaningful event in my life, because it was the first time I felt different from other people. Others were no longer just an extension of myself — I was separate, which meant that I could be hurt by others. After school I told my mother about the teasing and she gave me sound advice. It was the first time I'd heard the word *ignore*. Funny though, when I first heard the word, I associated it with a giraffe. Why the image of a giraffe would pop into my head is unclear. At that age, our minds are still making neural connections and maybe sometimes the connections get a bit crossed. Even now, whenever I hear *ignore*, the image of a giraffe pops into my head. But I did clear up its meaning with my mother. I was to act as if nothing was happening when people tried to hurt me and I would remember to follow her advice almost all other times I was threatened during my later years in Compton. I'm not sure that was the best advice, though.

The parsonage had two bedrooms and one bath, too cramped for the eight of us, so the following year my parents bought for $24,000 a more spacious three-bedroom, two-bath house with a granny flat behind it (where my father's grandmother, mother, and teen-aged brother moved later on) and a large back yard on Compton's east side. Being a bedroom community for L.A., Compton was largely residential, with single-family ranch-style homes complete with front and back yards, lining most streets. It must have been hard for them to manage that on my father's meager ministerial salary. He earned about $6000 per year back then, equivalent to less than $52,000 today, approximately 19% over today's federal poverty level for a family of eight. At the time, I had no sense of our financial condition, but looking back, it's clear we weren't well off. At one point, we couldn't even afford to bail out our escape-artist family dog Pal yet again from the dog pound. I couldn't understand back then why we just left him there, and it breaks my heart even now whenever I visualize how excited he was to see us because it leads to thinking about his likely fate.

Having grown up during World War II, my parents were used to living frugally. My mom knew how to stretch meals — we ate plenty of what she called noodle casseroles and spaghetti with sparse amounts of meat, we drank milk reconstituted from powder, and we

Family Christmas photo in front of Lynne's childhood home on N. Bradfield Ave., Compton, 1963. All were dressed in their "uniforms" of the day, with Lynne (the one making the face) as a Bluebird

never ate in restaurants — and my father ate the leftovers, punished us for wasting food, and continually yelled at us to turn off the lights when we weren't using them. My mom also knew how to sew. When our clothes weren't hand-made, Ruthe Willey, a parishioner and a second mom to us girls, gave us seconds from her work in the garment district of L.A. I wore my sister's hand-me-downs, and those that I'd not demolished, my younger sister Leigh wore when she grew into them. The only clothes we regularly bought new were shoes, because they became so worn that they couldn't be passed down. We girls each had one pair at a time, black for fall and winter, white for spring and summer.

The house was conveniently located across a residential street from Theodore Roosevelt Elementary School, where I attended school for the next six years. Being on Compton's east side, Roosevelt's racial composition was very different from that of Rosecrans Elementary. As my class photos reveal, in my first-grade class, 26 of the 27 children were White and one was Hispanic. In my second-grade class, we had more "hard of hearing" students among the 36 children than we had non-Whites (Roosevelt was a magnet school for students with hearing loss). Only one student was Hispanic and only one was Black, and he was one of the hard of hearing students. In fourth grade, of 32 students, we had three Hispanics (one of whom came from Peru that year with no knowledge of English, but which he learned very quickly) and two Blacks. One of them was the same student with hearing loss from my class two years earlier. And finally, my sixth-grade class included only three Hispanics and no Blacks.

East Compton was safe back then, and I quickly grew competent navigating the surroundings on my own. I discovered Lueders Park three blocks away, and spent many days happily playing there. I loved the merry-go-round for making me dizzy while the swings helped me imagine I could fly. I'd give myself a running start, then saddle up, pump my legs, feel the air blowing my hair back then forward, back then forward, as I'd swing higher and higher until at the swing's apex, I'd suddenly break away to fly through the air, challenging myself to land farther away each time. On Rosecrans Avenue, three blocks from my house and adjacent to the park, Killarney's Liquor Store, a small family-owned shop with a large, neon, four-leaf clover on its roof, was a reliable source of candy and ice cream for us kids. To get to the store, my siblings and I always took a shortcut down an alley littered with cigarette butts and bottle caps that separated a row of two-story apartments from a Richfield gas station adjacent to Killarney's. That alley would become scarred with death in later years. A little farther away was the Compton Shopping Center bordering on the wide Long Beach Blvd. and smaller Bullis Road. Most Saturdays I would walk there with my sister Jeanne and sometimes my brother Dann. We walked past the row of stores, including Kinney's Shoe Store, See's Candies, and Sav-on Drug Store, to get to the Sears department store, our final destination and the anchor for the shopping center. The camping section of Sears became a routine stop for us to play in and around the tents until we were told to leave. We'd also check out the records and maybe once in a while buy a favorite 45 rpm vinyl record when they were discounted from 99¢ to 67¢. I bought "Hush Hush, Sweet Charlotte" by Patti Page for my mom because she told me once that she liked it. The first 45 I bought for myself was the 1966 protest song "For What it's Worth" by Buffalo Springfield. We always stopped by the candy section to buy ¼ lb. of Spanish peanuts or chocolate malt balls with some of our $2.00 weekly allowance earned after cleaning the house. Sav-On's had the best deals, three candy bars for 10¢, which we'd buy before heading back home with one of their ice cream cones for 25¢. Sometimes, though, instead of candy bars we bought suckers at See's Candies. These were idyllic times, when kids were free to go anywhere they could walk to as long as they were home by dark.

In the opposite direction on Compton Blvd., the library was only five blocks from our house and we frequently spent summer days reading books there or checking them out to read at home. The

Angeles Abbey and Mausoleum, built in 1923, was also nearby. The large grounds were carefully manicured and the buildings, always unlocked, resembled a Moorish castle, complete with minarets and domes. It was a beautiful place where adults could, with honor and respect, permanently place their departed loved ones. For kids, though, the mausoleum was spooky and thus called for sneaky investigation within its cavernous Italian-marbled hallways and crypt-filled rooms. Our voices and footsteps echoed as we looked at names and dates, all the while trying to avoid the mausoleum's manager.

But I spent most of my free time playing sports. At an early age I learned from my older brothers and sister how to handle a ball, bat, and glove. When we couldn't field two softball teams from the neighborhood, we played other games. "Three Flies Up" meant that the person who caught three fly balls first got to bat next. "Hit the Bat" was more complicated. It required the fielder of a grounder to roll the ball back in. If the ball hit the bat, now placed on the ground, the fielder would become the batter, but not if the ball bounced up and the batter caught it. If it was a fly ball, then the fielder would automatically switch places with the batter. The game called 500 got us practicing our addition without even knowing it. Catching a fly ball was worth 100 points, a line drive 75 points, a one-bouncer 50 points, and a grounder 25 points, and balls that were missed or that had stopped didn't count at all. The first person to collect 500 points would become the next batter. Other neighborhood games included Hide-and-Seek, Red Light-Green Light, and Mother-May-I. We always played so long and hard that by the end of the day our lungs would ache whenever we took deep breaths. I didn't learn until years later that painful deep breathing is not actually normal. Kids are meant to run around a lot, but they're not meant to breathe in smoggy air, which grew thicker throughout southern California as the population increased and its car culture expanded. The smog often lingered so dense and low that buildings just down the block would be obscured from view. In 1963 Congress passed the Clean

Air Act and in later years vehicle emissions were better controlled so that now, even with many more cars on the streets, the intensity of pollution is not as bad as it was when I was growing up. Still, for today's southern California residents, views always get clearer and sharper when the Santa Ana winds coming from the desert blow the smog out to sea.

During the school year, every day as soon as I finished my homework, I would run across the street back to the school to play with the "after-school" kids, children whose parents worked and couldn't be home for them but could afford the cost of adult supervision. Kickball was big, as was a game called Red Rover, where teams took turns chanting "Red rover, red rover, send Lynne on over," and then I or whoever else they named would run at and try to break through the human chain of the other team. Success meant that we could grab someone from the opposing team's chain and add him or her to our own. Failure meant being added to the opposing team's chain. The winner was declared when one team lost its chain.

I also loved foot races, especially sprints such as the 50-yard dash. Our fourth-grade teacher once went around the room and asked each of us, one by one, row by row, what animal we would want to be if we could be one, and why. Most of the students responded with "a cat" or "a dog," or another domestic animal and I could tell she was getting irritated at the lack of imagination in her students but no one deviated from the pattern until she got to me. I was the last person in the last row and so I had plenty of time to think. As a lover of animals, I knew a bit about what else was out there in the world from my years of poring over picture books of animals and so I said, "A cheetah." Everyone laughed because they thought I meant Cheeta, the chimpanzee from the popular Tarzan movies. Their laughter didn't hurt me; I knew they were laughing from ignorance. When the teacher asked me why, I replied, "A cheetah is wild but it can also be tamed, and it's the fastest animal." My romantic, ideal way of living was to be completely free while also being civilized, and of course, being able to outrun everyone. In my last year of elementary school, the coach for the after-school kids worked with me to improve my chances of winning the 600-yard "walk and run" race in the school's annual track meet. I was so tired of losing to Rosa Coverdale every year! His efforts didn't pay off, unfortunately. The coach was visibly disappointed when I told him the bad news that I'd lost to her yet again, and so I didn't tell him the worst of it. At one point I was so far ahead of her that I thought I could afford to walk. It was a strategic blunder. As she drew nearer, I was so fatigued that I just couldn't start running again. She passed me and I ended up in second place yet again, and I would never have another chance for a do-over.

I made some good friends during my elementary years. Sharleen Watson became my best friend in second grade and we continued to be friends until she moved away after ninth grade. Sharleen had blond hair, was cute, and loved to draw. We were regular recess partners, spending our daily 30-minute and twice-daily 15-minute recesses on the blacktop playing hopscotch, jumping ropes, and chasing Raymond Geller. We stayed after school to help Mrs. Keith clean up the classroom, talked during class breaks about the original McDreamy, intelligent, handsome, dark-haired Adam on the TV show *Bonanza*, wrote poems to submit to the *Roosevelt Times*, the school newspaper, so that we might be noticed by the cute editor Gary Henderson, who was several years older than us, drew horses and weeping willow trees to accompany our poems, and practiced for the school's annual spelling bee by spelling words out loud as we walked home from school. Sometimes on Fridays I spent the night at Sharleen's house where we often read from the Book of Mormon before falling asleep. My father was a Methodist minister but it was never an issue that I was learning about another religion.

Sharleen's home was always a warm and welcoming place for me, and very different in character from the goings-on in my home. When I started first grade, my mom returned to college to learn to be a nurse and we were on our own when we came home from school. The house was always unlocked and we would make ourselves snacks, do our homework, and then entertain ourselves one way or another until my mother rang the dinner bell. That fostered independence and individualism in the six of us kids. We Isbell kids had learned to become independent operators, but it also resulted in a degree of disorder. We did a lot of things together as a family, including dinners, vacations, church paper drives, and the ritual of folding church bulletins on Saturday nights, but we also often bickered about, among other things, which television shows to watch and what radio stations to listen to. The house itself was always a mess inside; my mom just couldn't manage cleaning up after six kids and the inevitable dog while also trying to study or work. Apart from the boys mowing the lawns and taking the garbage cans to the curb on Sunday evenings, and the girls occasionally washing dishes and cleaning the house on Saturday mornings, we kids were no help at all. And we girls were also a mess. Bath time was a Sunday evening ritual; other than that, it was hard to get us to wash, and it didn't help that I had found enjoyment in the peculiar pastime of pouring sand onto my head from under the merry-go-round at school and then scraping it back off my scalp with my fingernails. Since my father's hours were more flexible than my mother's, he would get us ready for school in the mornings, but I don't think he was happy about it and it seemed he took out his frustrations on us. Arming himself with a hairbrush to battle our tangles, he yanked our heads back hard with every stroke as he put our hair up into ponytails. But that only revealed how caked on the dirt really was. He reacted by so vigorously scrubbing our necks and behind our ears that our skin turned red and felt raw as we left for school.

Sharleen's family life was much more orderly. Sharleen and I would wake up on Saturday mornings to a neat house and the smell of pancakes that her dad would make for the whole family, complete with maple syrup and powdered sugar on top. We'd all then sit down for a relaxing breakfast together. It was during one of those Saturday breakfasts that I first heard of "going on a mission." Sharleen's brother had just returned from his mission to Australia with souvenirs for her and the rest of the family and she explained that it was something all older teenaged Mormon boys did. Sharleen's family was just one of a large contingent of Mormon families in Compton. On many Saturdays Sharleen and other school friends invited me and several other classmates to their church where we watched kid-friendly cartoons and movies such as Laurel and Hardy, and ate popcorn, snow cones, and cotton candy. It was a lot of fun for us kids.

Mary Surwillo, a freckle-faced girl with a brown bob, was my friend in fifth grade until her mother put an end to it. One day Mary told me we couldn't spend time together anymore because her mom said she just thought it would be better that way. I couldn't understand why and was puzzled by how unfair and arbitrary adults could be. Now I wonder if she might have worried that, as obvious tomboys, we could be gay. Mary introduced me to Sandy Sherriff, who claimed that her family kept wild cats in their garage. One day we went to Sandy's house and she opened the garage door. Sure enough, there they were, a lion and two other large cats, chained down with massive collars around their necks. Like everyone in Sandy's family, all the cats had names starting with "S."

After Mary, I shifted over to Irene Rueda. Irene was a pretty, black-haired, cheerful girl who was good in softball. I had a pattern of developing one strong friendship at any given time, usually with a girl from the class I was in at the time.

I also spent a lot of time with my cousin Chip, who had moved just before first grade to Compton from Pennsylvania with his mother. We were the same age and sometimes in the same class, but we couldn't have been more different. Among other differences, he was an only child whereas I was one of six, and he was pale-skinned even in summer whereas I tanned easily. Still, I fell under Chip's spell early. Shortly after he moved in next door, Chip convinced me to call in false alarms to the fire department. I'd dial the phone number and say, "Help, help, come quick! My house is on fire!" Then I'd hang up. One time I did it, though, I stupidly gave them my home address and they came with sirens blaring just as the older kids were getting out of school across the street. When I heard the sirens, I grew frightened and ran next door to Chip's back yard, where I hid in the pen with his geese, hoping that the firemen wouldn't find me. No such luck. With no smoke or flames but only a large crowd of older kids gathering, a fireman discovered me and took me back to my house. In full view of the crowd of students across the street, he went down on one knee and talked to me at my eye level. He told me gently but seriously that they would let me go this time but that if I ever did it again, I would get a police record. It was exactly the right posture and tone to take with a frightened little girl who was not used to getting in trouble. He was kind and showed me my mistake, knowing that I was just a kid and not a criminal. I'm lucky I was born when I was. In today's world there seems to be far less tolerance of children making mistakes and I suspect a kid doing that stunt today might very well be handcuffed and arrested. The next day at school I was embarrassed to be there. Third grade classmates of my sister, especially, two years older and who otherwise would have not bothered to talk to me, gave me dirty looks and told me how stupid I had been. Their disapproval stung. Knowing how much trouble I could have brought upon myself, I caught a glimpse of how blindly I could be influenced by peer pressure. I wanted to be a good kid and a good friend to my cousin. I thought doing the right thing included pleasing the people I cared about. I suddenly realized that the two desires could conflict. Sometimes pleasing them wasn't in my best interest and even got me into trouble.

Once Chip and I auditioned in the parking lot of our local supermarket for *Fun for All,* a children's talent show on Saturday daytime TV, and we were offered a spot in the "potpourri" portion of the show. Chip played the clarinet and I played the flute, and before we went on TV, we practiced over and over again the one song we would play until we had memorized it. Despite all that practice, I was very nervous as we were driven to the set in Hollywood because I knew we would be performing in front of a large, live audience.

Whenever we watched the show on TV the audience was filled with cheering kids in a huge auditorium. The odd thing about it was that when we actually performed, there were only two rows of benches, just enough for the families of the performers. I didn't understand then that images on TV could be manipulated and so in my curiosity I asked the host how come the audience looks so different on TV. What I could understand, even at the young age of 10 years, was his patronizing tone. When he brushed me off without a straight answer, I lost respect for him.

Chip also found a marching band for us to join. I thought it would be fun and it was, more or less. I didn't realize how strict they were about the uniform, however. When I was getting dressed for my first parade, I didn't have any black shoes to wear so my mother gave me her own black shoes that had a bit of white on them and she assured me they would be fine. When had my mother ever steered me wrong? But as we stood in position ready to begin, I knew it was not fine when the adult supervisors came along one at a time and tried to look surreptitiously at my shoes. They didn't pull me out of the parade but I had violated their rules and hurt their chances of winning an award. After that I stopped marching with the band, all because I was ashamed that I didn't have the right color of shoes.

Although early on I developed a strong sense of loyalty for those I cared about, perhaps acquired through sports, I also supported myself. When the desire to support both conflicted, it would take me a while to stand up for myself, but I would get there eventually. I finally stopped feeling loyal to Chip four years after he moved in next door. It was during another foot race with the after-school kids. In the past, whenever we ran in a race, he would tell me not to run so fast so that we could stay even, and I had always done that. This time was different, though. I'd finally had enough and I decided that it wasn't right for Chip to expect me to hold back. It suddenly hit me that I didn't WANT to do it anymore. As we lined up to begin the race, he reminded me once again to run more slowly so that he could keep up with me. Then the after-school coach yelled, "On your marks! Get set! Go!" and I was off. I sprinted as fast as I could and left Chip behind. It was liberating. From then on, I felt free of his powers of persuasion. I also won the race.

Not only was I highly competitive, I was ambitious and fearless. In sixth grade I decided to run for Student Panel president. I had been class representative to the Student Panel in previous years and Student Panel secretary in fifth grade so it seemed logical that I should try for the top position in my last year. My opponent was David Kieselburg. He was one of those friends who attended Saturdays at the Movies at the Mormon Church and sometimes we would go back to his house, a standard one-story, stucco Compton house, after the movies to talk or even, once, to chastely snuggle together on his couch in the back-porch room. I always felt very comfortable with David but, as an independent and driven sixth-grader, I wasn't going to let that stop me from running against him for president. Unusually and to my surprise, I had a lot of attention and support from my father. In hindsight, his interest likely stemmed from his own desire and plan to run for Compton City Council. My father would come home in time for dinner and we would talk about events of the day at the dinner table, including my election campaign. I knew I was required to give a speech in front of the entire school, and I knew that I would have to promise to do things for the students. Most importantly, from previous years I noticed that those who gave funny speeches invariably won so I knew it had to be funny. My father said that after greeting the students, I should say, "The first plank in my platform …" which he thought was very funny. I didn't get it but since he laughed, I thought it must be funny so I included it. My many campaign signs also included a goofy-looking character I borrowed from my older brother Rand, who was always drawing cartoonish people. She wore a shapeless "shift" dress, and had spiky brown hair, a grin with missing teeth, gangly arms and legs, and bony elbows. On the day of the school assembly, I was not at all nervous. After all the students were gathered in the school auditorium to hear the candidates' speeches and it was time for me to give mine, I strode purposefully to the lectern on stage and spoke confidently. People laughed at my jokes and I did indeed eventually win the election. I had no power to change anything because I was really just a figurehead but it made me feel important and successful anyway. I think David was disappointed but we stayed friends. In our college years, long after he'd moved away, we caught up with each other at a mini-reunion of Compton junior high school friends, and then again, after reconnecting through Facebook, over lunch a couple times when we were in our 40s and his work brought him near to where I lived.

In addition to being elementary school president, I was one of the captains during our annual girls' softball tournament. I always looked forward to the tournaments. Unfortunately, I had no control over my roster and, as it turned out, most of my teammates were fourth- and fifth-graders, skinny, tiny girls who lacked the skills to hold their own against other teams. We couldn't win for anything. Simple plays at first base ended up being bobbled, with the runners going to second base. Easy fly balls to right field were misjudged and uncaught, sending the runners home. Ground balls rolled past the infielders even when the girls were directly in front of the balls. When we were at bat, strikeouts came with feeble swings so obviously far off the ball that they were painful to watch. It was like watching the Keystone Cops, except that it wasn't funny to me. They couldn't do anything right. Everything was bungled.

I have done a lot of things in my life that I am not proud of, and what follows was one of those moments. I was so competitive and so frustrated that I went to the teacher in charge of the tournament and told her, "I want to quit. We haven't won any games and I am really embarrassed by how bad we are. And it's not fun at all." Well, she would have none of that. Chastising me for my poor attitude, she said angrily, "Stop feeling sorry for yourself. I expected more from you. You cannot quit. You have to finish the tournament."

Here I had thought that I would get acceptance and understanding. I expected her to say, "You're right, Lynne. They're terrible." But she was disappointed in ME. As someone who always tried hard to win the approval of my teachers, I was not used to being scolded and called a quitter. That hit me in the gut. Then, as I walked out to play another hopeless game, I overheard two players talking ahead of me, one of whom was on my team. The girl asked my teammate whose team she was on and when she heard, she said, "Oh! I'm so sorry, she's always yelling at you guys!" It was true, my competitive nature clearly revealed its negative side when I took out my frustrations on my teammates, which happened pretty much every time someone failed to hit a ball or get the runner out. That overheard bit of conversation was what we might today describe as "a defining moment" for me. Had I not been so humiliated by the teacher's anger, I might have been less receptive to it. But I was disheartened, and in that vulnerable state I was able to see how awful I was to others. I vowed right then that I would no longer yell at my teammates but would only cheer them on. While we still lost most of our games, our performance improved and I also enjoyed it more when I wasn't making people feel bad. I learned a simple lesson that my father never seemed to have learned with his own family: when you want the best performance out of someone, you don't yell at them.

At age 11, I also had the opportunity to join a citywide Bobby Sox girls' softball team. I was thrilled to be in a real league with uniforms. We were the Fillies and our colors were purple and white. Before I was recruited by a fifth-grade girl from my school to play with them partway through the season, the team hadn't won a single game. After I joined them, we won a total of three games. Coincidentally or not, they were my first three games with the team and they were the only games in which I played shortstop. With the regular shortstop returning after her injury, I moved to left field. When we started losing again, I thought the coaches would adjust and put me back in at shortstop to see if it would turn things around, because I'd proven myself. I was wrong. I had never felt quite like a full member of the team but, I wondered, was it because I joined after the season began or because I was one of only three White girls on the team? Did the coaches not put me back at shortstop because they were sensitive to a White girl displacing an older Black girl and the captain of the team or did they just favor her because she was the daughter of one of the coaches? I never learned what went into their decision but either way, it didn't

Lynne, proud member of the Fillies, 1967

seem fair or smart to me. We all liked winning.

In fact, adults continued to let me down with their capriciousness and bad decisions. We lived directly across the street from the kindergarten-to-third grade section of my school, and until sometime in the fifth grade I could simply walk directly to the section that housed the fourth through sixth grades by crossing over to the street running perpendicular to mine and that also bordered the school. One day the teachers told me I couldn't do that anymore, that I would have to walk a block down to the next street over and then go for several more blocks to enter the school from the main entrance. All right, but the kids whose houses directly faced the kindergarten through third grade section were still allowed to continue taking the shorter route. I'd heard that a kid who attended the pre- and after-school program had been hit by a car at the back entrance to the older grades' section but their decision made no sense to me because those students would still have to walk past that spot. If safety was the concern, why they did they think the risk was acceptable for those other kids but not for me? Their decision seemed arbitrary to me since only a crosswalk separated my house from their street. I implored the teachers to let me continue on as I'd done for over a year and as my siblings had done for several years before me, or to just let me walk across the kindergarten-third grade blacktop and avoid the street entirely, but they wouldn't budge.

In all fairness to adults, as I grew older it didn't take much for them to fall short of my expectations. When my sixth-grade teacher, Mr. Armistead, shared with us in his southern voice that he once worked at a Texas oil field and had only recently begun teaching, I thought so much less of him that I felt equal to him, never mind that he had all those years on me. It didn't help when he excused my mispronunciation of the word *gridiron* by saying that I wouldn't be expected to know it because I was a girl. He may have just been trying to make me feel less stupid but at that time it made me angry, as if being a girl handicapped me. I always kept my disappointment to myself, though, except for one time when Mrs. Mortimer, my fifth-grade teacher, made us redo the fire drill multiple times because she didn't like our disordered way of leaving the building. I liked her as a teacher, normally, but she just seemed to be mean-spirited this time so I shared my feelings with Rudy Avila, who was next to me in line, telling him under my breath that she was a witch. He betrayed me by immediately telling her what I'd said. I was shocked that he did that, embarrassed that she knew, and certain that she was disappointed in me. Fortunately, by the end of the school year she seemed to have let it go. On my final report card, she described me as a "fine responsible girl" who was a pleasure to have in her room.

One of my jobs in sixth grade was to collect milk money in the mornings from the classrooms on the main campus and take it to the school office, which was probably about 30 yards from my house. At some point I decided to simply take a break from school and go home for a short time every day before finishing my job. I just felt confident and I really enjoyed the self-granted freedom. Maybe I was a little Ferris Bueller in the making. One day I came home while my father was there. He asked me if leaving the school was acceptable to the school administrators but I justified it by saying I wasn't missing anything because I was on the milk money run and that I'd go back soon. He didn't push it then or any of the other times.

I believe I got my sense of fairness from my father. In Gardena he was involved in the Spanish-American Institute and that gave me the opportunity to meet several young men from Latin American countries as they learned English and other skills. They were incredibly kind to me and I accepted their accents as normal. My father then moved us to Compton because he said he felt called by God to help smooth the process of integrating White with Black. One of the first steps he took as the new minister of the First Methodist Church in downtown Compton was to fully integrate it. Before his sermons, he would ask the few Black parishioners to move from their seats to sit among the White parishioners until one day they felt comfortable with each other and did it on their own. Not everyone approved of this. A number of White members of the church decided to leave and go to Temple Methodist church on Compton's east side. It made a very strong positive impression on the Black families, however, and more Blacks began attending my father's church.

In the summer of 1961, my father and 140 other concerned citizens in Compton met and voted to create the Compton Council on Human Relations in response to what the local *Herald American* newspaper described as a near-riot involving 400 students on the Compton High School campus that required police intervention to end. With my father as this organization's first president, its statement of purpose was developed:

> We are deeply concerned with the racial tension and conflict that have manifested themselves in our community. We believe that prejudice, intolerance, and discrimination against any individual or group because of race, religion, national origin or cultural background promote tension and conflict, and that such tension and conflict are seriously present in our community. Therefore, we call for the formation of a Compton Council on Human Relations which will work with the purpose of creating a wholesome community atmosphere conducive to the well-being of all the citizens of Compton.

Because of the groundwork they laid, with emphasis on dialog and honest communication between citizens of all backgrounds, the Compton Council on Human Relations would later be credited for their role in the sparing of Compton during the Watts Riots in 1965.

At home my father was a strict disciplinarian about things that mattered to him. He held regular family meetings in the living room, and most of the time they were designed to determine who was at fault over a minor infraction. During one particularly memorable family meeting he demanded to know who had left a glass of milk out on the counter to spoil. I was the culprit but wouldn't admit it, so the meeting went on and on for what seemed like hours. Finally, Jeanne took the fall after I secretly offered her a penny to say she did it and put us out of our misery. Those family meetings sometimes seemed worse than the spankings we got. As his father did to him, he forced us to eat everything on our plates, even when it would be vomited back up. Dann couldn't stomach beets and I had particular difficulty keeping down my great-grandmother's pot pies, which smelled like dog poop to me. In response, we kids developed strategies to minimize the discomfort. An especially effective strategy was sneaking unwanted food under the table to our ever-present and eager dog, Pepe. There were also times when we just thought it would be fun to play with our food, and that included pretending that we needed to stretch our arms high over our heads and then flinging spaghetti noodles as far as we could when our parents weren't looking. I don't know how they missed seeing the noodles stuck on the ceiling and walls. We were also all expected to help fold the church bulletins on Saturday evenings and then had to be very quiet for the rest of the night while our dad struggled to write his sermon for the next day. Also difficult for us young kids were Christmas mornings when he made us wait to open our presents until after he preached at us about the true meaning of Christmas, which was definitely not about receiving presents but about the love of Jesus, and then ending the sermon with a long prayer, all while the tempting presents were in full view of his six fidgety children.

Normal is whatever we grow up with. Normal for me included interacting with people of different cultures and races as well as my own. Normal also included expecting justice and fairness, and doing something when the situation was not right. As a physically active child, my solutions sometimes involved physical responses. Once I kicked Tom Walker in the groin during recess because he kept stealing the basketball from Sharleen and me. I was surprised that it hurt him so much but I wasn't sorry, even when I was sent to the principal's office, because I thought he deserved it. So, one evening when I told my family at dinner that I had arranged to fight a different boy after school the next day, I was surprised at how they responded. Dann, my youngest brother but four years older, was especially vocal. He said, "That's no way to solve problems, and besides that, you're school president. How would it be if the school president got into a fight? You need to set a good example for everyone else." That was a different way of looking at leadership than I had done in the past. Until then, it had not occurred to me that fighting wasn't an appropriate alternative for dealing with major conflict. It was another defining moment; I didn't fight the boy when I went to school the next day and from then on, I only ever slipped up once more, in high school.

In those years I was fairly oblivious to events that didn't directly involve me. I knew about a bomb shelter on school grounds but had only the faintest idea why it had been built. I learned about the World Series in third grade when the Dodgers played the New York Yankees. In 1963, baseball games were still played in daylight and our teachers let us listen with transistor radios to the World Series during recess, and kids all over the playground could be seen holding the radios up to their ears. "Who are you for, the Dodgers or the Yankees?" the older kids demanded to know. I had no idea then what they were talking about but I replied, "the Yankees." I didn't know that allegiance to teams was based on geography; I just liked the name. Of course, others were not so ignorant and, as we were living in L.A. County, greater Dodgertown, not that far from Chavez Ravine where Dodger Stadium had been built, my response was immediately rejected. That was how I learned the right answer was "the Dodgers," and in subsequent seasons I followed their games regularly, falling in love with Vin Scully's mellifluous voice, graceful phrases, and fairness to both teams as he did the play-by-play over the radio. I eagerly anticipated games when Sandy Koufax or Don Drysdale was scheduled to pitch, but my favorite was No. 28, Wes Parker, their first baseman. He had it all — he was handsome, intelligent, and superb as a fielder, winning the Gold Glove award six of the nine years he played. My lifelong dislike of the San Francisco Giants began in the summer of 1965 when Giants pitcher Juan Marichal, up to bat, turned on Dodgers catcher Johnny Roseboro, my fellow Comptonite, and clubbed him with his bat. I believed the Giants were truly evil after that, and their ghoulish black and orange Halloween colors only reinforced that image in my mind.

About six weeks after the 1963 World Series (which the Dodgers won), my teacher tearfully told our class after lunch that President Kennedy had just been shot. Until then, I had no inkling who our President was. But when the teacher said these words with such sadness, and when the TV was wheeled into the room so that we could hear the news updates, it was clear something was terribly wrong. In the following weeks, I became as wrapped up in the mourning as everyone else. I cut out a portrait of him from the cover of the *Saturday Evening Post*, got my mom to buy me a picture frame for it, and I put his picture up on a wall in my bedroom. I felt it was the least I could do to honor and remember him. Soon after the assassination, Lee Harvey Oswald (everyone always said his full name) was arrested but then two days later he was shot and killed by Jack Ruby, a nightclub owner, right there in the Dallas Police Department, so we never really ever knew Oswald's motivation. A week after Kennedy's assassination, new President Lyndon Johnson established the Warren commission to find out how the tragedy happened and why Oswald acted. There were lots of conspiracy theories that blamed the Russians, the Cubans, or the mafia, but in the end the Warren Commission decided that Oswald (and Ruby) had acted alone.

Music played a big part in my family life, and old songs heard today easily take me back in time to my childhood. Although my mother didn't like most of the music ("too noisy"), my father embraced it. He even brought home for us a 45-rpm record of Chubby Checker's 1960 version of "The Twist." With the British invasion, the Beatles and Rolling Stones became very popular, and on the playground we were pressed to take sides again as if it was another World Series: "Who do you like, The Beatles or The Rolling Stones?" This time I could state with assurance, "The Beatles" because it was well known that only the bad kids liked The Rolling Stones. Some of my favorite songs during my elementary school years included Shelby Flint's "Little Dancing Doll" and Johnny Crawford's "Cindy's Birthday" in 1962, The Beatles' "All My Loving" and Kyu Sakamoto's "Sukiyaki" in 1963, The Four Seasons' "Dawn (Go Away)" and Gerry and the Pacemakers' "Don't Let the Sun Catch You Crying" in 1964, Barry McGuire's "Eve of Destruction" and Herman's Hermits' "Mrs. Brown You've Got a Lovely Daughter" in 1965, and The Shades of Blue's "Oh How Happy" and Johnny Rivers' "Poor Side of Town" in 1966.

Although as I grew older I became more aware of financial inequity because it was clear my family had little material wealth, my concern was pretty much limited to who at school had stylish clothes. Wendy Miller not only dressed nicely, she owned horses, and I was incredibly envious of her, although I was shocked to hear her talk back to her mother. And while protest songs were becoming more popular as the fighting in Vietnam became more intense, the war didn't make a dent in me in elementary school. I was oblivious to crime until my bike was stolen when I left it unlocked in front of the house overnight, despite regular reminders from my parents, and I knew nothing of politics because I never watched the news. It was boring to listen to dry-talking, serious men. My parents also made a point of not talking about politics (for instance, my father never revealed his political party) or negative news around their kids, perhaps to shield us from discord, so I was unaware of the riots in 1965 that occurred in Watts and Willowbrook next door to Compton.

Social and economic inequity was at the root of the riots. Most residents of Watts and Willowbrook were Black, many of whom moved from the South to Los Angeles during World War II with the dream of employment in the defense industry and a better life in the California sunshine. Unfortunately, with the end of the war, jobs became harder to find while more and more people poured into the area. Housing for Blacks at that time was limited to a few areas in L.A. County, including Watts and Willowbrook. Without good jobs, over time people in those areas grew poorer, living conditions deteriorated, including access to medical assistance, and the L.A. police were viewed as being biased against Blacks after several other incidents occurred over the years. For many, a defeatist attitude, coupled with either a sense of hopelessness or a sense of rage against the inequity, eventually replaced the optimism. Then, on one warm August night, a simple misunderstanding of the interactions between a family and the police was the match that lit the conflagration, and many people vented their frustration and anger by looting, burning, maiming, and killing for six days.

The threat of violence spilling over into Compton was very real but because good communication between Black and White citizens and between citizens and police had been established years earlier through the efforts of the Compton Council on Human Relations, the police trusted its citizens, both Black and White, to arm themselves with shotguns in protecting their businesses and homes, and the citizens helped the police wherever they could. Unlike Watts, poverty was not as a big problem in Compton. Most of Compton's residents, Black and White, were middle-class and owned their homes, even if they were largely separated by the railroad tracks into West and East Compton, respectively. They had a lot to lose if the riots spread into Compton so they were unified in their desire to protect and defend their city. Compton Police Captain Harold Lindemulder recounted in an interview recorded only five months after the riots and broadcast by local radio station KFPK that

When the riots started, hundreds of people, both colored and Caucasian, called the Police Department to ask what they could do. It was not a divided city, and I think when people looked north and could see the smoke and fire, every single citizen decided they didn't want it to happen here, and that Compton was a community that was sticking together. Colored people on many occasions helped the Caucasian officers, and Caucasian people helped the colored officers throughout the entire riot. We don't feel that there was any problem with the

Compton newspaper front page headline during the Watts Riots, 1965

average citizen. Hoodlums gave us trouble — some hoodlums that were chased out of Los Angeles gave us trouble — but the average citizen, Caucasian or colored, stood by the Police Department and helped defend his city.

In the end, most of the damage in Compton was limited to burglary of liquor stores in the wee hours of the night by opportunistic, drunken men, many of whom were arrested. Others were arrested for carrying concealed weapons, and still others for throwing rocks at fire trucks. About half of the 150 people arrested in Compton were not even from Compton.

According to data compiled by the Bureau of Criminal Statistics for the State of California, in 1960, there were 574 adult felony arrests in Compton, or eight per 1000 citizens, and 539 juvenile arrests for major law violations, also eight per 1000 citizens. By the time I finished elementary school and started junior high in 1967, there were 1007 adult felony arrests. Assuming the 1967 population was halfway between that established by the 1960 census and the 1970 census, that meant 13 arrests per 1000 citizens, an increase of 62% in seven years. Juvenile arrests for major law violations also increased, climbing up to 827, or 11 per 1000 citizens. Of course, I was oblivious to the changes that were going on at the time.

My elementary school years were what most parents want for their children: largely carefree, energetic, educational, and full of friends. My innocence and ignorance would begin to fade in junior high as other national and local events affected racial interactions among the students of Compton's schools.

<u>2</u>

Can't We All Work Together?

In 1967 I was promoted from elementary school to Whaley Junior High School, the neighborhood junior high serving seventh through ninth grades on the far eastern side of Compton. The school was built in 1951 and named after Dr. Franklin S. Whaley, who arrived in Compton in 1870 as the town's first physician. The demographic shift from White to Black was beginning to approach East Compton, street by street, as Whites moved out, convinced that their property values would decline the longer they stayed, but Whites were still in the majority in that part of town when I began junior high. In my seventh-grade class, roughly 57% were White, 23% Hispanic, 19% Black, and 1% Asian. We were organized into homerooms where we went for the first 15 minutes of each day when roll was taken and we heard the daily announcements over the P.A. system. Homerooms also provided the structure for teams that played against each other during the annual "Fun Day." I was in 7-5, the homeroom of Mr. Fish, otherwise a gym teacher. It was very easy to adjust to junior high, partly because in every class the first day the teacher singled me out during roll call, saying something along the lines of, "Another Isbell, I see. Well, I'm sure you'll do just as well as your brothers and sister." I think their preconceived notion that I would do well did, in fact, help me to do well.

Life at Whaley in seventh grade started out fun and carefree, a lot like my years at Roosevelt. I continued to be involved in the things I had been interested in before: academics, school government, and sports. The high points of seventh grade for me were serving as my homeroom's representative to the student council and being in the Girls' Athletic Association (GAA), an after-school sports program available in all Compton secondary schools. Through the GAA I made new friends from other elementary schools, including Bonita Bradshaw and Joyce Neely. Irene Rueda and my other softball buddies from Roosevelt were also members. In fall we played softball, in winter we played in a bowling league at the bowling alley just down the street from my house on Rosecrans Ave., and in spring we had volleyball. I also always looked forward to the annual girls vs. boys softball game in P.E. and the spring all-school track meet. These events gave sports-minded girls, tomboys as we were called, a common goal that helped solidify our friendships. In contrast to elementary school, team captains in junior high had more control over the membership of their teams. As a captain of one of the softball teams, I quickly determined who was good and tried to get them on my team regardless of their skin color. The ultimate goal of the GAA teams was to win the championship for

Seventh grade Girls' Athletic Association (GAA), Whaley Jr. High, 1967. Becky, first row, fourth from right; Lynne, third row, fourth from left; Bonita, not pictured

their respective grade and go on to represent Whaley against other junior high schools in Compton in what was known as Playday. My softball and volleyball teams won the championships and went to Playday all three years.

My friends were also the high academic achievers in school. In seventh grade, this included Sharleen, Irene, Bonita, and Becky Rivera. I was one of 28 European-American seventh graders in Whaley's California Scholarship Federation (CSF) group that year. Bonita was one of four Black students in the group and Becky was one of three Hispanics. We also had a Japanese-American student, Steve Sugita, in our group. The membership didn't mirror the overall racial representation of the seventh-grade population: Whites were over-represented in CSF (78% in CSF vs. 57% in school) whereas Blacks (11% in CSF vs. 19% in school) and Hispanics (8% in CSF vs. 23% in school) were under-represented.

Sharleen and I slowly drifted apart as best friends after fifth grade, and then we lost touch entirely when she moved away after ninth grade. Joyce Neely became my best friend in seventh grade. We spent a lot of time at her house, talking and listening to songs on the radio. Merrilee Rush's version of "Angel of the Morning" was one of our favorites. The beginning of junior high also marked a change in us girls — we became more interested in the boys around us. One of the perks of spending a lot of time at Joyce's house was that she had a brother who was two years older and he had friends. One of Joe's friends was the mysterious and handsome Julio Orozco, one year older than me. My sister and I both had multi-year crushes on Julio that went unrequited. Neither of us could quite put our fingers on what made him so attractive to us, although his quiet demeanor and straight posture clearly helped.

On Thursday, April 4, 1968, when I was still in seventh grade, a watershed event occurred for the U.S., for Compton, and for those attending Whaley Junior High. On that day Martin Luther King, Jr. was assassinated. Before that day I had not heard of him, so engrossed was I in my own small world. I had room only for school, family, friends, and pets. That day was my awakening. I had been working on my homework in the dining room when my dad rushed into the house. His face was pale and anguished and I could see immediately that something terrible had happened. He had the same look that I would later see on so many faces when 9/11 happened. He never talked about politics or current events with us but this time he blurted out, "Martin Luther King's been shot!" I asked, "Who?" and he just repeated it and then continued on to another room in the house. Well, I quickly learned who. I listened to the news that night and began to see why this turn of events was so devastating to my father given that his life's work was fully in line with King's goals.

The reaction to King's assassination was felt at school the next day. A newspaper article mentioned that all Compton secondary schools were planning to hold assemblies. My father was asked to speak at Dominguez High School and there he talked to the students about meeting and shaking hands with Dr. King, about looking up to him and his method of non-violence, and feeling his loss as one would a brother. My father said he hoped the students would follow Dr. King's lead in non-violence at this very sensitive time. I wish he had spoken at Whaley. With Blacks still in the minority on campus, the mood nevertheless grew threatening. A rumor floated around campus that anyone with blond hair would be jumped after school. As a blond, that made me nervous, but I was also puzzled that certain types of people should be targeted; we had nothing to do with King's death. I made it home that day without incident but from then on, life at Whaley was far from carefree. Some Black students seemed to react to King's death in a way he would not have wanted. I was harassed at my locker so often and it was broken into so many times during my junior high school years that I stopped using it unless I absolutely had to (and this was before daypacks were available for carrying books). I was angry about this. I didn't know these kids and they didn't know me but somehow, they thought it was acceptable to be hurtful to me. It was not right. As my mother had taught me to do back in kindergarten, I ignored them, but I still reported it to the school administrators. They did nothing to help.

Then, just two months later, on June 6, Senator and presidential hopeful Robert F. Kennedy, brother of former President John Kennedy, was also assassinated. Kennedy had been campaigning to be the Democratic nominee for United States President and had just won the California primary. After he gave his speech to his supporters in the Ambassador Hotel in nearby L.A., he proceeded to leave through the kitchen and that was where he was gunned down. The first doctor to attend to him was Ross Miller, Jr., a Black Comptonite and a member of my father's congregation. Dr. Miller would later sew up my much less serious wound after I was attacked in high school. Within the span of two months, gunmen had killed two important people, two people who wanted to do something about injustice and inequity, two people who were strong proponents of civil rights and who could have done something to fix our social problems if only they'd lived. How could anyone have a problem with those goals? What was happening to our country? School ended that year on a sad and confusing note.

And the violence, albeit in different forms, just kept on coming. On the morning of August 14, 1968, a little over two months after Robert Kennedy was assassinated, my brother Dann was walking to his job at McDonald's while I was home in the kitchen making biscuits for breakfast. At the same time that he heard a loud, slow, wop-wopping sound and looked up to see the blades of a helicopter struggling, the helicopter wobbling and then plunging straight down to the ground, I heard a loud sound from some kind of engine that seemed right above the house. I could only stand still and listen as I tried to understand what was making such an unusual noise. Then suddenly, there was a deafening explosion. Jeanne and I ran outside to see what had happened and we saw black smoke coming from the direction of Lueders Park just three blocks away. We ran there and were confronted by helicopter parts and luggage scattered all over. So much devastation! The helicopter crash was an accident, not like the riots, assassinations, school threats and fights, stabbings, drive-by shootings, and suicides that I was exposed to growing up, but it was traumatic violence all the same. The violence of racism, tragedy, trauma, and loss acted like a hammer, repeatedly pounding into me the view that life is fragile and sad for reasons often out of our control, and the best we can do to protect ourselves is to try to plan ahead and cover our bases.

By crashing in the only open space in the area, the pilot saved lives that day but 21 people were on board the helicopter, including three children, and not a one survived. They were on their way to Disneyland and had just left the L.A. airport, undoubtedly

Newspaper front page headline about the Disneyland
helicopter crash, 1968

anticipating how much fun they were going to have in the "happiest place on earth." Although I didn't know any of them, I felt the loss of their hopes and dreams for them. The sad irony of a Disneyland helicopter crashing and burning was not lost on me. How could the world be so cruel? I also learned that evening to be wary of what's reported on television news stations. One supposed eye witness was a student at Whaley. I knew him as a mentally challenged kid, relegated to taking the remedial classes at school. He told the reporter that he heard screams as the helicopter was coming down, but I was skeptical after having heard for myself the loud roar of the helicopter as it was going down.

That summer Jeanne and I were also accused of shoplifting from Sav-On's, our local drugstore, not once but twice. The first time it happened, the store walkers approached us before we left the store and simply asked if we'd taken anything. When we said that we hadn't, that was the end of it. It did give us something to talk about on the way home and to our parents, though. The second time was different. The two store walkers waited until we left the store and then, as one man darted out ahead of us, the other stayed right behind us as if to seal off our exit route, and said in an authoritative voice, "Stop where you are, keep your hands at your sides, turn around, and follow me back into the store." When we heard that, we both made the innocent mistake of giggling and saying, "Oh no, not again!" We didn't know it then but in their minds that was a confession. They thought they'd nabbed repeat offenders! We were marched to a back room where they demanded that we give up the goods. What goods? We had no idea what they were talking about. They insisted that we had shoplifted; we insisted just as strongly that we hadn't. They asked us if we dye our hair or drive a car. Couldn't they see our hair wasn't dyed? Couldn't they see we weren't yet old enough to drive? These were puzzling questions to us. Of course, our answer was "no" for both questions. They patted us down in the little room and then they brought in a female store employee to look down our blouses. Just becoming a teenager, I was mortified by her invasion, an emotional form of violence because it was done without my permission. The men made me unroll the newspaper I had been holding and dump all of my chocolate malt balls onto the table. When they touched every single one of the malt balls, that's when my indignation swelled beyond my control and I challenged them back. "What are you doing that for?" I protested. After getting only silence from them, I then asked them why they thought we'd stolen something. One of the store walkers finally said it was because we were standing in a "classic V formation" against the jewelry counter. What? What was a classic V formation? And then they showed us. We had stood shoulder to shoulder while leaning our other sides against the counter. That was the goofiest thing I'd heard. Don't two girls often stand like that when looking down at the same small thing such as a piece of jewelry? Maybe that's why it's "classic." They also said they knew we were repeat offenders when we admitted outside to getting caught again. We tried to explain what we meant but they weren't buying it; they clearly thought we were just trying to cover our tracks. Then I asked them what they thought we'd stolen. They told us we'd stolen hair dye and a key ring, that they had been watching us for a long time, and they would find the stolen goods. I thought they were idiots. I replied, "Well, if you'd been watching us, then you would have seen me unroll the newspaper to read while I was standing in line for ice cream so I couldn't have hidden anything in the newspaper. You won't find anything because we didn't steal anything." Finally, after more threats and a fruitless search they let us go without any apology. We went home and complained to our father, asking him to use his contacts in the police department to not let them get away with their rude behavior. He was upset that they searched us without our permission but to my great disappointment, nothing came of it. From then on, we added another bit of entertainment to our Saturday visits to Sav-On's, a game we called "Spot the Store Walker." For this game we wandered the aisles looking for people we suspected might be store walkers. When we settled on someone, we followed them around just as they did the store's customers, spying on them for clues to determine if we were right. We were pretty good at it; an easy clue was whether they eventually left the store or continued to stay inside.

Being young and still innocent, we thought the store walkers' accusations and invasion of our privacy were serious affronts. To others with a broader view of the world, it would have been completely understandable that the police didn't bother with such a minor issue. There were many other more serious crimes happening in Compton at that time that we didn't know about. The police actually did help us out once, though. One day a police officer called my mother to ask her if she knew where our car was. She told him, "Well, it's in the parking lot of the church." In fact, they had found it dumped in a ditch on the outskirts of Compton. It had been stolen while my father was in his office and he hadn't even missed it.

After the unrest that followed Martin Luther King's death, the exodus of White families with long ties to Compton increased dramatically during that next summer and beyond until I became a minority student in a minority town. I lost many of my long-time Roosevelt friends as they scattered to the adjacent city of Lynwood or to cities in Orange County. Some students still living in Compton used the addresses of friends or relatives in Lynwood illegally to attend schools there. In September 1968, when I started eighth grade, the percentage of White students in my grade had declined from a majority of 57% the year before to 48%, while the percentage of Blacks increased from 19% to 24%, and Hispanics, from 23% to 26%. I was elected Student Body secretary the first semester, but that may have been because no one ran against me. For the first time in the school's history, the Student Body president was not White.

These changes didn't affect me personally at first beyond the locker harassment and losing my good friends, and I continued to take part in school activities. That year I added cheerleading to my interests. Although most of the cheerleaders were in ninth grade, eighth-graders were allowed to try out. Joyce and I made it but it was a bit awkward interacting with the ninth-grade girls. I underestimated the social challenges of being around girls who were good friends with each other and a year older but Joyce and I hung in there. One of the friends of Angel Sims, our yell leader captain, was Nancy McPherson. I had gotten to know Nancy a little through Angel, and Nancy's younger brother Don was in my grade. One awful day we learned that Angel, Nancy, and some other girls from Whaley had been in a bad car accident. Angel suffered a broken jaw and had to have it wired shut for a long time, obviously crimping her cheerleading activities, but Nancy died. Knowing someone whose life was taken too soon, and in that way, was yet another form of violence I had to process and deal with emotionally. Many of us attended her funeral as another rumor floated around the school, that the driver was underage. If that was the case, maybe the accident could have been avoided with an experienced driver and Nancy would still be alive.

****

I'm not sure how it happened that I switched "best friend" status from Joyce to Becky. As I did with Sharleen, Mary, Irene, and Joyce, I spent many days after school and on weekends at Becky's house where we talked and played softball in the street with her other neighbors. She had lots of siblings, including Patty, who later attended Caltech, Carlos, whose beautiful girlfriend Francesca was a year ahead of us in school, and little Oscar, who had the longest eyelashes I'd ever seen on anyone. I wondered about a bumper sticker Carlos had on his car. I knew enough Spanish to know "raza" meant race but I thought it meant a foot race, so when I read "Viva La Raza," it didn't make sense to me. I was still innocent.

At 13 years old, after the condescension of the TV host, the nonsensical decisions of my elementary school teachers, King's and Bobby Kennedy's assassinations, what I thought was false reporting on TV about the helicopter crash, and the store walker incident, I began to question even more the blanket authority of adults. Much later, my mother would describe me at this time in my life as "prickly." One of the victims of my new attitude was my father. In the past year after I'd aged out of Sunday School, I'd begun to attend church and the Methodist Youth Fellowship, or MYF. The MYF of my older brothers was a harmless group of young people, both Black and White, all doing good deeds such as running paper drives to generate donations to worthy causes, but the social atmosphere had changed by the time I joined the MYF. The music played at MYF changed from benign folk songs such as "Kumbaya," "He's Got the Whole World in His Hands" and "If I Had Hammer," to soul that had more strident lyrics, such as Aretha Franklin's "Respect" and James Brown's "Say it Loud! I'm Black and I'm Proud." I doubt it was their intention to isolate me but some of the songs emphasized the differences in appearance and attitude between us, not our similarities. Also, several times boys tried to talk me into kissing them despite the fact that (or maybe because of it?) I was the minister's daughter. I didn't tell my parents about this. I stopped going because these things made me feel uncomfortable. Then I stopped attending my father's services. He was surprisingly tolerant, saying only once, "I didn't see you in church today." When I responded with, "Yeah, I didn't go," he said no more. I actually felt more pressure from my siblings telling me, "If we have to go, you have to go!" I replied, "You don't have to go." But they were more considerate than I was. They kept going to church while I enjoyed the rare freedom of having the house all to myself for over an hour every Sunday.

The summer before ninth grade was a luxurious time in retrospect. My girlfriends and I were often driven by Becky's adult friend Dah to Hermosa Beach, where we spent the days slathering ourselves with cocoa butter or baby oil to tan more quickly, and thinking we were cool. We listened to Stevie Wonder's "My Cherie Amour," Bob Dylan's "Lay Lady Lay," and other top 40 songs on transistor radios and we talked, mostly about boys. I believed then that we were quite mature. One day, while walking four abreast across the sand in our bikinis to buy our lunch, we passed by some young men

I estimated to be in high school or in college. I just knew they would find us appealing. So, of course, I was surprised to hear one of them put us down as "teenyboppers" as we passed them. I wondered then how is it that different people can experience the same situation in such different ways?

Ninth grade was a complex year of anger and sorrow mixed with a little glory. White flight continued unabated, as reflected in our changing demography. Whites declined in my grade from 48% the previous year to 35%, whereas Blacks increased from 24% to 35%. Hispanics increased from 26% the previous year to 28% and Asians remained at 1%. Although I believed the changing demographics meant that the doors had closed on me to be elected a student body officer, they opened up for some of my friends. I was happy that Becky was elected student body president in ninth grade.

In CSF, however, Whites were still over-represented relative to their numbers in the general student population, and for the first time Hispanics were also over-represented, with each group contributing 44% of the members. Asians were also over-represented, contributing 6%. Blacks were still highly under-represented, however, contributing only 6% of the members. Several of my good friends, including Sharleen, Irene, Becky, and Bonita, were also yell or song leaders. Bonita was the only Black student among them. I was elected yell leader captain that year, probably because Joyce had moved away and I was the only one remaining with any experience.

One of the traditions in Compton was its downtown Christmas parade and we cheerleaders were proud to represent the Whaley Warriors in the parade. Becky and I carried the banner in the front, while Bonita marched directly behind us. We were also all in the girls' elite service group called the Maidens, we wrote for the *Smoke Signal*, the school newspaper, and we continued in GAA. As a ninth-grader, and with all my friends and activities, I should have felt on top of the world, and I did feel that for a short while.

When softball season came in spring, I didn't care what color my teammates were, I just wanted to win, so again I recruited the

1969 Compton Christmas parade, with Lynne (L), Bonita (C), and Becky (R) in front, representing Whaley Jr. High

best players without any other concern except that I didn't want any rowdy girls (they wouldn't have joined the team, anyway). My teammates felt the same. Our fully integrated team won the ninth-grade championship against an all-Hispanic team and an all-Black team. We showed everyone that when it comes to sports, not only is it possible, but even more, it is advantageous to pay no attention to skin color or cultural background. Unfortunately, some of the girls on the all-Black team didn't like that lesson. They were definitely sore losers. While we were changing clothes for the next class, several of them approached one of my Hispanic teammates and threatened to beat her up. She maneuvered out of it by going on the offensive. She told them, "Fine. You come and get me but first I'm going after Niecy." She'd been taught by her brothers how to box and they could tell she meant what she said. They backed away from her and then headed over to me. I had an entirely different and naïve approach. Having been taught that taunters should be ignored and that fighting isn't the right way to deal with conflict, I thought my only option was to try to get to my next class as quickly as possible. I walked out of the gym with them following close behind and heckling me. I was halfway to the classroom when one of the girls yanked my hair from behind, forcing me in a "limbo" position. Clutching my books with one arm, I extended my other arm to the ground behind my back, knees bent but feet still firmly planted on the ground. If I'd fallen my fate would have been sealed, but somehow, I bounced back up and made it without further incident to my class where I knew my Spanish teacher, Mr. Lombardi, would protect me.

That experience, the first of several threatening situations, did not teach me how to survive in Compton; it only confirmed that adults, the teachers, were valuable as protectors. I didn't find out what I had to do when left to my own devices. Pacifism was regarded by other students at my school as a weakness, not a strength. The non-violence that was espoused by Martin Luther King was not appreciated in my school. In that environment, my parents' and siblings' guidance and teaching through the years put me in danger. I only learned by trial and error to go on the offensive, and almost too late. My family's experience and knowledge about how to live safely applied to a different world, not mine.

In ninth grade, John Adams, our new principal, was Compton's first Black junior high school principal. He seemed especially eager to encourage events that celebrated Black culture and pride. Music by Black singers was regularly played in the cafeteria while we ate. I still hear Eddie Holman's "Hey There Lonely Girl" and The Five Stairsteps' "O-o-h, Child" in my head when I recall standing in line for my food. We had a dress-up day and fashion show in which students were encouraged to wear West African-inspired outfits. Somebody in the office created a photo board display of "Great Black Americans." Although I didn't have the perspective to understand the depth of history and what was fueling their need to feel empowered, I thought I understood it because it seemed we all have the need to feel empowered. But I knew of no similar events held for Hispanics who were also common on campus, and there certainly weren't any for Whites, who were as numerous as Blacks. One can argue that the White kids didn't need to feel empowered because they already were but that would be taking the broad strokes of history and applying it to individuals who were still maturing emotionally and who thus would have benefited from any kind of adult support. Non-Blacks just seemed inconsequential to this new principal. And it appeared to me that within the Black Power movement there was implicit approval of violence toward non-Blacks, as if empowering one group required disempowering another. The principal also seemed to have no idea of the importance of tradition at the school. Every year before us, as a special treat the ninth-graders were bussed to a county park for one day of carefree fun at the end of the year. In our year, though, he decided the entire school should go. That just wasn't right!

So, despite my upbringing and my father's best efforts, I began to resent the principal and those Black kids who I thought were being encouraged by the principal and segments of society to be "in your face." As early as 1965, the local Compton *Herald American* newspaper reported school windows throughout Compton being broken at an average rate of 1.8 per day. By the time I was in junior high, so many windows had been broken at my old elementary school across the street from my house that they were now just boarded up with plywood. As the years passed at Whaley, fights became more and more common and inevitably, they grew more violent. On December 10, 1970, the year after I left Whaley for high school, an Hispanic student, Robert Valdez, was stabbed and killed by a Black student, Johnny Jones, neither of whom should have been on campus that day because they were actually Dominguez High School students. The following Monday nearly half the student body stayed home from school as parents pressured school officials to reduce the violence.

My resentment even boiled over to a new dislike for any music sung by Blacks, even love songs. Talk about prickly, I disliked it when groups such as the Watts 103rd Street Rhythm Band pronounced words in their songs incorrectly. In "Do Your Thing," they sang it as "Do Your Thang." So, imagine my surprise to find that, despite my resentment, there was a song on the radio by a Black singer that I really liked. Whenever I heard "Feelin' Alright," I liked it all — the tune, the gravelly voice, the back-up singers, the lyrics. Then imagine my greater surprise to find out that the singer, Joe Cocker, was actually White, and British White at that! Admittedly, at that time I was relieved because it meant I could still hold on to my resentment.

My only African-American friend at school by then was Bonita. I felt she was the only Black person who treated me as a fellow person. While I was pretty sure we had different perspectives, we never talked about them, and our strong shared interests in sports and academic achievement overrode whatever differences might have existed.

For the annual track meet in the spring of ninth grade, Bonita, Becky, Evita van Schravendijk, and I formed a team for the 440-yard relay race. We knew we were fast, and we were also highly competitive. More than anything else, we wanted to win. Before the race I was jittery not knowing what was going to happen but also giddy with anticipation. I was to run the first leg of the race. When the coach fired the starting gun, I ran as fast as I could down the gravel track and then handed off the baton to Evita, my job now done. We all literally kicked butt, running so fast and hard that our heels sometimes did hit our butts, and when Bonita ran the last leg, it

Ninth grade Whaley Jr. High yearbook photos of Lynne (L), Becky (C), and Bonita (R),1969. Note that the camera was not adjusted for different shades of skin color.

was clear we were going to win. It felt great to be the fastest team in the school! We were especially proud that we won as an integrated team. Black, White, Hispanic, and a combination of Dutch and Indonesian, we represented geographical lineages from Africa, northern Europe, southern Europe, and Asia. It seemed we were as integrated as one could get in Compton. We showed everyone that the race is won by not caring about race.

Toward the latter part of ninth grade, I lost Becky as a friend. We had an argument in class one day but, strangely, even back then I didn't know how it happened or what it was about. I was surprised when she became angry with me while we stood there among the desks and chairs. I wondered afterward if it was about her boyfriend Mike, whom I didn't like. That may have been part of it, but I also wondered aloud to my sister if Becky might be becoming more militant about being Hispanic and didn't want to hang around me anymore; the Civil Rights movement was not just for Blacks. Over the next few months, I tried asking Becky what was wrong but got no answer. I apologized for anything I might have done to make her angry with me. I tried to show her, awkward though it might have been, that I appreciated her background. I practiced writing in the stylized script of the Chicano graffiti artists, and I told her about a guy from Mexico I had become interested in when he started visiting our next-door neighbors. He didn't speak English and when I asked her once to help me translate his letters, it just seemed to make the situation worse. It was a very painful and confusing time for me. I'd been harassed by Blacks and now I was being rejected by my best friend. In the end I turned toward the White kids who were still left in school, but they weren't the type I was usually drawn to.

Jeanetta Yanni, a fellow cheerleader, introduced me to them. She'd gone to elementary school with some of them, so she knew them from way back. The boys were more physical than intellectual, but most of my more academic friends had moved away by then. One of my new friends was Del Floyd, a square-jawed blonde. He was definitely more physical — he was the first person I ever knew who lifted weights and his efforts showed! Over time we got to know each other better and enjoyed each other's company. We had just decided to "go steady," which at that time pretty much meant the guy gave the girl a necklace with a St. Christopher's medal and they said hello to each other in the halls at school, when another variation on violence hit me emotionally. While my friends and I headed off to our GAA bowling league competition after school, Del and several other friends stayed around to do a little track and field practice. At one point Del took a fateful run over the high jump. He landed wrong, breaking his neck and becoming paralyzed from the neck down. That night our mutual friend Terry Swift called to tell me the bad news. I was stunned at first, and then I cried off and on for days.

Del's friends all did as much as we could to rally around him while he was in the hospital and later when he was moved to the rehabilitation center. Our attempts were feeble. None of us knew how to deal with this kind of loss other than to keep showing up and trying to cheer him up. It became more difficult as he grew angrier at his condition. He either refused to speak or he struck out at us with his words, hurting those trying their best to help him, and eventually pushing most of his friends away. I found some comfort in talking about the situation with Terry, who became like a brother to me. Terry joined me on the walk to school and back every day, helping me to feel a little safer in a world that had stopped being safe in so many ways.

I continued to visit Del out of loyalty and because I could understand why he was bitter at what had happened to him, but it didn't seem that I deserved his anger. Nor was I sure I deserved the guilt he tried to put on me to remain his girlfriend. Should I be expected to stay with him through thick and thin at this early age and when we were barely committed to each other to begin with? I'd vowed to keep seeing him, but I just couldn't persevere, and I did feel guilty. Long afterwards, I learned that Del had boasted to his friends on the day of his accident that he was going to dump me after bowling and move up a notch to Kathy Snavely, a very pretty half-White, half-Japanese friend of mine. When I heard that, I felt no more guilt about walking away from him.

Sixteen years later, I met up with Del again when a number of old junior high school friends, including Becky and Bonita, attended a reunion dinner at Jeanetta's house. I was glad to see that he was no longer bitter. He introduced us all to his girlfriend, who seemed very nice, and he told us he had earned a Master's degree in counseling. But six months or so after that, Jeanetta wrote to me when I was in Kenya that Del had been killed in a car accident while his girlfriend survived. As I lay on my bed 10,000 miles away, reading her letter over and over, I broke down in tears and thought again about how unfair life was. Hadn't he already suffered enough? Why take more from him? Decades later, the memory of Del's first accident would return with a vengeance. Whenever my son cleaned the gutters of

Whaley Jr. High School mini-reunion, 1986, 16 years after finishing ninth grade. People mentioned in the text: (back row, first three on left) Mr. Lasley, David Kieselburg, and Steve Sugita; (front row, l-r) Del Floyd, Lynne, Bonita, Becky, and Jeanetta Yanni

52

our house, I had what to me was a very reasonable fear but that others thought irrational, that he would somehow trip over the blower cord or slip on the shingles and fall from the roof, breaking his neck. Each time, I admonished him to be careful for as long as I could stand to watch, and then went inside the house and hoped for the best but waited for the accident. The emotional scars of our early years often persist long into adulthood.

After Del's first accident, my parents somehow managed to buy a horse for me from a local stable owner even though we didn't have much money. It was a heroic stopgap effort. Since I had lost so many of my friends, they thought that a horse, which I had wanted for years, would occupy my time and help make up for those losses. I named him Floyd in honor of Del. But getting the horse was a mistake. My parents didn't know anything about horses, and what I knew I gleaned mainly from reading. We were sold a highly spirited young horse that I couldn't manage and Floyd clearly knew it. He liked to step on my feet when I brushed him, and he repeatedly brushed me up against fences to try to dislodge me when I was riding him. The day he bucked me off I decided I was in over my head. We returned him to the stable owner; after that I got a rabbit.

Over time, my friendship with Terry developed further. I was comfortable being around him because he had a nice disposition and, as one of the physical types, I felt he could protect me. This was to be my first serious relationship with a boy. When the time came for the ninth-grade dance, I went with Terry. My mom had sewn together a baby blue mini-dress with opaque long sleeves for me to wear to the dance, but what to do with my hair? The only thing I knew was how to put it in a ponytail. Then Bonita and Jeanetta came to my rescue. They came to my house that day after school, and as I sat in a chair in the bathroom, I felt them give me all their attention to expertly transform my hair into a fancy updo. That day I felt cared for, surrounded by love, just like years before when my mom took her time to roll my hair in curlers for kindergarten, wonderful feelings that are memorable because I so rarely felt them.

At the end of the year, Whaley held its annual awards ceremony. It gave recognition to three years of academic, athletic, and service effort and I really wanted to win the top award, a gold watch given by the Kiwanis Club for the person with the highest GPA. My oldest brother, Scott, the widely recognized star student in our family, had not even gotten the Kiwanis Club gold watch. If I could be awarded that watch, my parents would also see me. It was a simple analog watch that just told time, with a knob needing winding every day to keep it going. It was one of the last awards to be handed out and when the time came, I was both thrilled and relieved when I heard my name called to go onto the stage to accept it. My name was even engraved on the back of the watch. I felt on top of the world! I proudly wore that watch until Casio watches, with their greater functionality, became popular in the 1980s.

Although I was very happy to receive the gold watch, there was another award that came with more wonderment. Mr. Lombardi, my Spanish teacher whose mere presence had protected me from those mean girls, gave me an umbrella-shaped petit-point pin from Vienna handed down to him from his mother. He gave it to me for a "perfect score" in Spanish all three years. He also gave Becky an award, a gold watch for "high grades" and for substitute teaching for him on occasion. We were the only ones to whom he gave awards and I'd not heard that he'd given out awards in the past. Perfect score? I don't think I was the only one to get A's in his classes for all three years if that's what he meant. High grades? A number of other students also earned high grades. It was true, though, that Becky did substitute for him several times and it was indeed unusual for a student to serve as a substitute teacher. After pondering it for a long time, I decided he gave us these awards because we meant something to him for some reason. He was a gruff teacher but these awards came from his heart. I still have that pin.

I was the designated student speaker at our graduation ceremony. I knew I was expected to come up with something hopeful and inspiring even though our years at Whaley were fractured by harassment, frequent fights, and deadly accidents. I felt I couldn't express the truth I perceived, that Whaley had turned into a stressful place, so unfavorable for learning over the three years we were there. But I couldn't lie, either. How could I come up with something worthy of a graduation speech that I could also live with? At first the only thing I was certain of was that, unlike my sixth-grade President's speech, there would be no jokes in this one. The past three years had not been funny.

In the end, like many writers, I drew my inspiration from what I knew — my friendships with Becky, Bonita, Evita, Kathy, and Jeanetta, and my experience of being targeted for being White. To that I mixed in a bit of wishful thinking with the goal of encouraging the students of different races to see each other not as embodiments of an entire race but as individuals worth getting to know for themselves. I also felt that because of the distraction caused by social upheaval, I needed to remind the students why we were in school. Finally, after being subjected to so many long sermons from my father, I knew I wanted to keep it short. This is what I said, mistakes and all, unedited by teachers:

> When considering the topic about which I will speak today, I find that there are three areas which I feel are most important: namely race relations, the task of understanding others, and the goals which have been made clearer by our three years at Whaley.
>
> Whaley is concrete proof that people of different races can live and work together successfully. Naturally, through the years, there have been little outbursts of temper because when a group of people get together, there will always be differences of opinion. However, in our three years at Whaley, there has been nothing so threatening as to disrupt the entire student body of our school. I have seen much more unity between the people at Whaley this year than the past two years combined. I think we are finally facing up to the fact that people cannot be

changed unless they want to be changed. I think we are finally accepting people the way they are and not how we want them to be.

If one has different kinds of friends, he can learn how they feel and act in certain situations. By understanding each other, we can break the line that separates us; the line which consists of cultural, religious, racial, and ethnic barriers. Our goal to break these barriers at Whaley is a much harder task than that of other schools around us, because we have a greater mixture of different students. However, I believe that we are succeeding in this goal more than other schools because we are trying harder to understand each other as an individual rather than as part of a group.

These past three years of mental, physical, and emotional growth have prepared us not only for high school, but for life in a larger world, where there will be harder problems and decisions waiting for us. We will be called upon to take care of tasks which do not exist today and there will be new occupations springing up as a result of inventions. We must be able to keep up with our rapidly changing world and to do that we must have a good education. It is said that there is a certain time for everything. The time for learning is now — for everybody.

These past three years of our lives have made us aware of our troubled world, and formed our characters. As we go onto high school, we will take with us the knowledge that we have learned — and I am sure that all of us, the 9th grade class of Whaley, 1970, will use that knowledge to the best of our abilities.

It was not to be.

3

What Did I Ever Do To You?

With conditions in Compton and its schools continuing to deteriorate, my mother grew increasingly worried for the safety of her children who still remained in Compton, all of them daughters. My father didn't want to move, however, because it would go against his conviction that Blacks and Whites can live and work together. If we left, he would be seen as hypocritical and we would be just another "White flight" family. With moving out of the question, my mother felt she had no other choice than to break up our family. While my younger sister Leigh stayed in Compton because she attended a special needs program outside the Compton school district and needed extra care at home, Jeanne moved to Virginia to attend high school while living with Mom's brother, Uncle Bill, and Aunt Bea, who was from Ecuador. I was offered a place with old family friend Joyce Sears and her three kids in Saugus, California. Fifty miles northwest of Compton, Saugus was subsumed in 1987, along with three other communities, to create Santa Clarita, perhaps best known for being the home of Six Flags Magic Mountain, which has more roller coaster rides than any other amusement park in the world. When I lived there in 1970, however, Saugus was a small town with little racial diversity, if any, and plenty of opportunities for outdoor recreation on its edges. I used to ride horses where Magic Mountain now sits.

As a single mom, Joyce had her hands full with her own kids my age and younger. At the time her generosity didn't occur to me but now I'm amazed. And on paper it all should have worked out. Joyce's oldest daughter Joanne and I had spent a lot of time playing together when we were very young and back then we got along well. Now, however, we were both teenagers and we quickly learned that we had grown into very different people. Whereas I was a studious, athletic type, she was a big partier. When I first arrived, she took me to a couple outdoor parties in the hills but people seemed just to want to smoke and get drunk. It wasn't who I was, and I felt uncomfortable being there, but I was dependent on her or her friends for my rides back to her house, so I had to wait them out until my ride was ready. When I wouldn't drink, I felt irritation from her. She and her best friend might have seen it as a rejection of them, and they turned on me as many girls of that age are able to do so well. I may as well have been in Compton for all the harassment I got. I rarely had the peace and quiet needed to study, several 45s in my precious record collection were scratched, but they denied doing it when I asked them, and her friend often obliquely aimed a barrage of malicious comments at me as we rode on the school bus to and from William S. Hart High School every day. Captive on the bus, I sat there gritting my teeth while enduring the trash-talk. She thought I thought I was too good for them because I wouldn't cuss or drink with them. But the truth was that I wasn't judging them, I was just trying to be a good person, which in my mind included not breaking the law and drinking alcohol before I was legally allowed to. Again, as my mother had taught me, my response was to try to ignore her. I sat on the bus never saying a word back, but a person can take only so much. One day when I stepped off the bus, I howled my frustration to the skies, like a banshee. Releasing that energy made me feel better but it also put off a boy I liked, and the only friend I felt I had at the school. I thought he would be sympathetic to me but he wasn't. I thought he would stand up for me but he didn't. Instead, he looked at me with disgust and asked without expecting an answer, "Jeez, what's wrong with you?" before walking away to catch up with his actual friends. I now realized I couldn't even trust him.

So, there I was in an all-White environment, still having problems. My new problems were probably more the norm for teenage girls, the pressure many feel to conform to rigid social expectations, but they were problems nonetheless. The person with whom I shared a bedroom disliked me, as did her friends, and yet I couldn't make friends with the more academic students because they associated me with the partiers. I was stuck between a rock and a hard place. With no friendships developing in Saugus, I stayed in touch with my friends in Compton and on many weekends took the Greyhound bus home, but that provided no respite, either. During that time, Jeanetta's boyfriend Anthony Foglesong shot himself in the head, as his father had done before him. Anthony's best friend had found him on the floor of his bathroom, and Jeanetta fell into a tailspin that, as much as we tried to help, she couldn't get out of for years.

I felt like a misfit in Saugus. I decided to go back to Compton where I still had at least a few friends and wouldn't feel any pressure to conform. I didn't even last three months in Saugus.

When I withdrew from Hart High, I had to go to each of my teachers to get my grades. This was when I confirmed how helpful it had been for my siblings to go before me and develop a collective Isbell reputation. My Hart High Spanish teacher seemed to notice me for the first time when he saw that I was getting an A. If I'd stayed around, I might have made a name for myself independent of my siblings. My biology teacher, a crusty old man who behaved as if he took pleasure in berating students, looked up from behind his glasses and his desk and said begrudgingly, "Well, I guess I have to give you a B." Since I had nothing to lose in standing up to this man's bad attitude, I looked him in the eye and replied, "You didn't give it to me, I earned it!" He returned my gaze and made a noise like *hmmf*, but I could see that I had also earned a little respect from him. It was uncharacteristic of me to challenge an adult directly but it felt really good, and right, to stand up to this bully. I had worked hard, and I needed him to give me that credit. I learned then that I could stand up for myself without any repercussions. I didn't have to ignore bad behavior and I wouldn't be punished for dealing directly with it. But of course, experiences later on taught me that this was actually a rare moment. Later on, I learned that there are risks in standing up to a bully, and anyone who takes a stand for what is right has to be prepared for things to go wrong.

In 1971, according to the *Herald American*, Compton had a population of 78,611, with 71% Black and 26% White. There was no mention of Hispanics or Asians so I think at least Hispanics were lumped in with Whites. Thus, I returned to Compton as a minority in a minority town.

Dominguez High School was even more racially skewed. In 1972, my last full year in Compton and not even four years after Martin Luther King's assassination led to growing school unrest and White flight, Blacks made up 76% of the eleventh-grade class, Hispanics, 19%, Whites, 5%, and Asians, 0.6%. On school forms that asked us to identify our racial or ethnic background, I was by now an "other"; they had no box for Whites. It was amusing in a way because I wouldn't have been an "other" elsewhere, but it also allowed me to understand how under-represented people may feel demeaned to be placed in a grab-bag category even if the purpose of gathering racial/ethnic data on such forms is benign.

As at Whaley, I signed up for GAA and focused on academics, but school was not fun anymore. Dominguez High had clubs and lots of events focusing on Blacks and Hispanics but there were no events for Whites. I understood that, too, because there were very few Whites left, but I felt left out. And imagine, had there been a club for Whites, it would have appeared exclusionary and racist. No, the school encouraged celebrations of traditional minorities, but it would not have been possible to do the same for the traditional majority given our country's history of marginalization of people of color by Whites.

I spent most of my free time with Terry, who taught me how to ride motorcycles, unbeknownst to my mother, who called them murdercycles after she'd seen so many people mangled by them at the hospital where she worked. Terry and I had no classes together but we met for lunch every day. Lunchtime was always noisy. Students always seemed to be shouting, if not at someone, then to be heard above the din of other voices. Terry and I found a nice quiet place near the classrooms to eat in peace and it worked well until one day when a teacher told us we had to move away. We moved to a spot farther from the buildings and people, and sat together on the grass eating our lunch. Within minutes, six boys, all of them Black, approached us. As we stood up, they surrounded us. One boy began accusing Terry, saying, "I heard you hit my cousin Rufus." Terry replied, "I don't know anybody named Rufus and I didn't hit anybody." The boy acted as if he hadn't heard Terry and he repeated it again more loudly and insistently, "I heard you hit my cousin Rufus!" Again, Terry denied it. Another boy suddenly spoke up, proclaiming, "We're gonna have a trial, we're gonna put you on trial." Then all at once the boys all began shouting in turn, "Guilty!" "Guilty!" "Guilty!" Guilty!" That's when Terry told me to go and get some help. I left the group and ran to a classroom because I knew from experience that teachers were protectors. I stopped in the doorway and calmly said to the teacher, "I think there's going to be some trouble outside." When the students in the class heard me say that, they all rose in unison as if I were their choir director, and rushed out to see the excitement. The teacher stayed inside, no protector, just a coward. I returned to find Terry straddling one of the boys on the ground, pounding the boy on the head with his thermos. It was chaotic with all the students running around and jostling to get a good look. Disgust and anger at what was happening were so palpable in me that who I had been since sixth grade vanished and I became as animalistic as those boys who started the whole thing. Obviously, I had no experience as a fighter; I drew instead upon my grade school kickball experience and simply kicked one of them in the rear. I wasn't thinking and I didn't have a plan, I just wanted to help Terry and stop the mess. One kick was all I was able to pull off because then the boy turned around and hit me in the head with his fist, his ring opening up a large gash over my left eye. That knocked some sense into me. Returning to my former pacifist self, I began shouting at the top of my lungs, "Stop it! Stop it! Stop it!" As I was shouting, I turned and came face-to-face with a Black girl I knew from my classes. She had been laughing but when she saw my face and our eyes met, her jaw suddenly dropped and her eyes widened in surprise, the happy creases at the corners of her eyes disappearing. My shouting was just as ineffective as my kick in the rear but right after that, two teachers, a Black woman and a White man, who also happened to be the shortest teacher on campus, finally broke up the fight. The male teacher came to me, put a handkerchief up to my face, and led me away to the nurse's office. Within no time at all, he withdrew the handkerchief from my face, and I saw that it was soaked in blood. Suddenly I understood why that girl's expression had changed so abruptly and dramatically.

In the nurse's office, I sat and waited, for what I wasn't sure. I was no longer making decisions. I just sat there, dazed by what had happened and by the intensity of emotion surrounding it. A Black girl from the GAA, one of the rowdy girls on campus, stopped by and told me that if I knew who had done this to me, I should tell her and she would go after them herself. I was surprised and touched. Bonita also showed up, tears streaming down her face, and she stayed with me until my mother, who had to leave her teaching job in Torrance 11 miles away, could come to pick me up. I stayed overnight at a hospital where Dr. Ross Miller, a friend of my father and the first doctor to attend to presidential hopeful Senator Robert Kennedy after he was shot, stitched me up. Dr. Miller was also by now a Compton city councilmember so his attention, and those stitches, meant a lot to me.

When I returned to school, I saw one of the original instigators in the hallway during passing period. As we passed each other, I looked hard at him and gave him the meanest look I could muster. He kept his eyes straight ahead but I know he saw me. He couldn't miss me with the large white bandage above my eye. I didn't see him again after that. The boy who hit me admitted he had done it, but he claimed it was with an open hand, which he apparently knew was a less serious offense than a fist. Eventually he was called to appear in juvenile court. My father took me out of school and drove me there so that I could testify about what had happened. We sat on a wooden bench and waited for hours just outside the courtroom doors. In the end, however, they never called me to speak. I was told the fight never came up because they focused on a different charge, that of breaking and entering. I don't know why they didn't cover both crimes. Maybe they thought I was just as culpable because I had actually hit him first and they didn't want to penalize me, too, or maybe they thought they were doing me a favor by not asking me to refresh the event in my mind. In fact, I needed to tell my story in order to heal completely.

After the fight Terry's family moved two cities away to South Gate, and then, despite my pleading for him to remain in school, he dropped out as soon as he turned 16. We continued to see each other while I further withdrew socially at school, lying low in the hope that, even though I stood out like a sore thumb because of my color, I might not attract any more attention. Garnering attention was a bad thing, punishable by emotional and physical abuse. I began to feel highly vulnerable around large numbers of people and I developed a wary vigilance, my eyes always scanning the crowd, my body always on guard. I perceived lunchtimes as particularly dangerous because there seemed to be no semblance of adult control over the students at those times. Fights were common and the rumor was that both girls and boys regularly hid razor blades in their afros as a form of defense. I also began to feel disgust toward the students as I replayed in my mind over and over again how a mob of them crowded around during the fight, all hyped up and laughing like hyenas swarming around a kill. My revulsion deepened when I learned that on another day a student's mother actually drove a van filled with her daughter and other girls onto the athletic field at Dominguez. The girls piled out, armed with nail-studded two-by-fours that they planned to use as weapons against some rival group. A mother did that! Dominguez was no place to get an education.

I went through the motions of going to school, but I talked to few people. I was in the Spanish Club and I was still involved in GAA, which seemed a world apart largely because of the support I had received from that girl in the nurse's office, but I attended no football or basketball games, no dances, and no other school functions that become a major part of the memories of high school for fully engaged students. My world had revolved around school from first grade until high school. Maybe I could have been one of those with good memories had I grown up somewhere else but Compton. For the first time ever, I didn't buy the school yearbook because I felt so disenchanted and disconnected to Dominguez. Mix fear in with that and it might be understandable that when the opportunity arose to graduate from high school a year early, I jumped at it. I learned that by taking just two classes during the summer after tenth grade, I could earn the minimum number of credits to graduate the following year.

Just before I finished tenth grade, an article in the *Herald American* on June 6, 1971, reported a statement made by city councilmember Lionel Cade that an average of 32 major crimes (homicide, rape, robbery, assault, burglary, larceny, and theft) occurred in Compton every single day. The McDonald's restaurant where my brother Dann, and later on my sister Jeanne, worked was robbed three times while she worked there. On one of those occasions, one man who was pretending to stand in line for food grabbed a co-worker who had just finished her shift and was talking to Jeanne at the front counter while the other jumped over the counter and yelled for everyone to put all the money in the registers in bags. They then both went to the back, and Jeanne looked to make sure they couldn't see her before she stuffed a lot of $20 bills in her pockets while putting the $1 bills and change in a bag she puffed up. The workers handed the robbers the bags while a gun was aimed at Charlie, the manager, as he nervously opened the safe for them. Fortunately, at that point, a co-worker who was just about to start his shift saw what was happening through a back window and went away to call the police. Once the safe was opened, the robbers forced everyone to get into the freezer and then they drove away. By the time the police arrived, Jeanne and the others had been locked in the freezer for about 15 minutes. Although it was risky to stuff her pockets, she did save the store a bit of money. I can't help but wonder if her experiences with thugs helped inspire her to become a police officer later on in life.

Others in my neighborhood were not as fortunate. A classmate of mine was stabbed as he walked down his street. He lived but a woman who was stabbed in the alley we used to walk through to get candy at Killarney's liquor store did not. And Larry, the owner of the bowling alley near my house where we GAA girls bowled in junior high, was shot to death. This was at the beginning of the violent gang activity that made Compton notorious as the murder capital of the U.S., most notably by the Crips, who started out from a couple high schools in L.A., and the Bloods, who started out from Centennial High School in Compton. Today, the area where I grew up is centrally within the territory of the Lueders Park Piru street gang, a violent gang affiliated with the Bloods.

The one bright spot in my life was Levi. Our Black next-door neighbors, who moved in after my cousin Chip moved out, had two vicious German shepherd dogs that they believed kept them safe, and they gave a long-haired throwback pup, the runt of the litter from their two dogs, to my grandmother and uncle. Before Levi came into my life, my family had had a series of dogs, the latest being Pepe. Pepe was short with curly gray hair and we thought she might have been a mix of poodle and something else that was even harder to tell. Her behavior suggested to me that she might have had some terrier in her; she really didn't give up when it came to strangers. She never bit anyone but if we weren't careful and opened the door more than required to talk to someone, she would squeeze out in escape and would run up and down the street terrorizing the neighborhood, barking at and chasing anyone she saw. We never could cure her of her bad behavior but it did come in handy at times. One day I deliberately let Pepe out to chase away Squeaky, Jeanne's awful boyfriend. Pepe chased him across the street and deep onto the Roosevelt school grounds before we could get her back. Jeanne was furious with me for a long time after that but I felt justified because I was trying to protect my sister from a low-life guy. The fact that the guy was Black was not an issue for me but his character was. My mom was certain that Pepe kept us from harm; soon after my parents finally moved out of Compton, the house was burglarized.

My grandmother and uncle named the pup "King" but I didn't know that at the time. They lived in the granny house behind ours, and because the two houses shared a backyard, I had ready access to King/Levi. When I first started playing with him, he was covered in fleas and he practically bit my fingers off when I offered him a piece of hot dog, so I washed and fed him. Then I continued to spend much of my time after school with him, teaching him basic manners and fun commands such as "roll over" and "beg." My mother was not happy about having another dog around the house, though, perhaps because she expected that, based on our history with other pets, it would quickly fall on her shoulders to take care of him. In a rare moment of assertiveness, my mom told her mother-in-law that the pup would have to go. The problem was that she had not known how attached I'd become to Levi. When I heard that he would have to leave, it broke my heart and I pleaded with my mom to let him stay. I promised I would take care of him and that I would cover any veterinary costs that might arise. As awkward as it was for my mother to tell my grandmother she couldn't have the puppy and then in a few days turn around and allow me to have the very same, she did it anyway because she saw how serious I was and how important he was to me. My parents knew I loved animals, and that's why they thought getting me a horse would help counter the loss of my friends who fled from Compton. When the horse didn't work out, I bought a rabbit, but I had him for less than a year. One morning I found him untouched but dead in his hutch after a night when I had heard a lot of barking. I think he might have died of acute stress. I had Levi for 13 years, and he became my companion, protector, and emotional savior.

I learned about Levi's power when he was just five months old. I was playing with him in the front yard of my house when two girls walked toward us from down the street. When they saw him, they made a sharp right 90° turn off the sidewalk, crossed the street, and continued in our direction on the other side of the street. Wow! That was amazing! From then on, I felt safe whenever I had Levi with me, and I took him everywhere I could.

Lynne's dog, Levi, in front of Theodore Roosevelt Elementary School, 1970

Unfortunately, I couldn't take Levi to school but I took his picture and proudly showed it to Becky and a few other people who knew me, while talking glowingly about him. I loved him! He was the best dog ever! So incredibly smart and obedient! A complete joy to have around! I had started driving by then and we would often go in my mother's car to Houghton Park in North Long Beach with a stop at McDonald's for a bag of fries to share on our way. Once there, I would relax on the grass, enjoying the serenity of being away from Compton, and Levi would get to chase balls to his heart's content. Even that place was marred, though, when one day I watched as a woman's body was pulled off the island in the middle of a pond at the park. Was there no place I could go to escape the violence?

My final year in high school was unremarkable. Since leaving Whaley, I felt I had not learned anything, and I continued to learn nothing of academic value except perhaps a little bit of English composition. Dominguez offered no AP classes and in my chemistry class we covered a paltry three chapters during the entire first semester. The teacher was new out of UCLA and she wanted to make sure she didn't leave anyone behind. Inexplicably, I'd been put in a class with slow learners and class clowns but there I stayed. I doodled my way through that class and have hated chemistry ever since. Jeanetta, on the other hand, was in a more advanced chemistry class with the same teacher and she loved it so much that she ended up with a career in pharmacy.

I saw Jeanetta, Becky, Bonita, and my other long-term friends less often since we weren't taking any of the same classes. I found a new friend in Loretta Sifuentes, who had also taken the summer school fast track out of Compton. The following year she attended the University of Redlands and I attended Johnston College, part of the U of R, and we spent a lot of time together before she transferred out that year. She left because she was unhappy and wanted to go to a college with more Hispanics. I tried to talk her out of it to no avail, and was sad to see her go.

I continued in GAA in my final year of high school but with new teammates. The Compton school district was one of the few districts in southern California to offer field hockey. That year our field hockey Playday was at Centennial High School, a school long known for its violence, and the home of the founders of the Bloods. I was probably the only European-American student on Centennial grounds that whole year, not just that day, and I went there nervous but I made the decision not to show it because experience had taught me that it would signal weakness and place me in another tough situation. So, I prepared to act with false bravado. When a couple of Centennial boys trailed behind me and began to hassle me as I walked to the field, I warned them, "If you don't shut up, Ah'ma beat you upside the head with this stick!" The boys were apparently impressed with how tough I was, especially for a White girl, because they said a few words to that effect and backed off. Some days after our visit, the Centennial teachers boycotted to draw attention to the rising level of violence at their school.

Girls' Athletic Association (GAA), Dominguez High School, 1972. Top photo: Lynne, first row, third from right; Bonita, third row, fourth from right. Bottom photo: Becky, top row, last on right.

The president of the GAA that year was a Black girl named Frankie. She was also senior class president. I really admired and looked up to her for her skill in sports and her work in student government. In another place I might have been her! I also appreciated that she treated me with no racial prejudice. She did not discriminate, unlike so many others in our school, and like my friend Bonita, she seemed to look beyond color to see the individual. Maybe she did, but she was also a product of her environment, and the environment of Compton schools in the early 1970s was unfailingly racist against Whites. One day after gym class the pedestal I had put Frankie on crumbled and she came tumbling down. I was walking behind her when I heard her call someone a "honky," a derogatory name for Whites. After she said it, she turned and saw me. Her eyes opened wide and she quickly covered her mouth with her hand in surprise or embarrassment. Then she apologized. The disappointment I felt was not because I hadn't heard that word before, it was because she wasn't the person I thought she was. She clearly knew she should not have said it; I couldn't even fool myself into thinking she was just ignorant. I relegated Frankie to human status and over time forgave her for her slight. The following year Frankie also attended Johnston College and we lived in the same dorm. I spent a lot of my free time during my first several weeks there with Frankie and her roommate, Phyllis Leggett, a fellow Dominguez student and a member of my father's congregation. I knew they would understand when in the first few days of the school year I asked them, "What do I say to all these White people?"

At the end of senior year, I decided to buy a yearbook for no other reason than the pure vanity of having a keepsake documenting that I was among the top five seniors having the highest GPAs. Every year in the past, as I'd seen from my siblings since 1963, the Dominguez yearbook devoted a page to the photos of those five students. My GPA was third highest in my adopted class and so I expected to be on that page. Nope. My particular year broke out of the mold by including photos of just the valedictorian and salutatorian, while listing the names of the top 20 seniors with the highest GPAs. These were listed alphabetically, with the editor-in-chief's name listed first because it started with "A." I felt burned but also not surprised; it seemed par for the course. The yearbook does serve as a keepsake, but not in the way it was meant. There are so many misspellings, typographical errors, and awkward sentences in the yearbook that it is a strong reminder of just how poorly educated we were coming out of Dominguez.

I received the Bank of America plaque for academic achievement in liberal arts, an award that meant a lot to me. Teachers nominated students to receive these awards, and I believe Mrs. Taylor, my English teacher, nominated me. Perhaps she was predisposed to like me; she was one of the longest-tenured teachers at Dominguez, now ready to retire, and she had taught all my siblings before I came along.

In addition, I was recognized as a CSF sealbearer, reserved for students in the senior class whose grades were consistently high for at least two of three years. The number of sealbearers is a useful index of academic interest among students. There were 17 seal bearers in Scott's graduating class of 1966, 14 in Rand's class of 1967, and 13 in Dann's class of 1969, and then the number plummeted to five in Jeanne's class of 1971, marginally improved to seven in my adopted class of 1972, not counting myself, and settled at six in 1973, the year Becky, Bonita, and I would have all graduated together had I not accelerated my departure. The downward trend wasn't because students faced stronger academic rigor. No, this was clear evidence that during the short nine-year span of my family's attendance at Dominguez, student interest in academics had declined, and did so most dramatically for those who were entering high school the fall after Martin Luther King was assassinated, when Compton's schools became more violent and White flight had begun in earnest. This should be a warning to those parents whose kids are attending school anywhere in the U.S. today, because no place is immune from

Dominguez High School yearbook photos of Lynne (L), Becky (C), and Bonita (R), 1972-73.

the threat of school violence, including mass shootings, anymore — academic learning almost always comes in second in the minds of students perceiving threats to their survival.

Dominguez is better known for its athletics, having developed numerous professional baseball, basketball, and football players over the years. During my time there, Dominguez produced Kenny Landreaux, who went on to play baseball for the California Angels, the Minnesota Twins, and the Dodgers. I was also proud to be recognized for my athletic ability during the awards ceremony but that recognition came with an asterisk. That year, the trophy for top senior female athlete was, unusually, given jointly to two girls, a Black girl and me. Since Dominguez was all about recognizing and empowering Blacks in the early '70s, my guess was that the gym teachers were sensitive to the image that would be conveyed if the top athletic award were to be given to a White girl, one of only two Whites in the GAA, and the joint award might have been their solution.

As the school year came to an end, someone drugged one of the school secretaries by putting a hallucinogen in the milk that was on her desk while she went to grab a bite of lunch. Three weeks later she was still suffering from flashbacks. Go Dominguez!

****

The early 1970s were the beginning of affirmative action and there was a big push to get promising students out of Compton and into good colleges, which were finally opening their doors to students of color. That was great for them and I was especially happy for my friends; anything to get them out of Compton. I applied to some of the same colleges that others at Dominguez did, thinking my chances would be really strong with my academic record. But they got in and I didn't. The inequity bothered me. It wasn't because my credentials were not as good. There wasn't as much focus on extracurricular activities by college admissions as there is these days. We had all gone to the same crappy high school in the same crappy town, and we had all gotten the same crappy non-education. I could only explain it through affirmative action. A couple years later Alan Bakke, a White applicant to the medical school at UC Davis, challenged their admissions procedures in court and eventually won. I certainly understood his frustration.

It all worked out well in the end, though. My father was the one who told me about Johnston College. I was fed up with school and needed something different. He'd heard about this new experimental college during his annual Methodist ministers' conference at the University of Redlands where the college was located. We checked it out and although I thought it was strange in some ways, those ways seemed good to me, including the policy of allowing pets in dorms. I could keep Levi in my dorm room! I applied and they accepted me, which meant I would be able to leave Compton in less than six months. The thought of that gave me hope.

The summer after I graduated from high school I worked at McDonald's with Dann and Jeanne. I had a lot of fun earning $1.65 per hour with two of my siblings and Denise Leos, another friend I made as a new senior. I was supposed to be saving my earnings for college but when Levi developed an acute case of hip dysplasia, it was fortunate that I had the money to pay for his veterinarian bill, as I'd promised my mother I'd do. For $100 the veterinarian severed a ligament in his inner thigh that fixed the problem until Levi was very old.

I had just turned 17 when I went off to college a couple hours' drive from Compton in the "Inland Empire," approximately 60 miles east of L.A. This region includes, among other cities, Riverside, San Bernardino, and Redlands. With its Victorian homes, palm tree-lined streets, and numerous orange groves, Redlands was a vacation destination for rich Hollywood actors in the earlier 1900s before Palm Springs took its place. The University of Redlands still had remnants of orange groves on its campus when I arrived. When I started at Johnston College, I felt as though I was going there academically straight from junior high. Thankfully, Johnston's unique educational system allowed me to catch up without the shame that getting low grades would have wrought on me. Classes were small discussion-style seminars for which we drew up individual contracts that detailed what we wanted to accomplish. Success in the seminars was determined not by tests and grades but by written self- and faculty evaluations of how well we students achieved those goals. I was able to get rid of most of my academic deficiencies as time went on and I learned more, but I was never comfortable in seminars, especially those in which we discussed literature. By definition, the seminars were discussion-intensive but I was always afraid to speak up, partly because I was insecure about my poor educational preparation and partly because I had been punished in junior high and high school for standing out. I felt very uncomfortable drawing attention to myself.

Terry continued to be in my life until shortly after I left for college. He'd become more demanding and possessive after he moved away from Compton and dropped out of school, and I was fearful about the change in him. Sometimes he even seemed jealous of Levi. Toward the end of our relationship, I was no longer so compliant with his demands and I backed off emotionally from him in my need for self-preservation. One weekend I came home to get my hiking boots because one of my classes was scheduled to go on a weekend hike in the nearby San Bernardino mountains. I knew he would react poorly if I told him about the trip and so I tried to sneak my boots into my luggage without his knowledge. Ever vigilant, he saw the boots anyway and demanded to know why I needed them. When I told him I had to go because it was part of my class, he questioned what kind of class would go on a multi-day hike with both young men and women present, and he forbade me to go. We left it at that and I returned to college with my boots. As the weekend approached, I told him over the pay phone in the dorm that I was going, and then he gave me an ultimatum: it was either the trip or him. Well, by then it was an easy decision. In my mind I wondered how he could think he had the right to dictate what I was going to do in my life. It was such a trivial thing to go on a weekend hike and yet there he was, trying to con-

Lynne and Levi at a college retreat in the
San Bernardino Mountains, 1972

trol me. His possessiveness had changed him from a protector into a bully. I decided I could no longer put up with that; I would be in charge of my life, not him. When I told him my decision, he tried to withdraw the ultimatum but it was too late; I had my out and I took it. I had a wonderful time that weekend laughing and bonding with my new friends as we hiked our way up toward Mt. San Gorgonio, the tallest peak in southern California.

My last visit to Compton was over the Christmas holidays in 1972, my first year of college, and it was marred by yet another death. At 6:30 on Christmas morning, Ramón, with whom I had worked at McDonald's the summer before, was getting the place ready to open. He was taking out the trash when a car passed by and someone in that car shot and killed him. When I heard about it, hatred permeated every cell of my body. He wasn't part of a gang; he had a wife, a young child, and another child on the way. He was just minding his own business, being responsible, doing his job. It was the first drive-by shooting I'd heard of in Compton, a cowardly tactic that would become commonplace soon enough. I doubt it was the first in Compton. The fact that it happened on Christmas day, a day that was supposed to represent love, kindness, forgiveness, and charity to all made it too hard to bear. At that moment Compton was defeating me. I told my parents that if I had a gun and knew who had done it, I would go and shoot him myself. I thought of what would happen to me if I'd had the opportunity and I just didn't care, I was willing to throw away my whole future. That's what hatred does. It makes a person not care about the consequences of one's actions, even when they may be self-harmful.

One final insult from Compton: as my father began to drive me back to college, someone standing in front of a house on the street I had lived on for 12 years threw something hard at our car, a rock perhaps, as if to say good riddance. The sudden loud bang surprised us both but we kept on driving. After that incident I told my parents that I would never return to Compton even if it meant never seeing them again.

I finished my first year at Johnston College while Becky and Bonita finished their last year at Dominguez. As had been the case for me in elementary school and for Becky in junior high, Bonita was elected student body president in high school. The doors that closed for me in that short span of time had opened up for my friends, and I couldn't have been prouder for them. After they graduated from Dominguez, we all scattered to the winds, with Becky going south to UC San Diego and Bonita, east to Notre Dame. True to my word, I avoided Compton after that Christmas holiday, fearing I would be shot if I ever returned. Although, as fate would have it, I didn't have to give up seeing my parents. That next summer, the summer of 1973, my father was transferred to a church in Orange County and our family's time in Compton was finally, thankfully, at an end.

PART 2: THE BROWN GIRL'S STORY

<u>4</u>

I Am No Different From You

My life, based on how far back I can remember, started before the summer of 1960 when I was five years old and my mother flew my four siblings and me to the United States. We had been summoned by my father who had been in the United States for over a year. He traveled north from Mexico City, seeking stable employment and a home for his family before sending for us. We flew out of Mexico City's International Airport and landed at LAX in Los Angeles, California.

In Mexico I was surrounded by family and feelings of peace and happiness. We lived at Americas #57, Colonia Moderna, Mexico 13, D. F. (Distrito Federal) in an upper middle-class community. Our large family was part of another large family on my mother's side and we lived in close proximity. We visited our grandmother next door quite frequently, enjoying the bullfights on Sunday morning on her TV. I enjoyed playing hide-and-seek in her house, always hiding in her bureau. It smelled of cedar and fresh, clean linen, a scent that when I smell it now always takes me back to those Sunday morning bullfights on TV.

Living near a large family, there were always celebrations and festivities to participate in. There was always a birthday, graduation, or wedding to attend. My mother always dressed impeccably and so did we, even on normal occasions — little dresses and patent leather shoes, hair combed and curled, and possibly a bow to top it off for the girls and stiff white shirts and pressed black pants for the boys. Women never wore pants in those days, at least not in our neighborhood. Especially when going out.

My father was born in El Paso, Texas and had two siblings. The eldest was his sister Amparo, the youngest, his brother Guillermo (Uncle Chuy). Few stories were shared about their childhood and how they got along. I suspect that life was difficult for them and that they lived in poverty. When my father was 12 years old, his father threw them all out of the house,

Becky, four years old in Mexico, 1959

including his mother. His mother took the oldest and the youngest with her to a home she had in Mexico City. My father was left to fend for himself.

Armed with only a third-grade education, he worked the fields when harvest season rolled around or he took on odd jobs fixing things for homeowners and landowners. He learned carpentry and construction. Living pretty close to the U.S. and Mexico border, he went where the jobs were and repeatedly crossed back and forth. He was never stopped or questioned at the border because he had learned to present himself as a solid citizen. He always made sure he was bathed and his clothes were clean and pressed. He learned to differentiate himself from the other farm workers and illegals crossing the border. He used the practice of cleaning up before crossing the border to his advantage for many years. He rode the trains on occasion, jumping onto empty cars to get from one place to another. At the age of 13 or 14, he was attacked by an adult while he slept. He was startled awake by a pain in his neck; he had been stabbed in the back between his shoulder blades. Somehow he managed to fend off the attacker. He pulled the knife out of his back and noted that none of his possessions had been taken.

The distance between El Paso and Mexico City was extreme, approximately 1,136 miles. Unsure if his intent had always been to follow his mother into Mexico City, he eventually traveled across the border into Mexico one last time and continued on his journey of survival. Traveling from town to town he took on odd jobs and stayed just long enough to make enough money to eat, wash his clothes, and have a safe place to sleep. I suspect he spent a lot of nights sleeping on the streets. His primary mode of transportation was his feet and he was in no particular hurry, yet eventually between the ages of 12 and 15, he arrived at his mother's house. She was living with a man, Mr. Aramburu, who happily took him in and put him to work. Mr. Aramburu had money and he owned a welding and gate-making shop that was located on the first floor of his house. My father started working for him in the shop making steel gates. Most of the homes in the area appeared to be made of stucco with long driveways and steel gates. There was plenty of work for the two to keep them busy and profitable. Here he learned machining and welding, skills that helped him find substantial work when he eventually returned to the United States. But for now his travels across the border had stopped and he committed to working with Mr. Aramburu in his shop.

The Aramburu house was on Americas Street, around the corner from Bismarch, the street where my mother lived. Colonia Moderna, where my grandfather's mill was located, was across the street from the Aramburu house and shop. That is how my father and mother met.

My mother was well-to-do. She completed the equivalent of an Associate's degree, majoring in music, and she worked in the family-owned flour mill. She grew up in a household where live-in maids did all the cleaning and cooking and where she could dedicate her free time to her piano and singing. She was an accomplished soprano and the family had hoped she would pursue a career with the opera. When she met my father, she was smitten by his good looks and charm. He was mysterious and had a quick smile. He was nothing like the men she had grown up with and she was enthralled by the stories of his travels. He was not afraid of hard work or of getting dirty. He took pride in his work and gave it his all. He was a blue-collar worker with no pretense of being more than that. He did not try to impress, not that he had the means to do so anyway. He also looked forward to the weekends when he could enjoy some downtime. Both my father and mother loved to dance. The '40s were known for the big bands and energetic swing dances such as the Lindy Hop and the Jitterbug. I can envision them dancing their feet off. Waltzes and ballroom dancing were also popular at the time and I know they enjoyed dancing to them as well. They went on double dates with my mother's sisters and their boyfriends or just joined them at outings and parties. In later years, they oftentimes danced together in the living room when they thought no one was looking. In later years after having children, she would blast her Mexican music throughout the house while she cleaned the house and washed our clothes.

Once her family realized that their relationship was becoming serious, they decided to put a stop to it. My father was not well received as a prospective suitor for my mother. He was poor and had nothing to offer her, but she fell in love with him and didn't see beyond that. Her father told her to abandon the relationship or forfeit her inheritance. She would be disowned and the family would not support her any longer. It didn't sway her or stop her from marrying him a couple of years later. She gave up any inheritance that would have come her way. She was ready to venture out on her own, no longer to be under the thumb of her father and older brothers. She was never paid in all the years she worked at the family mill. She was taken care of financially by her parents, she never went without, but perhaps she was ready to make her own way. Perhaps she saw adventure and greater opportunities with my father. Her story is so similar to my own — she gave up everything for the guy who was different from everyone else.

After my parents got married in 1948, they moved next door into the two-story house that was owned by my mother's family, constantly under my grandfather's scrutiny and evident disdain. My mother continued to work at the family mill until she got pregnant with her first child. From that point forward, my father would not allow her to work. First to be born was my brother Carlos. Then came Richard, Celia Patricia, whom we called "Patty," and then me. Rosa came next, the youngest of the Rivera children born in Mexico. We were all about two years apart.

By the time I was born, my father was a machinist by trade. My father made a decent living working for Mr. Aramburu so we lived comfortably. We didn't spend much time with our father and we were able to run about the neighborhood to visit our cousins as we pleased. We also had live-in maids so my mother did not worry about cooking for us or cleaning after us. My brothers tell stories of how they teased and taunted the maids, how they ran through the house creating havoc and making messes. For no apparent reason, one of them once threw a fork over the railing from the second floor and it struck one of those poor ladies in the forehead!

Longing to go out on his own and get out from under his in-laws' scrutiny and control, my father decided to travel to the United States to start a new life for all of us. He began saving money for a trip north of the border and back to where he was born.

When I was 4 or 5 years old, my father returned to El Paso, Texas, traveling to his father's house. He was hoping to stay there while he looked for a job and perhaps a home for his family, but this was not to be. His father was very unhappy to see him and did not hesitate to let him know. He sent my father way. Realizing that he had no prospects in Texas, my father decided to make his way to California. He was about 29 years old by then and willing to take on any job. He ended up in Los Angeles and cleaned tables and washed dishes for a while; he even became a chef. He moved in with someone he befriended at one of the places he worked, which helped him save more money for his family. At some point he was hired as a machinist at Byron Jackson Pump Division Borg-Warner Corporation in Vernon, CA. Vernon was known for its orchards and green landscape in prior years, but after a corrupt land deal, factories began to take the place of the trees. By the time he started working there, Vernon was a large contributor of pollution in California. Vernon became an industrial city consisting of factories, transfer stations, and refineries. At Byron Jackson, my father worked as a machinist, making parts for airplanes and bombs. This was where he worked for the rest of his career. In later years after Carlos and Richard graduated from high school, he helped them both get jobs there as well. They both became very accomplished machinists, making a good living. Carlos is still in the field, while Richard ended up as an engineer at McDonnell Douglas, now called Boeing.

After about a year, he'd saved enough money to purchase a house in Watts on E. 120th Street, a block from San Pedro Ave, and he could now send for his family in Mexico. So, it was time for us to prepare to meet my father in America. My mother had to get a visa and of course passports for everyone, but it wasn't that easy. When my father moved in with his mother and Mr. Aramburu as a teenager, he took Mr. Aramburu's name as his own. When we were born, all of our birth certificates reflected the Aramburu last name. This was inconsequential, until we went to get passports for travel to the United States. My father's true surname was Rivera, which is the name that we all had to memorize and repeat should we be questioned at Customs. I can only assume this was to prove that we were in fact his children. For weeks before our travels my mother would quiz us as to what our names were to ensure we became accustomed to our new name.

Watts was a low- to middle-class White neighborhood, a surprise to us and a major change from what we were accustomed to in Mexico. When we moved to Watts, we also had no idea how our father would be. Our household was traditionally Mexican —

autocratic and abusive. My father ruled with an iron fist, his belt, and demoralizing words. From what we had learned from my mother, he was physically abused as a child by his own father so when I thought about it in later years, it made no sense to me why he would perpetuate this treatment on his children.

My mother became the traditional Mexican wife, subservient and catering to her husband's requests and demands. He managed the money and only gave her enough for weekly grocery shop-

Becky's growing family, 1960. Becky is front left

ping. Everything to do with the home was her responsibility. And our brothers were raised to think the same way. Her responsibilities consisted of cooking, cleaning, washing, and taking care of the kids. This was a dramatic change from what she was used to. I often wondered later on if she regretted leaving Mexico or giving up everything to be with my father. She went from being wealthy to living in poverty in Watts. She had to learn how to cook and clean and did so through trial and error. Her primary responsibility and focus, however, was my father and we all knew it. She responded promptly to his beck and call, as we all did. If he whistled, she came running.

I grew up in fear of bodily harm, but didn't think twice about it. Because of our father's violent temper, I learned to cry at the drop of a hat. He would beat us until we cried so I got smart early on. Rosa was not as smart or just too stubborn. She refused to give him any satisfaction and refused to cry. I could never understand how she tolerated the beatings. One Saturday morning we were watching cartoons on TV in the living room and we were starting to get a little too loud. It was Rosa, perhaps Oscar, and me. I fretted that he may wake up and I shushed them a couple of times in an effort to quiet them down. What I didn't realize was that he had already awakened and was on his way into the living room with his belt. He yelled at us for making so much noise and swung his belt and struck me a couple of times before I began to cry. He then went for Rosa who as always, refused to cry. I went into my room crying and listened as he beat her and beat her again and again. Still no tears. He put the belt down, picked her up and threw her against the front door. He picked her up again and did it a second time with such force that she finally cried. He turned around and went back into the bedroom, slamming the door behind him. I went back into the living room to check on Rosa. She was sitting on the floor with her back against the front door that was now partially open, her knees pulled up to her chest. She was crying like I'd never seen her cry before. The force of her 10- or 11-year-old body against the door had knocked it off its hinges. This was the only life I knew, and I assumed every household was the same.

It wasn't until I was in third grade and I started visiting the homes of school friends that I realized how different our household truly was. My friends never came to my house; I would always go to theirs. Not that I had a lot of friends. I was an odd kid who wore old clothes and didn't speak English very well. It was hard to make friends.

My brothers Carlos and Richard struggled socially because of the language barrier. They were made fun of at school and bullied as well. They got into a lot of fights, coming home from school with bumps and bruises. They were smart boys, but they struggled staying on top of their lessons because they didn't understand the teachings. When we first came to the United States Carlos was 11 years old and Richard was nine. Although Patty was seven, I don't remember her struggling as much as they did. She went into second grade and was lucky to get a teacher who was willing to work with her. We were lucky when our teachers had a basic knowledge of Spanish which helped us progress in our studies.

My brothers quickly became friends with the Plant boys, Michael and Harold, part of a White family who lived across the street. Those boys were worse than mischievous, they were downright mean. They would put firecrackers in frog's mouths and light them or pour gasoline on grasshoppers and watch them burn. I couldn't understand how they derived pleasure from doing such horrible things. So, my brothers didn't start out with the best influences in life. Carlos and Richard always got into fights. Initially I assumed it was because they were picked on for being different; however, after the White exodus and influx of Blacks into the neighborhood, the fighting didn't stop. Then I realized they were just trouble waiting to happen.

Carlos and Richard didn't get along well with each other, either, from my perspective. My mother was constantly breaking up fights between them. She would step in with a broom, or if they were outside, she would turn the water hose on them. During one of their routine fistfights my mother found herself without a broom or hose in her hand and tried breaking them up. She ended up with a right hook to the chin from one of them. We never learned who hit her because neither one of them was willing to confess. They both got into a lot of trouble for that one; getting whipped by my father with the belt was something neither one of them would forget for a while.

As we all grew older, my father had high hopes for all of us, yet in time we all disappointed him in one way or another, except for Patty. Patty was fairly quiet and shy, but she was very smart, too. In later years we learned that her IQ was at genius level, which made my father very proud. She was the gleam in his eye, and he made no attempt to hide that from the rest of us. After high school, in 1970 she was one of the first 39 women accepted to Caltech in Pasadena, and on full scholarship. She was definitely the anomaly in our family. I attribute my drive to be better and to do more to the fact that she was smarter than me and was the only one who had my father's admiration. I also attribute my struggle with self-confidence to the same. Never being good enough in his eyes was devastating.

I would bring home A's and B's on all of my report cards, yet they were never good enough. He would ask, "Why can't you get all A's like your sister Patty?" All I know is that the animosity between Patty and me grew and grew as we got older. It wasn't uncommon for the two of us to get into fistfights ourselves. Either she would antagonize me or I would her. There was no love lost between us. Looking back, it really is sad that none of us were very close growing up. I blame my father for most of it; he derived pleasure from seeing us at each other's throat. He also loved taking off his belt and ending our brawls for us.

Rosa was the next closest in age to me, born in 1957. I don't remember much about her younger years; I was too young and she was still the baby of the family. She and I didn't really do much together other than sleep in the same bed. She would walk and talk in her sleep, which was really scary. My parents had three more kids once we settled in. My brother Oscar was born in 1961, Lydia, in 1962, and finally Martha, in 1964.

I truly loved our house in Watts. It was a two-bedroom with a formal dining room that we converted into a third bedroom. There were bunk beds in every room to sleep all of us. We had a large living room and I loved the nights when we all sat together to watch *Bonanza.* We weren't allowed to make a sound, but it was nice sitting in the same room with everyone. We were a large family, but not very close at all. So, these rare moments that we spent together gave me the feeling of "family" and connection. Carlos and Richard usually couldn't be bothered by us, the younger kids. We were a nuisance at best, which is why I treasured those moments together. They were too caught up with their friends and putting together model planes and aircraft carriers in those days.

My favorite place to be was in our huge back yard. This was my sanctuary. We had fruit trees down the middle of the yard, apples and figs mostly, and the entire property was surrounded by tall eucalyptus trees. When the wind blew, they swayed and swished and made such a racket. I loved running in the back yard on windy days, feeling the air blowing around me and the eucalyptus trees swishing and snapping, making so much noise. Heavy branches broke from time to time. Patty once just barely avoided being smashed by a large one that snapped off and came down fast.

Way in the back, we had a pigeon coop. Carlos and Richard took great care of their birds and spent most of their time back there during the summer. There were different kinds of pigeons. Some flew higher than the rest and one breed would start rolling down from the sky and then, just before hitting the ground, would flap their wings. It fascinated me to watch them. Unlike the chickens and rabbits we kept, the pigeons were definitely pets, and we never ate them. Of course, our little farm wouldn't have been complete without roosters, dogs, cats, and an occasional duck. I will always treasure the many adventures that took place in that back yard, although some adventures were a little scary.

Our back yard was inhabited by a feathered bully. When he got out of his cage, he would chase and try to peck anything that moved, and that was usually us kids. One windy winter day, the eucalyptus trees were swaying and rustling and enticing me to go outside and play. I ran out the back door to the swing my father had built for us. It was located past the garage and down to the middle of our yard. I was standing up and pumping the swing with my legs to go higher and higher. I was soaring and feeling the wind around me when I happened to look down at the ground and see the rooster just watching me. Oh boy! I was in trouble. As I let the swing start to slow down, he began jumping at me, trying to peck my legs. I tried to maneuver the seat of the swing to hit him, but I kept missing. Finally, I realized I had no choice but to make a run for it. I pushed the swing at him and as he jumped into the air to avoid it, I hopped off and sprinted toward the back door. Terrified, I screamed at the top of my lungs all the way to the door, knowing that it was just a matter of time before he caught up to me. As I took the first step up to the back door, my mother opened it, allowing me to run in the house without slowing down. She slammed the door shut behind me. The rooster, just inches away, ran smack into it. For weeks after, I so quietly and delicately ventured into the back yard waiting to be ambushed, but it never happened again.

In fall of 1960 I started my school life at 118th Street School. I spoke not a word of English, but Mrs. Coleman, my kindergarten teacher, was willing and able to work with me. Lucky? Maybe. She taught me basic English expressions and words but was not very forgiving. She let me wet my pants when I couldn't say "May I please go to the bathroom," entirely in English. She allowed me to go to the bathroom after the fact. I don't hold it against her. I can only imagine that I was a nuisance for her, having to take extra time with me to ensure I was learning the lessons she was teaching the entire class. I suppose I should thank her for allowing me to experience the very first of many humiliating experiences of my life.

Starting school at the age of five was the best thing to happen to me. I watched as my older siblings struggled with keeping up with their lessons and fitting in socially because of the language difference. I had the added time to master the English language before getting into junior high school or high school. Our lifestyle and cultural differences were hard enough for others to understand; the language barrier only added to the discomfort of being different. We didn't dress the same as everyone else. Our clothes were mostly hand-me-downs. For lunch, every day, my mother would pack for me an egg sandwich wrapped in wax paper and stuffed into a recycled paper bag. Everyone else had bologna or peanut butter and jelly sandwiches wrapped in cellophane. Some kids had lunch boxes and fruit or other snacks. Kids would look at me at lunch time and pinch their noses with their fingers implying my lunch smelled. I didn't understand what they said, and I knew they wouldn't understand me so I didn't even bother conversing with anyone. Kids would stare at me; I was not what they were used to.

Still, school served as an escape from the reality of my home life. I enjoyed learning and everything else school had to offer, except for recess. Recess is where I mostly felt out of place and sensed how different I was from everyone else. Besides my hand-me-downs, my shoes and socks always had holes in them, and my ankles were always scabby because I constantly kicked them when I walked. My feet turned in slightly, just enough to attract ridicule. I never felt like I fit in. Even as my English got better, kids were not open to letting me into their circle of friends. I was pretty pathetic as a kid and received a lot of grief for it. I learned early on how cruel kids could be. On rainy days we would play 7-Up in our classrooms, a game where we would lay our heads down on the desk with our eyes closed and put our thumbs up. If someone touched your thumb, you had the chance to get up and chase that person down before they made it back to their desk. It looked like a lot of fun, but I was never picked, ever! All I wanted was to be accepted; I wanted friends. I wanted to blend in and feel like I belonged. Most of the kids grew up in their neighborhoods and knew each other because of it. It always takes a while for new kids to start to fit in and find friends with similar interests, but I was the exception. Even after I was no longer the new kid, I was still the weird one.

During my years in elementary school, English as a Second Language (ESL) or Special Ed classes were not available to students, forcing me to learn English in an English only environment. My teachers helped me along the way as best as they could and my desire to fit in made it a priority that I grasp the language sooner than later. I believe I learned pretty quickly, with a few bumps in the road. I remember vaguely in second grade being asked a question by a fellow student and not knowing whether to say "can" or "can't" because I didn't know which was which. I struggled with words containing the letter "s." Should it sound like a "c," "s," or "z"? Is it decision, desision, or dezision? My second-grade teacher, Mrs. Lambert, was astute in recognizing my problem early on and recommended me to the speech therapist on school grounds, whom I met with two times a week. What I remember mostly are the magic tricks he performed for us. He did the old pulling his thumb off from one hand to the other. He would also make shadow animals on the blackboard with his hands against the light from his desk.

I am asked from time to time if I believe that all school systems should offer bilingual or ESL programs for non-English speaking students, especially since I was deprived of this opportunity in my elementary school years. Unfortunately, I don't usually give the answer people are looking for. Yes, my siblings and I struggled in getting a foothold on the English language, especially since our teachers were not prepared to work with us in that capacity. However, I believe that I mastered the English language quicker because I did not have a choice. I often wonder if we are not doing today's non-English speaking students a disservice by keeping them segregated in ESL classes, adding to the stigma that they are different, and allowing them to prolong the learning of the English language. I would recommend that teachers know a second language and help students assimilate and encourage interaction among all the classroom students. Creating a separate class for ESL students creates a stigma. In my opinion, assimilation is not a bad thing; it doesn't mean one has to give up old traditions or beliefs. It means you are willing to incorporate the basic fundamentals to fitting in and contributing to your new country of residence. It also gives one the feeling of belonging, of being accepted, something I longed for my entire life.

My father worked nights so he was not available to drive us to school in the morning regardless of the weather conditions. In August, every year, my father would drive all of us to Sears at the Compton Shopping Center to shop for school clothes. We girls were allowed to buy three dresses, one sweater, one pair of shoes, socks, and underwear, and that was it until the following August. My mother would walk into the store with us and help us select our clothes. My father did not participate in the selection process. He would go to the candy section and buy himself a bag of popcorn and wander around the store while we shopped. When I was in third grade, Mrs. Johnson, my teacher, noticed that I arrived to school wet every day during the rainy season. She asked me why someone didn't drive me to school and I told her that my father was asleep and my mother did not drive. Noticing the holes on the bottoms of my shoes, she had me take my shoes off and stand on construction paper. She traced my wet foot for reasons unknown to me. A few days later, when I returned to school, she handed me a new pair of saddle oxford shoes. I was embarrassed, felt ashamed, yet loved the shoes immediately. Of course, the following day, my father DID get up to take me to school and to return the shoes to Mrs. Johnson. He explained to her that we did not want her charity, that he could take care of his family without her help. To this day I do not know what she told him, but she was able to convince him to allow me to keep the shoes. That same year, my sister Rosa received a waterproof jacket from her kindergarten teacher and my father paid a visit to her class as well. Rosa got to keep her jacket, too.

Some days, as my sister and I walked to school in inclement weather, parents of some of our classmates would pick us up and take us to school. We never thought twice about accepting a ride from anyone who pulled over for us. It was better than getting to school wet to the bone. One rainy day, someone pulled over and offered to drive us home, and we accepted. My mother happened to see us get out of the car and demanded to know who that was. Who drove us. "I don't know," I answered honestly, "there weren't any kids in the car with her." My response shocked her. "What were this lady's intentions in picking you up?" she asked, clearly upset with us for accepting a ride from a stranger. I guess compassion couldn't have been the motivating factor. You would think she would be more upset that her kids walked around at school in wet clothes all day long.

I attended 118th Street School through the middle of third grade while a new school was built behind our house on 122nd Street. I transferred to the brand new, beautiful school during the second half of third grade and stayed through the fourth grade. It was during these years that we began to notice a change in the demography of our community. Our White neighbors were slowly moving away and their homes were purchased by Black families. As more Black families moved in, more Whites moved out. By the end of fourth grade, our neighborhood was predominantly Black.

Most of my early elementary school years are a fog and I attribute this to the struggle with the language and inability to make friends. Kids shy away from others who are different and this was certainly the case with our family. Perhaps I just didn't notice it at the time, but I don't remember any other immigrant children attending school with me. My family was probably the exception in our neighborhood, which made us stand out even more.

I have fond memories of some of my teachers at 122nd Street School. One May Day celebration when I was in third grade, girls were asked to wear a white shirt and red skirt to participate in the Maypole activity. Not having either, nor the money, to buy a shirt and skirt, I showed up on May Day wearing a dress. The teacher who had coordinated the event had obviously anticipated my dilemma because she had sewn a red skirt and bought me a white shirt to wear. To this day I cannot understand the motivation for so many of my teachers to be so compassionate and giving. My fourth-grade teacher, Mrs. Nakashima, seemed to like me and allowed me to go to Mrs. Masaki's class at the end of the day to help sort the weekly readers for each classroom. Mrs. Masaki, from Hawaii, was probably a teacher's aide who helped out in the office. She taught lei-making and I was allowed to attend her class after school. I loved Thursdays at 122nd Street School! That was the day of the week when we could buy our lunch for a quarter. Lunch would consist of a hot dog, chips, and carton of milk, a welcome change from my usual scrambled egg sandwich.

Fourth grade is when I met Lynette Hardiman, my first real friend in life. I cherished our friendship. Lynette was always kind and never treated me any differently than she treated anyone else at school. In addition to not speaking English very well and dressing differently than everyone else, I did strange things. I was the girl who chased a butterfly during recess one day. It's not surprising that kids kept their distance. We didn't have encyclopedias at home and sometimes our homework required research. Lynette would invite me to her house to use her encyclopedias and we would do our homework together. Her house was always neat and clean and her parents were pleasant to me. I thought her house was like a palace; the furniture looked expensive and her house appeared so big to me. But what mainly caught my eye was the bookcase filled with books and a set of encyclopedias. I always went to the library if I needed to do research for an assignment; who could afford encyclopedias? In retrospect, it was a normal middle-class house, with a big couch and nice chairs. Living in a two-bedroom house with 10 people, there was no way our home would ever be as orderly with everything in its place.

That year I also met Marquita Ray. The three of us would do homework together at Lynette's house. They were the only two friends I had at the 122nd Street School. We moved out of the Watts area the summer after fourth grade so I lost touch with both of them, but years later while at Dominguez High School, I saw Marquita entering the girl's gym as I was walking out. I knew her immediately and called out to her, but she didn't recognize me. I had to tell her who I was. I reminded her of our study periods at Lynette's house. She remembered Lynette, but she did not remember me, and I do not blame her. I felt invisible for so many years that I really was not surprised.

That same year I hurt my eye trying to open a window in my bedroom. The window opened inward and as I tried to open it, it would not budge as I pulled and yanked on it. I grabbed the handle with both hands and pulled with all my might. The window pane gave and as it swung open, the corner hit my eyebrow just above my right eye. It hurt so badly that I actually saw stars. My mother put ice on it which helped sooth the pain. The next day my eye was swollen shut and the right side of my face was puffed out to the edge of my nose. I was a frightening sight! My father rushed me to the doctor. There was nothing to be done but he gave me a tetanus shot and told me to keep cold compresses on it and wait for the swelling to go down. I missed about two weeks of school because of it and I was glad not to go. I was ridiculed enough as it was and did not need to add fuel to the fire. The swelling would not go down and I could not open my eye for the longest time. The doctor was concerned that I would lose my eyesight, but after about a month the blurriness went away. I walked with my head looking down in hopes to avoid eye contact. The few kids who laughed at me was more than I could bear. For years thereafter I continued to walk looking down. It helped me avoid uncomfortable situations and kept me from seeing the ridicule in the faces of kids walking toward me.

In the summer of 1965 we experienced a record heat wave. The unrest of the South had made its way to California, and it was rearing its ugly head in Watts. I had just completed fourth grade and was enjoying summer months of freedom before starting up again in September. Temperatures reached into the three-digits and lasted for days at a time. It was difficult to escape the heat, which made people more hot-tempered and impatient.

This was a time of unrest in America as it was. We heard frequently on the news of violence in the South against Blacks. In January, 1965, African-American religious leaders and other activist groups planned three marches from Selma to Montgomery, Alabama to campaign for voters' rights. Although African-Americans were allowed to vote after the passage of the Civil Rights Act of 1964, they were often blocked from placing their vote by local authorities. The marches were to encourage Americans to register to vote. Being only 10 years old, I could not comprehend the extent of what this meant.

The marches were non-violent but this did not deter the local White officials from brutalizing the protesters and spraying them with tear gas. There were two deaths associated with the marches, which only fueled the desire of African-Americans across the United States to do something about it — to retaliate, to confront the authorities. Martin Luther King, Jr. had joined in on two of the marches and encouraged other church leaders and clergymen to join in. Martin Luther King, Jr. spoke often with President Johnson, who appeared to believe in and support the civil rights cause, although President Johnson wasn't successful in stopping the violence by the local authorities. The visions of beatings and handcuffed Blacks were on TV nightly, further igniting frustration and anger across the country.

This was a time when minorities, even in southern California, were limited to where they could work, go to school, or live, which aided in creating hostility between the races. Laws were in place to protect against discrimination but areas redlined their communities so Blacks could not buy homes. It was against the law to do this, but redlining was prevalent. Segregation was no longer acceptable; laws were in place to protect against discrimination but it did not stop White Americans from doing their best to keep minorities out. Discrimination was not limited to the South. In the Los Angeles area, minorities were limited to where they could live as well. Los Angeles was predominantly a White neighborhood from the 1920s into the 1940s. World War II created opportunities in the defense industry, which drew African-Americans from other states to the Los Angeles area in hopes of acquiring decent jobs. The United States needed to make tanks, guns, ammunition, and planes to be used to fight the war. President Roosevelt signed Executive Order 8802 banning discrimination in the job sector, which was promising for minorities. California also became a major ship and aircraft builder. McDonnell Douglas was located in the Los Angeles area and was hiring by the thousands. The Black population in Los Angeles went from around 63,000 in the early 1940s to over 350,000 by the 1960s. They came in search of jobs, jobs that were not necessarily being offered to Blacks. And with limits on where they could live, South and East Los Angeles only, over the years these areas, such as Watts and Willowbrook, became home to Blacks who were underemployed and/or poor. Unfortunately, violence and crime increased as the population grew.

The tension could be felt in our neighborhood as well. The days being so hot, we spent a lot of time on our front porch, looking for relief from the heat. One scorching day my father was sitting on our front porch when a car sped by, the occupant in the back seat firing a gun in the direction of our house. Once the reality of the event sunk in, my father got up to see if there was any damage to the house. Two bullets had entered the front of our house, just inches from where my father had been sitting. Even though I was only 10 years old, I will never forget the events of Friday, August 13, 1965. It was nearing dusk and in order to cool off a bit from the heat, I went out to water the front yard. I watched as an army truck drove by slowly and dropped off a fully uniformed and armed soldier in front of each house on our street, including ours. I remember trembling and feeling a sense of foreboding that something terrible was going to happen.

I went back into the house to tell my mother what I had seen. We were all home, with the exception of my father who worked from 4:00 PM to midnight. My mother insisted we all stay indoors the rest of the evening for our protection. The National Guardsman did not speak with us so we were completely in the dark as to what they were doing there. As the evening progressed, we watched the news and learned quickly that we were certainly in harm's way. On TV we saw the effects of what had started out as a normal traffic offense two days earlier on August 11th and had now turned into the "Watts Riots" of 1965.

A 21-year old Black man suspected of driving under the influence was pulled over by a White California Highway Patrolman in a densely populated area of Los Angeles. As he proceeded to handcuff the young man, bystanders watched as the police officer roughed up the 21-year-old. This being commonplace in Black communities, some of the observers became angry. The 21-year-old's brother who had been in the car had gone home to bring their mother to the scene. An argument broke out which resulted in a brawl with the police. The Highway Patrolman called for backup and by the time they arrived, the crowd had gotten larger and before long people started shoving and pushing each other. Rumors spread to community members that the motorist had been beaten up and a pregnant woman kicked, resulting in angry mobs running rampant. One officer pulled out a shotgun and that was it. One officer was hit, the crowd began to throw rocks, breaking windows, and beating up non-Blacks, and the looting began. This continued off and on for the next 4-5 days. White motorists were targeted; some cars were flipped over.

It is said that the looters focused on White-owned businesses and did not damage or burn down homes that were in their path. Unfortunately, this is not completely true as our home was destroyed. First Responders were also pelted with rocks and chunks of concrete. A couple of police officers were shot by friendly fire; 23 of the 34 deaths were caused by the police. An 8:00 PM curfew was put in place and anyone found outside after this time was subject to arrest. Between 31,000 and 35,000 people are believed to have participated in the five days of rioting. Almost 14,000 National Guards were deployed and Watts sustained damages in the amount of $40 million. Community leaders tried to diffuse the situation and were eventually successful, but not until after many lives were lost and many buildings and homes were looted and/or burned down.

As we watched TV the night of the 13th, we saw the local White Front store catch fire and burn down. A large mob was coming down our street and getting closer by the minute. The destruction was unreal; the fact that the rioting was approaching our house was surreal. My mother couldn't call my father at work, we didn't have a phone. She didn't drive, plus, my father had the only car we owned. We hunkered down and hoped for the best. We watched TV as we waited patiently as the hours passed and the mob got closer. Watching the news, we saw our neighborhood being overrun by looters and people just marching down familiar streets. We could faintly hear loud voices and screaming, and breaking glass, unsure if they were coming from outside or from the TV. My father was nowhere in sight. I didn't learn until a few years later that my brothers had taken places on the roof of our house with guns, waiting for someone to approach. In later years when we were older, we sometimes talked about the events of that day, and every time we relived it we realized more how close we were to being harmed.

My father finally arrived shortly after midnight. He slowly pulled the car into the driveway and loaded us all in. As we pulled out of the driveway, we couldn't help but notice the large mob of people walking swiftly down the street. The soldiers were nowhere to be found, making us feel alone and vulnerable. We drove down the street quite slowly in the direction from which they came, making sure not to hit or bump anyone on the street. We'd wait for people to move out of our path before accelerating forward. On his way home, my father had witnessed a motorist trying to drive through the mob at too fast a speed and his car had been flipped over by the mass of people.

We stayed at our uncle's house in Hollywood for three days. My father's brother, Uncle Chuy, Aunt Socorro, and our two cousins, Rosalia and Javier, lived across the street from Paramount Studios on Gower street. It was a modest home, definitely barely large enough for the four of them. At the end of the third day, he told us that he couldn't handle having the 10 of us there any longer. He could barely manage his wife and two kids. With us not having anywhere else to go, my father's boss, Mr. Moore, who lived next to Compton in Paramount, offered up his home to us.

He lived with his wife and three kids in a beautiful three-bedroom, two-bath home. We girls slept in their daughters' room, two to a bed. The boys slept outside in the backyard in tents. It was actually a fun adventure for them. We stayed with the Moores for three full weeks, the time it took my father to find us another place to live. He finally came across a fixer upper in another low- to middle-class neighborhood in East Compton.

My parents were heartbroken by what they found once they were allowed to return to our house in Watts. The house had been looted and everything destroyed. All the mirrors and windows in the house had been shattered, clothes and furniture destroyed, ripped, torn, ruined. People had defecated throughout the house in every room possible and feces had been smeared on the walls. The worst of it all was finding our pets in the backyard. At that time, we had chickens, roosters, pigeons, and dogs. Our dogs had just had puppies. The chickens, roosters, and pigeons were gone; only the little dead bodies of our puppies remained. My mother learned to hate Blacks that very day. She could not fathom anyone being so vicious and cruel. We lost everything. We couldn't sell the house so my parents ended up walking away from it. Our move to Compton was fairly easy; we didn't have much to take with us.

Our new house was small, a two-bedroom with one bath and a second house in the backyard. My father was pretty handy and in time he converted the garage into another bedroom, dropping two beds in there and adding a toilet and shower. Moving during the summer months gave us the opportunity to get acclimated to our new neighborhood and neighbors, and them to us. We were the only non-White family on our street, besides the Garcias who had evidently lived there for many years. It was not easy getting acquainted with our neighbors; it was evident we were not welcomed by all of them. Across the street lived a police officer with his wife and two kids. He didn't waste any of his precious time speaking with us, but his wife was quick to show her contempt.

Vicki lived at the end of the block with her mother and father. We became close friends right away because we both liked to climb trees and read. Across the street from her were Lorraine and Beth with whom I became close as well, although they liked to make fun of me and some of my sisters from time to time. Beth, the younger sister in particular, was not a nice person. Her mother would give us their hand-me-downs and anytime Beth caught any of us wearing any of their old clothes, she always made a point to comment on it, especially if other neighborhood kids were with us. She would ask directly what it felt like to be poor or to be Mexican. She was devious; she liked making the distinction evident to anyone around her. I spent a lot of my childhood feeling ashamed or embarrassed for being poor and/or Mexican. In the end it taught me compassion and to appreciate the differences in others. I never wanted to make anyone feel the way that people had made me feel my entire childhood. My own children learned early on to show compassion and to not make fun of anyone for any reason.

Next door to us lived Peter and Kevin. Peter was the older boy, tall and thin with brown hair. He was probably our age, 11 or 12 years old. Kevin was shorter and not as thin, and his hair was lighter. They were foster kids living with Jack and Jackie, husband and wife. Their situation was odd; the boys did all the chores around the house and appeared to be very afraid of Jack. I know that Jack beat them because we could hear it from our house. It was the same at our house so it didn't seem out of the ordinary. Those summer months Vicki, Lorraine, Beth, Peter, Kevin, and I would play all afternoon after my father left for work. We didn't come in until parents started calling out for us. Peter and Kevin were usually first, then Lorraine and Beth, and then Vicki. I went home once Vicki had to go in.

In spite of the horrific events that brought us to San Marcus Street in Compton, that was the best summer of my life. Beth, Lorraine, and Vicki taught me how to ride a bike. Beth had a tall bike that required me to stand on the curb in order to reach the peddles. The three of them took turns holding the bike as I climbed on it and pushed myself into the street. It took a while, but after a few falls, I got the hang of it. Vicki and I spent a lot of our time at the local library which was just a few blocks down the street on Alondra Blvd. They had a program where you would read books from different genres and every time you completed one genre the librarian would place a star on our reading list. Vicki and I loved to climb the willow tree in front of her house and read for hours. Or we would lie on my bed or her bed and just read our afternoons away. We also loved to play war with the rest of the kids and get shot down off the willow tree. We loved falling and rolling off of the curb, dying slowly and theatrically.

We did a lot of running and playing softball on our street. San Marcus was a dead-end street so we didn't have to worry about oncoming traffic. Our block backed into the riverbed and the 7 freeway, which is now the 710. We would hit balls from the end of the block, where the riverbed started and in front of Vicki's house, toward Gibson Ave. We all got pretty good at it by the end of the summer and we could pop up fly balls all the way to Dah's house, which was about two-thirds of the way down the block. Dah's real name was George Henderson. He was Moya's grandfather and we all thought he was pretty old. Moya would spend her weekdays at Dah's house only during the summer. We spent a lot of time at Dah's house when Moya was there.

Dah would take us to 31 Flavors, which we now know is Baskin-Robbins. From time to time he would take us to the beach. He liked to swim the ocean so he would find us a spot to hang out and then he would disappear into the water. One time he was gone for a very long time. He got caught in a riptide and a lifeguard had to go out and rescue him.

When it rained, we would run around the block, like a track meet, around and around until we were tired. Or we would ride our bikes in the rain. When we finally went in for the evening my mother made us come in the back door. Our bare feet were so black from the dirt, we weren't allowed to walk through the house.

There was an unfortunate incident when my brother Carlos accidentally ran over a kitten when he pulled into our driveway. The policeman's wife came out of the house with her son and screamed at Carlos. She stood in front of our house and said, "See there, Randy, that's what Mexicans are good for." She had no idea how much Carlos loved animals and how much it hurt him to have this happen. This same woman slapped her son in the face so hard that her handprint remained on his face for three days. But we, the Mexicans, were the animals. She forbade her 5-year-old son to cross to our side of the street; our dead-end street was narrow, and we could hear everything that was said. Thank goodness for Vicki, Lorraine, Beth, Peter, and Kevin.

That September I started school at Theodore Roosevelt Elementary School on San Vincente and Bradfield, which was about a mile from my house. Beth, Vicki, and Lorraine went to St. Phillip Neri Catholic School across the bridge in Paramount. I was again going to a new school because of our move from Watts to Compton. I was in the fifth grade now. My teacher was Mrs. Burwell. The windows in Mrs. Burwell's class faced the front of the school and I remember this because a kid was hit by a car that year and I remember the commotion outside our classroom when it happened. I don't believe he survived the accident; he never returned to school. Fifth grade was uneventful as I see it in my mind. Same story, different school. I suspect that I pretty pathetic in those days because I certainly don't remember hanging out with anyone during most of my elementary school years. My pigeon-toed feet, my worn-out clothes, and my awkwardness. I would start a conversation in English and end it in Spanish. I would only become aware when the faces of my audience changed from understanding to puzzlement. It's funny now as I reflect on those times.

I was in fifth grade when I decided I wanted to be someone else. I wanted to fit in more than anything and had had enough of being an outcast. Using the dictionary, I would randomly pull up a word, learn its meaning and pronunciation and attempt to use it daily for a week. This helped me gain confidence in my communication and English language.

Tetherball and four-square helped me come out of my shell and get to know people. I was pretty good, which helped me get attention from some kids who enjoyed playing, too. I started to play softball and I even joined the track team, influenced by Lynne. While I met Lynne in fifth grade, I mostly remember her when I was in Mrs. Campbell's sixth grade class and she was in Mr. Armistead's. She was tall, thin, and blonde, definitely not what I was accustomed to. She seemed shy but projected confidence. She had an easy smile and seemed to have a lot of friends. I mostly liked that she was good at sports, something I also enjoyed. Making new friends and participating in games and sports were the beginning of a change within me. I believe I was finally learning to accept myself for who I was, but I still had a long way to go.

I did a lot of embarrassing things trying to bring attention to myself. I would call down a hallway and say something like, "See you tomorrow, Lynne," just to make it appear as though anyone really cared about seeing me the next day. I'm sure this didn't help my cause of trying to fit in with normal people. At a sixth-grade sock hop, I walked up to a boy and asked him to dance. He looked at me with contempt and turned me down; I was devastated, but managed to walk away with my head up. I am most ashamed of my sixth grade Back to School night. My mother, who didn't speak English at all, didn't drive, and dressed even more poorly than I did, walked from our house to Theodore Roosevelt, just to visit my class. I was so embarrassed by her being there. She never bought clothes for herself, instead she would buy bolts of cloth and make her own skirts. She was shy of 5 feet tall and after all the kids she had, she was chunky. She would wear the skirts she made for years. At times she would add a white lace trim to the hem of her skirts regardless of the print in order to change them up. At Back to School night she wore a skirt that had the lace at the bottom with a white top, and I was mortified. I was so embarrassed because she didn't look like any of the other parents there and she was unable to communicate with anyone. The other moms wore coordinated outfits, tops and pants, or dresses, with nice shoes, jewelry, and carefully done makeup. When I think back to that day, I feel so much shame. I neglected to consider how she must have felt. It must have been a very traumatic encounter for her, and yet she went. She did it for me. If anything, I should have applauded her courage and her belief in me that drove her to be there. Regrets ... there are so many…

In sixth grade, I became the editor of our school newspaper. I do not know how I pulled it off, but today as I look back on my life's accomplishments, being school editor is something I am very proud of, especially since I was still working at mastering the English language. This was at about the time that Lynne was Student Panel president. I had wanted David Kieselburg to win the Student Panel presidency because I liked him and he was in my classroom. In the end Lynne won.

Fond memories from sixth grade — running alongside Lynne during a track meet at school and playing softball during recess, realizing my athletic ability, being able to complete 35-40 sit-ups, and having the stamina to run long distances. My confidence was growing, I was making friends, things were looking up. In sixth grade I started to like myself, which helped me get through the next three years of my life.

<u>5</u>

Who Am I And Who
Do I Want To Be?

My junior high school years had to be the most traumatic and turbulent of my entire life. It's a scary transition from elementary school to begin with, and then we are thrown into an environment where we interact with eighth and ninth graders who aren't the most pleasant or welcoming. A tough transition for most, I suspect.

I started seventh grade in September 1967; I was 12 years old. It was pretty scary having to grow up and take ownership of myself, getting to classes on time and completing homework. During orientation when we decided what classes we needed to take, I wondered how I could possibly be qualified to decide what courses I should be in. Even with the counselor's guidance, it was intimidating. It's not like my parents could help me decide; neither one of them had a clue and my older sister or brothers weren't about to waste their time talking to me about which classes I should take. I had nightmares worrying about not finding my classes in time before the bell rang or not remembering my locker combination, or forgetting my gym clothes at home and getting detention for it. It all just seemed so overwhelming, but like everyone else who goes through this, I muddled along.

I struggled with a sense of identity in junior high school that didn't exist at Roosevelt Elementary. I noticed that at Whaley, White kids had White friends, Black kids had Black friends, and Hispanics hung out with Hispanics. Most of the kids I knew from Roosevelt were White, with few exceptions. I wasn't particularly concerned initially, but I started to sense a change in some of my friends' attitudes toward me. No one bothered with me or said anything about the people I associated with. I was a nerd by any definition and was probably invisible to most people anyway. I hung out with the "smart" kids: Lynne, David Keiselburg, David White, Steve Sugita, and others who transferred over from Roosevelt with me. We were a diverse group even then. Lynne, and the two Davids were White, Steve was Japanese-American, and then, of course, there was me. We took most of the same classes and we all got good grades. We weren't friends who particularly hung out, but I knew I could count on this group to support me. The kids from my neighborhood, Vicki, Peter and Kevin, Lorraine, Beth, and even the Garcias who lived almost to the end of the block, were more my friends than anyone else. The Garcias were Jehovah's Witnesses, but that didn't deter their kids from going trick or treating with us on Halloween. We played every day after school once homework was done and didn't usually go inside until it was dark outside. It was a blessing that my father worked nights because it allowed me to stay out until dark without fear of reprimand.

Gradually everyone in my neighborhood began to move away with the exception of the Garcias. My best friend, Vicki, went to Whaley for the first year but she was a casualty of the White flight as well that started about this time in Compton. This forced me to try to make better friends with my schoolmates. I only associated with my "school friends" at school and neighborhood friends while at home, but once Vicki moved away this changed. At some point, Lynne and I became closer friends and I would either walk or ride my bike to her house. She had a group of friends of her own so we really didn't spend all of our time together, yet I remember her being at my house quite often in the summertime. We would play softball in the middle of my street, popping flies up to each other and taking turns catching and hitting. We knew we were friends and maintained an active relationship while at school. I met two of her brothers at one time and knew her sister Jeanne, yet I never met her parents. I knew her mom was a nurse and her dad was a preacher and understood that they were professionals who were at work during the day. I didn't think much about it really. I was there to hang out with Lynne and that's what we did.

I met Gloria Morales in seventh grade and started spending more and more time with her. She was an A student as well and was in many of my classes. She was born in the United States and only spoke English. She and I joined the Spelling Club and were both Members of the Girls Athletic Association (GAA) along with Vicki and Lynne. Turns out Bonita was also in the Spelling Club, but I did not know her yet. We were also members of the Christmas Club at Whaley. In time Gloria and I began to spend time at each other's houses doing homework or just hanging out talking about school or watching TV. Her mom loved crossword puzzles, something that I also enjoyed, so we would help her solve them from time to time. Gloria was very quiet and shy at school, but when she was at home, she was different. Ignorant and naïve me, I thought she was boy crazy. She just happened to have a crush on an older boy who lived in her neighborhood. I had never looked at boys as anything other than people with whom to play softball, basketball, or football. I didn't understand Gloria's view of boys and what they represented. She was the first friend I made who didn't transfer from Roosevelt and didn't live on my street. She lived with her two sisters and her mom, and she had an older brother. Until then, I had not met anyone who lived in a single-parent home. This was unusual to me. Her mother was very independent and self-reliant, something else I was not quite familiar with.

I loved my Spanish class. Spanish being my first language, it was obviously a very easy class for me, but what really made an impact was how Mr. Lombardi, my teacher, showed an authentic interest in my learning. He took to me for some reason and would challenge me in class. I was struggling with who I was, where I belonged, and where I fit in, and I found myself changing my hairstyle, trying on new makeup, and wearing new clothes. One day I showed up in bell bottoms! Crop tops were popular in those days, but I only wore them at home. I couldn't imagine wearing them to school. My upbringing instilled some humility and modesty in me that kept me from being too outlandish with my appearance, but that doesn't mean I didn't try new things. When I put my hair up in a partial ponytail that hung down and covered half of my face, it didn't take long for Mr. Lombardi to approach me on it.

"What are you thinking?! Get that hair out of your face."

Looking back, I think he was watching to make sure I didn't go down the wrong path. I wish I had been mature enough back then to understand his motives so that I could have thanked him.

Mr. Lombardi held a contest once for the students in his class and the winner would get to teach one class during our class period. While I don't remember what the challenge was, I certainly remember the outcome: I won! I taught everyone how to conjugate verbs, a dreaded new skill for students of Spanish. I showed them how to distinguish between past, present, and future tenses. I could feel the support from them. They smiled and appreciated having me explain what was so difficult for them to understand. Mr. Lombardi sat at the back of the room beaming while I conducted class. For the first time in my life I saw my potential. I was no longer invisible. He made a positive difference in my life and at that moment I knew I could make a difference in the lives of others. I believe that's when I decided I wanted to be a teacher.

I met Susan Jacobo in seventh grade when she stepped out of Mr. Lombardi's class and we started to talk. We became quick friends. She was one of nine kids being raised by a single mom, which was especially hard in those days. Still, they always had enough for themselves and welcomed guests at their table. I was invited to eat at her house quite often. We only ate normal Mexican food like tacos and rice, but even then, I appreciated it as exceptional. With so many mouths to feed, they never hesitated to feed me as well and we dined together as one big happy family. They lived right behind the Compton Drive-In. We would watch movies from her house even though we couldn't hear everything that was said in the movie. I have fond memories of the times I spent with her and her family. Susan and I continued to be friends well into our high school years. We joined a Mexican folkloric dance group (Baile Folklorico) while at Dominguez High School and we performed at various venues including schools, senior citizen centers, and once at Olvera Street, a major tourist site in L.A. that has been around since before 1877 and is part of the El Pueblo de Los Angeles Historic Monument that preserves the Mexican culture so important in California's history. That was pretty amazing. We practiced weekly so our relationship developed during this time period. It was a large dance group and what we learned Susan and I later used to our advantage when we later taught folkloric dance together at the Paramount Community center to a small group of kids. Our kids performed at a Cinco de Mayo festival in downtown Paramount. We were so proud! Susan and I still keep in touch to this day. As the year progressed, seventh grade turned out to be a pretty good year. Classes were easy enough and I earned A's in most of my classes. I got along with everyone I met and felt good about myself. I liked being liked, I was walking with my head up, making eye contact with others, receiving smiles and "hi's" vs. sneers and disdain. I grew stronger and more confident in my abilities and in my knowledge. I stood taller and walked with a purpose while looking ahead, instead of at my feet. I felt a solid standing in my life again, with a great group of friends and motivated by my newfound confidence as a student. I was so unaware of the shifting ground I stood upon; unaware of how the changes in demographics in my community and school would implode into a social crisis that would transform my every day as I knew it.

I didn't see or feel the changes in the demography of school until Thursday, April 4, 1968. That was the day when Martin Luther

King, Jr. was assassinated. He was shot at 6:01 PM EST, which is 3:01 PM here in California. Once the news got out, which I suspect some of the teachers shared in their classrooms, the Black kids at school started rioting, running through the halls, yelling, banging and denting the lockers, and throwing trash cans. People were crying and running and punching at anything they could get their hands on and beating up anyone who wasn't Black. It was the end of the school day anyway and we were all leaving our classrooms to go home. As I walked across the lunch area to exit school, Beverly Poston looked at me and said, "don't you wish you were Black"? I didn't respond; I was as stunned as everyone else. It was either a threat or a challenge but either way it stung. I knew something had shifted and we were no longer equal in each other's eyes simply based on the color of our skin. Any progress that African-Americans made in bringing equality and fairness to Blacks certainly brought the same to Hispanics. I still believe this. I can never identify with what their ancestors went through and the struggles that African-Americans go through today, but any progress in reducing racism, bias, or bigotry is beneficial for all minorities and others who are viewed and treated as outcasts by right-wing Americans. I hurried home, looking over my shoulder the entire way. It was a very sad day for everyone of color, and for the world.

Unrest continued in school for days after the assassination. Martin Luther King, Jr. was a clergyman and civil rights leader of that time. He believed in nonviolent protest and became spokesperson for the Civil Rights movement. As a Baptist minister, his faith and vision led him to believe that one day there would be equality among all Americans regardless of color or race. He witnessed and endured for many years the mistreatment of Blacks by police officers, employers, and the government. I learned later that he first experienced racism when he was 5 or 6 years old. His best friend was White and one day he told MLK, Jr. that his father told him he couldn't play with him anymore. By 1968, the Black Panthers had become involved in the cause as well, but they didn't hesitate to use violence as a means to get results. Martin Luther King, Jr. believed that through diplomacy and peaceful means, the world would listen. He was the voice of freedom and he carried the country on his shoulders. When he died, we lost a champion of peace, love, freedom, equality, and humanity.

Returning to school the next day, I noticed the number of Black students who attended Whaley. I had not noticed the gradual change because it wasn't important to me; it didn't matter. I realized then it was going to matter what race we were, moving forward.

Beth, Lorraine, and their family moved out of the neighborhood, followed by Peter and Kevin. Peter and Kevin remained in Compton and ended up on Myrrh Street near Atlantic Ave. Vicki, my best friend in the whole world, followed everyone else by the end of the summer. I didn't know what I would do without her. She was my first true friend and I struggled with her leaving. We did, however, get a chance to have one last memorable summer together. The time with my friends made up for the dysfunction and disconnect of my family. As miserable as we were at home while my father was in the house, the things I experienced and learned on San Marcus Street made that time of my life one of the happiest. I cannot thank all those kids enough for all the great memories. I learned through them how different my life was compared to theirs, but I also learned the value of friendship.

As I mentioned, Peter and Kevin were foster children who lived next door to us. They appeared to be afraid of Jack and we noticed that Jackie had them doing all the household chores. They cleaned, cooked, washed, mowed the lawn, etc. Jackie would sit on the front porch with her cigarette while Jack would spend time in their above-ground pool in the backyard, naked. Vicki could see him naked in the backyard from the window in her den. She suspected that he knew she was watching. Her mom, Millie, complained to Jack and Jackie about it, but it never changed. Vicki would sometimes go to Jackie's house after school because Millie worked. When Millie witnessed Jack's nude adventures in his back yard, she told Jackie he should stop behaving like that.

"You have kids in the house! Jack should not be walking around with no clothes on! And think of Peter and Kevin — they're your foster kids and need to be protected. My daughter is there every day after school, too. It's not appropriate." Jackie would have none of it. She was offended by the mere suggestion of inappropriate behavior. "This is my house and I will do what I want. You are no one to tell us what to do in our own home!" A fight quickly started, and Jackie and Millie began pushing and pulling each other's hair. Jackie, a constant smoker, ended up with tousled hair and a cigarette snapped in half still hanging out of her mouth. She had to know what he was doing, but she defended Jack for the pervert he was. Vicki never went over again.

From time to time we would hear the boys crying or screaming at night. I assumed they were being whipped by Jack for doing something wrong. We would be beaten with the belt, also, or kicked around the room, so we attributed their crying and screaming to the same reasons.

A couple of years after they moved to Myrrh Street, we were invited to a birthday party for one of the boys. It turned out that Peter and Kevin were brothers and they had two sisters who were also in the foster care system. Jack and Jackie had become foster parents for their two sisters, Dorothy and Barbara, whom we met at the birthday party. They also had a baby with them who had to be less than nine months old. The baby was not related to the boys. Many years later when I was in high school, Jackie brought her dog, Tinker, to our house and asked my mother if she would please give it a home. We had dogs, cats, rabbits, and ducks already, so one more dog wasn't going to make a difference. Jackie informed us that she was moving away because Jack was in prison for sexually molesting the boys and their sisters. I could not believe what I heard. How could we have been so stupid? Why did we not ask them about those nights when we heard them crying? I felt so guilty and ashamed for my ignorance. All those years Peter and Kevin never said a word about it to us, but then it all started to make sense to me. The fear they had for Jack. How they jumped straight up when they were called into the house by Jack or Jackie. The nights we heard them crying and screaming. It was such a horrible revelation. It also made sense as a dark memory came to mind. On my twelfth birthday, I found myself at Peter and Kevin's house. One of the boys mentioned to Jackie that it was my birthday. Next thing you know, I was sitting on Jack's lap and he kissed me twelve times on the mouth. I jumped up, ran out the door, and went straight into my bathroom where I washed my mouth and face over and over again. I dared not say anything to anyone because I knew my dad would beat me for letting it happen. Jack was too bold; his wife Jackie had to know what he'd been up to. To this day, knowing the relationship that Jackie had with Jack, I believe that she knew what was going on in her home and had kept silent. I've tried to find Peter and Kevin through the years and have been unsuccessful in finding them. I assume they changed their last names at some point to protect their privacy. So often I think of them and want to tell them how oblivious we all were to their suffering. Jack got what he deserved, but not soon enough; he left too much carnage in his wake.

I had completely forgotten about my twelfth birthday until I was summoned to jury duty in 2013. I had been asked to appear in a case of sexual abuse of a child, and during jury selection, one potential juror, a young woman in her early twenties, asked to be excused because she had been a victim of abuse as a child. Then another potential juror asked to be excused. We started dropping like flies. It was at that moment when I remembered what Jack had done to me. I couldn't even speak. The judge excused me without me having to say anything. The look on my face must have said enough.

A few months ago, I was talking to Vicki, my old friend from Compton, and Peter and Kevin came up. I mentioned what happened to me with Jack and she said she had heard about it. She wasn't there at Kevin and Peter's house that day, but she had heard about it. She knew, long before anyone else, what Jack was capable of and that Jackie covered up for him.

Eighth grade changed my life forever. In June, 1968, when I was 13 years old, a Filipino family moved in across the street from my house. They were an older couple with two daughters, the younger one of whom had Down's Syndrome. I saw other people come and go from the house from time to time; they turned out to be older children of the couple. In total the couple had eleven kids, four of their own and seven from previous marriages.

Peter (Jr.) was my brother Richard's age and it turned out that they knew each other. They hung out with the same crowd in high school, which was a pleasant surprise for both of them. That first Christmas my mother gave them a turkey, which helped to bond our families closer together. Mrs. Edralin could speak six different languages and dialects, one being Castilian, which was basically Spanish, allowing her to communicate with my mother who only spoke Spanish. They were very kind, giving, and caring people who would end up being my sponsors for my citizenship application when I was eighteen.

On December 29, 1968 I noticed a new face at Mrs. Edralin's house. I was outside with the neighborhood kids taking turns with the baseball bat popping up fly balls. The new kid sat on a chair in their front porch and I thought it would be nice to invite him to join us. Boy was I caught by surprise! I asked him if he would like to play with us and he responded with an expletive. He said that he didn't want to look like a "bleeping" idiot like the rest of us. I stood there for close to 10 seconds not knowing how to respond. In fact, I didn't say anything, I just turned and walked away madder than heck. I had never heard that word directed at me and it really ticked me off, especially since I was just trying to be nice.

When we returned to school after the Christmas holiday, I found myself looking for him. I worked in the school office during one of my class periods and would look at the attendance roster to see if he was in school that day. Funny thing though, I didn't even know his name. Even after I learned from his grandmother that his name was Mike, I still didn't know his last name. I initially assumed it was

Edralin, but I never came across that name in the school absence roster.

In time, we began to talk after school sitting on his grandmother's front porch. My sisters Lydia and Martha would go across the street with me and we would just hang out. I realized that he was a punk kid with major attitude, but I could also tell that he was very intelligent. Since I didn't see him at school, I assumed that he probably went to Dominguez High School, and the fact that he told me he was 17 years old aided in my confusion. Turns out he was only 12 years old — a year younger than me. He was hateful and bitter and just plain mean, except around his grandmother and grandfather. It was evident that he had a lot of respect for them or he feared them. His grandparents called him "Pudgy," which I had never heard before and I asked him how he spelled it. He tore a corner from a grocery bag that was sitting on the chair next to him. We were sitting on the porch steps. He went in

Mike, Becky's boyfriend and future husband, 1973

the house for a pencil and sat back down beside me. After he wrote it down, I reached for the piece of paper and our hands touched. At that moment I heard a voice in my head say, "this is the guy I'm going to marry," which completely and utterly confounded me! I know my face turned red because I felt flush and heat come over me.

I learned quickly what a big mistake it was to have feelings for this guy. He hardly ever went to school; he was always ditching, getting high, or messing around with some girl from school. Somehow none of that mattered; I was already smitten. At the time I met him, he was living with his mother on Mulberry Street in Compton. He was from the Largo, a well-known Mexican gang in Compton, well-known by rival gangs in the area and the local police. Unfortunately, Largo's reputation as a dangerous gang was because of their reckless antics. They protected their neighborhood from outsiders by any means necessary. I'm sure he was involved in many of the gang-related activities that occurred in Compton in that era. He made a point of keeping me in the dark about anything he was involved in, like shootings and beatings, and today I appreciate NOT knowing. Mike's life was harder and more complicated than I would ever expect. He had been through so much at such a young age, as had his family.

Mike's Story

Grandma Edralin was born and raised in the Philippines. She was half Filipino and half Irish. She met her American (German) husband when he was stationed there at the army camp, and in time they had six children. When the Japanese invaded the Philippines the day after Pearl Harbor was bombed during WWII, she and Alice, Mike's mother-to-be, were at the marketplace in Manila while the other kids were home with their father. It took them three months to reunite with their family. Together they all went and hid in the caves above the village, protecting their children from being caught. Their skin was white among the dark-skinned villagers and they easily stood out. General McArthur fled and instructed the army soldiers to hold on until help arrived. It never did. The Filipino and American soldiers were forced to surrender. Thousands of soldiers were taken and marched to Batan. This was later called the Batan Death March because so many soldiers died.

Grandma was left alone to protect her six children. The Japanese had heard of the American family living in the caves and actively searched for them. Together they traveled many hundreds of miles on the island of Luzon staying ahead of the Japanese. Before his capture, Grandpa Light made arrangements with the Igorot tribe (native Filipinos) to protect his family. They did the best they could, some of them losing their lives in the process. Of all her children, Alice (Mike's mom) was the strongest and bravest. She was just 10 or 11 years old and would sneak into the local villages or Japanese camps at night to steal food, water, and medicine. Her younger brother Sonny, only eight years old, decided to leave the family and go off into the jungle on his own. As they traveled from village to village, staying ahead of the Japanese soldiers, they heard stories of a white boy who was fighting the Japanese alongside the guerrillas.

After the war, Grandma and the kids joined their father in Virginia where he was raised. In time Grandma divorced her husband and traveled to California with her kids. After a few years she met and married Grandpa Edralin and together they all moved to Hatchway Street in Compton.

Mike's mother, Alice, moved to Seattle, Washington, with her sister Evelyn when she was just 23, where she met and fell deeply in love with Mike's father. He was in the U.S. Navy, stationed there in Washington. They met in a diner on the waterfront in Seattle where Alice and Evelyn worked. Three months later, she realized she was pregnant and her mother, Grandma Edralin, told her to come back home to Compton. Alice asked Alfredo to join her. He couldn't accompany her at that moment, but he vowed to follow her to California on his next leave.

Alfredo visited her only once, when Mike was two years old. He left to return to his duty station, asking Alice to join him, but Grandma wouldn't let her leave. She never heard from him again.

Many years later Alice had a nervous breakdown and was unable to go back to work. Sadly, her mental state continued to deteriorate over the years and eventually she was diagnosed as paranoid schizophrenic.

Grandma took over raising Mike. She already had her children from Light and by now also had four children with Grandpa Edralin. She raised Mike as her own for the next eight years. The younger Edralin siblings were resentful of Alice and Mike and often poked fun at both of them.

Julianna was the most devious of the younger Edralin kids. She said mean things to Alice and Mike, letting them know that they didn't belong there and weren't wanted in the household. All of the Edralin kids were still at home and they made it quite clear that he was not one of them and didn't belong in the house. They took his toys and broke them and called him a bastard. Julianna was relentless when it came to harassing them. During one of her usual passive aggressive taunts, Alice grabbed her by the neck and started to choke her. Alice had survived WW II. She had kept her siblings and mother safe during the war, and knew how to defend herself. Julianna should have known better than to push her too far. Grandma ran in yelling and hitting Alice, forcing her to let Julianna go. Unfortunately, this resulted in Julianna convincing Grandma that Alice was too dangerous and should move out on her own. By now they were living in a larger house on Mulberry Street in Compton. There was a house for rent across the street, which was opportune for Alice.

Before he knew it, Mike and Alice were moved into that house. He could not believe that they would put him and his mother out on their own, knowing that she was not mentally well. He hated them so much, especially his aunts who were so smug about getting them out of the house. Mike was only 10 years old and forced to live with a mentally ill woman he really didn't know. He had been raised by his grandmother; hardly ever seeing his mom because she had worked nights. Already full of rage and bitterness over how he had been treated by his family, he felt abandoned by his grandmother. Living with his "crazy" mother, with no one to turn to, he turned to the streets.

With no supervision, he started running the streets. He met up with older guys 16-19 years of age, a mixture of White and Mexican guys, and hung out with them. They'd drink and smoke reefer (marijuana). They knew his older uncles and thought he was their little brother, accepting him into their circle of alcohol, drugs, and crime. On one occasion while hanging out behind Moreland Mortuary on Willowbrook and Rosecrans where they often went to get high, he met a guy who lived next door. This guy would later shoot at Lynne and me with a BB gun one Halloween when she and I were trick-or-treating down on San Vincente Street. He and Mike hit it off and began to hang out together. His family was affiliated with a Mexican organized crime syndicate known as the Mexican Mafia. They provided heroin, drugs, and weapons to the local neighborhoods and penal system. One evening when Mike was hanging out with the family, they were raided by the local and federal authorities. Numerous weapons and drugs were seized. Adult males were arrested and the remaining family, including Mike, were questioned and released. At the time members of various local gangs such as the Compton Barrio Three, Tortilla Flats, Willowbrook, and Largo were on semi-friendly terms. Most of them had known each other from school, church, and/or catechism. Based on the close proximity of the neighborhoods, it was inevitable that they would become mortal enemies in the future.

Mike for one was not into the "cholo" look, which was the way many of the gangs would dress; the Largo guys were more casual. They dressed in jeans, wallabies, and t-shirts, which was more what Mike was into. Although Mike knew guys from the other gangs, he was more in tune with the Largo guys. He did not feel inclined to join any of their gangs; he was content to hang out with them.

When he was 12-13 years old, Mike found himself cornered right in front of Whaley after school when two carloads of rival gang members jumped out and started beating him up. He fought them as best as he could, but there were too many of them. Just then a girl he did not know pulled up in her car, opened the door, and yelled, "get in!" which he did. It turned out to be an older sister of one of his classmates who picked him up then dropped him off at his grandmother's house. This all took place in front of the school as everyone was leaving for the day. Mr. Adams, our principal, like everyone else, saw the whole thing happen and went to see Mike at his grandmother's house. Mike told one of his Largo friends about the incident and his friend said, "you realize that would not have happened if they knew you from the Largo." It was shortly after this incident that he agreed to be initiated into the Largo.

Mike became more and more rebellious. He did not get the best education, but he was well-read. With his hatred for his father and anger for what had happened to his mother, he did what he wanted when he wanted, and didn't care about consequences. He was kicked out of Whaley in eighth grade for drug possession and ended up at a school for juvenile delinquents and criminal wannabes who had been kicked out of school like he had. He went to Harriet Tubman continuation school, located adjacent to Compton High School. There he met future convicts and murderers; he saw it as a mini-prison and school for how to become a criminal and how to survive. Kids in trouble for smoking reefer were thrown in with criminals who were already involved in serious crimes.

His reputation as someone to be reckoned with on the streets of Compton was solidified when he punched out a well-known drug dealer from the neighborhood. Wally was a major player in the distribution of Seconal (red devils) in Compton. Mike joined some of the older guys on a visit to this man's backyard. Feeling all-powerful and in control, Wally made a move to grab Mike, since he was just a 12-year-old kid. Reacting to the sudden movement, Mike swung up and hit him in the throat. Wally went down choking, and the older guys, knowing that there would be retaliation, told Mike to leave. Thereafter Mike started spending more time at his grandmother's house across the street from us, trying to lay low and stay out of sight. By the time I met Mike he was already from the Largo and well known on the streets and by the police. By the time I left to go to UC San Diego, he had already been arrested 16 times.

****

When Mike attended Whaley, we would walk home from school together and maybe meet up later in the evening on his grandmother's porch or mine. I started to like him a lot; I'd never felt like this before about any boy I had ever known. These feelings were new to me and I didn't understand them. Spring became summer and then school was out. That summer he spent about 90% of his time at his grandmother's house so we would spend a lot of time talking or visiting with his family. This went on most of the summer until my parents realized that there was more than just a friendship between us. I suspect I gave myself away by the way I looked at him or how much time I was spending with him each day.

Eighth grade was tough. 1968 was tough! Bobby Kennedy was assassinated, which was a tragic blow to America. He believed in equality for all and was highly regarded by minority groups. As always, someone who looked out for and cared about the plight of minorities was taken from us. During this time period Cesar Chavez was also in the news. During this time he organized a five-year strike by farm workers against table grape growers in California. He spoke on behalf of Chicano farm workers who couldn't speak for themselves. Along with Delores Huerta, he founded the National Farm Workers Association, a union for farm workers, fighting for collective bargaining with wealthy growers, and basic needs for workers, such as decent work hours, and pay, and medical benefits. He became their voice, especially since many of them did not speak English. He led strikes and boycotts, and brought attention to the "forgotten minority." Also in the news was talk about strikes by Chicano high school students in the Los Angeles area protesting treatment received from teachers and administrators after having had enough of the oppressive school conditions. Chicano students were not encouraged to go to college and were tracked toward vocational schools or the military instead. Spanish was not allowed to be spoken in classrooms, handicapping many Chicanos with their education. In 1968, 15,000 Chicano students walked out of L.A. schools in protest, putting their concerns in the spotlight. Cesar Chavez was the last well-known voice for Hispanics. The Hispanic community has not had strong leadership or support to encourage society to understand the plight of our people. Today Hispanics are viewed as pariah; society does not see all that we do for the U.S. and how much we contribute to its success and progress. We need a strong leader who will not bend to the tantrums of a wannabe dictator, but rather to stand up for what is right, moral, and beneficial for the country as a whole.

Hostility and anger was abundant in the '60s. Blacks didn't like Whites or Mexicans/Chicanos. Chicanos despised the White man, and the White man didn't trust either. We were all becoming more and more aware of racial tension and I for one had had enough. Walking down the hallway toward my next class, an Hispanic girl stared me down as she approached me. When we got close enough, she asked, "What are you doing hanging out with White people?" Or I would be asked by another random person, "Do you think you're too good to hang out with us?" I didn't know how to respond. I had my friends and race had no bearing on that whatsoever and it really upset me that others thought it should. I resisted and did not allow anyone to tell me who my friends should be. As Whaley became predominantly Black, we found ourselves looking over our shoulders from time to time. Although my close friends consisted of every race and nationality, it didn't protect me from the resentment of others who did not know me personally. At our school, we would hear about White or Hispanic girls or guys going into the bathroom and getting beat up by a mob, just for being White or Hispanic. You never knew when it was going to be your turn.

I joined the GAA, which required me to take sixth period P.E. We participated in intramural sports along with other junior high schools in Compton. We ran track, and played softball, field hockey, volleyball, and basketball. I really enjoyed sixth period P.E. because it allowed me to walk home in my gym clothes if I chose to. One of the best things that happened from my association with this group is that we all got to know each other better. By all I mean Blacks, Hispanics, and Whites. Some of the Hispanic girls who gave me lip were in GAA as well. We didn't associate with each other, but our teams would play against each other. We learned to get along or to at least leave each other alone. In spite of it all, it was a positive experience for me because people stopped hassling me about who my friends should be. They got to know me, what I was all about, which possibly changed their viewpoint of me. I was Mexican through and through, proud of my heritage, my culture, and hanging out with non-Mexicans did not change me in that regard. Some of the Hispanic girls would start saying hello when going to our other classes, others just stopped glaring at me or saying anything negative.

Lynne, Bonita, and I were usually on the same winning team, which allowed us to leave school to participate in the cross-school competitions. When we traveled to other schools, we were always the only school with a racially mixed team. Other schools didn't particularly like it and they made it obvious by saying things and looking at us with disdain. My favorite memory in GAA is when Lynne, Bonita, Evita, and I ran the 400 relay and won. When track season began for GAA, we decided to run together as a team. According to Bonita, there was a strategy involved in selecting who would start and who would be anchor. We were a force to be reckoned with. Lynne always took front position and Bonita, being the fastest, always came up last to close any gaps and take the lead. In my mind, the best part of our team was not that we beat the other teams, but that we were a diverse team of friends, something that was uncommon at that time. Lynne would pass the baton to Evita; who would pass to me, and I would pass to Bonita who always ran as if wings grew out of her heels so we finished strong. We were the best relay team; we just couldn't be beat.

Despite my close friendship with Bonita, because of what had happened during the Watts Riots, my mother would not allow us to bring our Black friends to the house. I wanted Bonita to visit with me, but I couldn't bring her home. So, I shared with Bonita my concern and told her what had happened to us during the Watts riot and that my mother might not be receptive to her visiting. Bonita did not let that deter her. She wanted to meet my mom in hopes of winning her over… and did she! Bonita brought a flower to my mom that first day she came to my house. My mother accepted it, but walked away without a word. Surprisingly, she did not forbid me from bringing her back. The next time Bonita visited, she again presented my mom with a flower, and this time my mom smiled, but still did not respond. She turned around and walked away. This went on for a few weeks until finally my mom's heart was warmed and she welcomed Bonita to our home. My mom came to love Bonita and appreciate what a wonderful friend she was to me.

Not necessarily on weekends but probably more often during summer months, the four of us would gather to play softball on my street. My mom would feed us sometimes, other times we just played, taking turns hitting and catching the ball. We did not talk about school so much when we were together, rather we enjoyed being with each other and playing softball, something we all loved to do. Just spending time together was important. I spent more time with Lynne than I spent with Bonita and Evita, but it was always a good vibe anytime we were together.

Compton was predominantly Black by this time and racial relations were increasingly turbulent. Mexican girls sneaking into the bathrooms by themselves to smoke were occasionally beat up by Black girls, for no apparent reason other than whimsy. Whites were definitely picked on and the focus of much frustration and anger. I didn't have any problems with the White or Black kids, nor they with me most of the time, but occasionally I'd encounter a handful of Black girls who were verbally abusive to me just because I was not Black. I was lucky in that I was never beat up while at Whaley, but I came close once. Lynne, Bonita, and I were leaving the gym at the end of sixth period one day. As we walked out, a mob of Black girls aggressively approached us. They were yelling and cursing at us. Their intentions were obvious and we mentally prepared for what was to come. Just then, Bonita — and a large Hispanic girl I didn't really know — stepped forward in front of Lynne and me. Bonita stated that if they wanted us, they would have to go through her. I was scared, but the lead girls in the mob stared at Bonita for a few seconds and then they walked away. I don't know if Bonita or Lynne remember this, but I will never forget it. I cannot imagine what possessed Bonita to stand up for us. She must have been just as afraid as Lynne and I were, but she was certainly more courageous.

I have to admit that it never occurred to me to ask Bonita or Lynne if they were ever attacked or taunted by anyone. They were both popular because of their academic status and because of GAA. I know that of the three of us, Lynne was the most outnumbered, but she had plenty of friends and was well liked. I would never have thought that anything would have happened to her. In retrospect, Bonita probably took the most guff because she hung out with Lynne, Evita, and me. I suspect she was told to keep away or suffer the consequences. If this was the case, she never shared with us.

My association with Mike brought a sense of awareness of me to others. People were curious about me, wondering why a goody-two-shoes like me would have anything to do with someone like him, and vice versa. People who knew him would make eye contact with me, but wouldn't say anything. His reputation as someone not to be messed with helped ME avoid confrontation with some, but not with others. In fact, some girls were out to get me specifically because of my relationship with him. Lynne and Bonita both thought I was smarter than to pursue someone that was not good for me.

He was not a very nice person, truly. He was bitter and angry most of the time. He cursed at everyone, which intimidated most people. He was tough and would challenge the toughest kids at school, which resulted in people staying as far away from him as possible. When we would sit on his grandmother's porch and talk, he was attentive, kind, and friendly. At school, he was insensitive to my feelings for him, yet he showed jealousy when he saw me speaking to other guys. I didn't get him at all. From the time I met him to the time I graduated from high school, he broke my heart repeatedly, more times than I care to admit. I can't believe I kept going back with him after each incident. What was wrong with me? I was a smart kid, I was a strong person, yet he had a hold on me that I cannot explain to this day. I was a lonely kid and I sensed loneliness in him as well. Sometimes I believe that he and I were both looking for something more or better in our lives and we found it in each other. I was a senior in high school when we stopped fighting our feelings for each other and accepted the truth.

One Monday morning when I arrived at Whaley, I ran into him in the office. He had the largest hickey on his neck and all he did was smile at me. Furious, I wrote him a letter telling him how much he had hurt me by being so callous and indifferent. I put the letter in his locker, knowing that he would get to it sometime during the day. Later that day as I was walking to the cafeteria, I came upon a group of kids huddled in the hallway near the lockers. They were laughing as a boy read something out loud to the group. As I got closer, I realized that he was reading the letter I wrote Mike! I felt so violated and embarrassed. Evidently, Mike read the letter, shrugged it off, and handed it to the first person to walk by. The letter, my soul that I poured out to him, meant absolutely nothing to him. Looking back, it is pretty funny, but it hurt me to the core then. I could not understand how anyone could be so callous and unfeeling. But as I got to know more about him through his family, I began to see the triggers and circumstances that made him what he was.

Ninth grade was when I felt a strong sense of confidence and felt comfortable in my shoes. I don't know what prompted it or why I pursued it, but I ran for Student Body president, and won. What I remember the most about this prestigious position is that I got to start every morning speaking over the intercom to the entire school to say the pledge of allegiance. I was also able to share the results of sporting events that our school teams participated in. At school meetings or performances, I led students in the pledge of allegiance and introduced the principal and the performing groups. Mike sang with the choir so there were times when we shared the stage.

I spent most of my time with Susan Jacobo or Gloria Morales the last two years in junior high school. I had gotten very close with each, but not with both of them together, which is an interesting dynamic that I had not thought of until recently. I don't know exactly why Lynne and I strayed from each other. She had her own friends as well, but we had always made time for each other. I suppose we were all growing up and changing during those years. Junior high was tough, but not due to peer pressure per se, it was just tough. We were all trying to find ourselves while looking over our shoulders, trying to decide who or what we wanted to be.

One day I brought to the attention of the principal the fact that we had never celebrated Cinco de Mayo at the school and told him that it would be nice to give the Hispanic kids the opportunity. We were given the OK and I proceeded to teach some of the girls from GAA a couple of Mexican dances. Bonita and our friend Evita also participated. I asked about eight girls to practice at my house in preparation. We rehearsed a few times before the performance. We were very proud to have a part in something that was intended to change the view and perspective of Mexican history and culture. It probably meant more to me than it did overall to the school or the community.

We were allowed to hold an outdoor assembly and we performed outdoors by the basketball courts. Our group performed a couple of old Mexican traditional dances and to my shock and admiration, another larger group of younger Hispanic girls also performed a type of line dance. I was not familiar with them, since they were seventh and eighth graders, but they must have solicited volunteers to participate. The girls did a great job performing their well-choreographed routine to a Santana song. To my amazement, it turned out to be a very successful event for the entire student body.

As I mentioned earlier, I loved school because it took me away from my dysfunctional personal life, so I never skipped a day. However, in ninth grade when I took an extra 15 minutes after my lunch due to a menstrual "accident," I was almost disqualified from receiving a perfect attendance award.

Gloria worked in the office for class credit and found out that I was being considered for a perfect attendance award for my three years at Whaley. She became aware that it was being discussed whether I should receive the award or not. I had asked for permission to go home and change and those extra 15 minutes had created the debate. I don't know what Gloria said, but she fought for me to receive the award. At the awards assembly for the graduating class, I received the Foreign Legion Award and a Perfect Attendance Certificate. I couldn't feel prouder. My parents had never attended a school assembly on my behalf until then. The school had contacted them and asked for their attendance as the Foreign Legion Award was one of the top awards given by the school. I was surprised to see them both in the audience. This was definitely a rare occurrence. My father never said so, but I saw pride in his face.

When I look back on my school years, I gravitate to my time at Whaley. I had the best friends and the best time. Although those years were wrought with personal pain from my family life, a never-ending ache in my heart because of Mike, I will always be thankful for the people who were in my life then. Vicki, Lorraine, Moya, Gloria, Susan, Lynne, and Bonita. My mother and father learned about my involvement with Mike around ninth grade and they were not happy about it. My dad forbade me to speak to him, but I wasn't having it. I snuck out of my house so many times just to spend time with him. I would drive around the block and pick him up on my way to the beach or the park with my younger brothers and sisters. We would have the best time, until he upset one of them. He always ended up upsetting someone. It was hard to lie to my parents, it was hard asking my siblings to lie for me. There was just so much emotional garbage lingering in my heart all the time. Everything had to be so secretive. Was that part of the lure? Was that part of the excitement in seeing him? I don't know. But I do know that as a parent, I would never forbid my children from seeing anyone that I didn't like. I would never want to further push them into a relationship that I hoped would diminish in time.

Graduation day at Whaley was one of the saddest in my life. I always dreaded the end of the school year because that meant I would be spending most of my days at home. I couldn't go outside and spend time with my friends until after my father left for work. What a blessing that he worked nights and that after 3:00 PM we could rest easy in the house. It was also sad to leave Whaley because I had grown into myself so much those three years. I had great friends and feared not seeing them again.

We were all dressed in white and the ceremony was to take place outdoors near the basketball courts. Susan Jacobo had made up her mind to let Carlos De Jesus know that she loved him. So, when the opportunity arose, she walked up to him. I don't know if any words were spoken, but next thing we knew, they were kissing. Of course, just at that moment, my mother and father walked down the hallway and saw the whole thing. I didn't think Susan would be allowed to come over to my house ever again. Actually, my parents never mentioned it and Susan and I spent a lot of time together that summer. So, we ended ninth grade with a bang!

6

Who Have I Become?

My summers have always been memorable to me. In spite of a dysfunctional home life, it was a blessing that my father worked nights. He left every day in the afternoon and did not return until midnight. This gave us the entire evening to hang out with the neighborhood kids, play, ride my bike to Lynne's house, or walk to Gloria or Susan's house. It also gave me the opportunity to spend time with Mike when I wasn't supposed to.

By the time I was a sophomore in high school, my parents had found out about Mike and me and, once they learned more about him, they decided that I was not to spend any time with Mike. When my brothers and sisters saw me with him at parties and dances, they did not hesitate to share the news with my parents. They would threaten to tell my father that I had been with Mike at a party, but they never involved me in their conversations — not that it made any difference. I was forbidden to see Mike, which was very difficult to do, especially since he usually spent his summers across the street with his grandmother and grandfather. That's not to say he spent all his time with me. His priorities included hanging out with his friend Ben Herrera and the guys from the Largo. He and Ben, who lived close to me, would listen to music or just talk. Ben was very bright and taught himself to play the guitar. I envision Mike and Ben taking turns strumming the guitar and trying to make music.

Mike's evenings were usually spent down at the Largo, which was in close proximity to the Piru gang. These two gangs got along well for most of the early years, but later the Piru Street boys expanded to other areas, split up, and became Crips and Bloods. Mike never allowed me to drive down to the Largo to see him. He said it was dangerous; he didn't want me to get caught in the middle of a "drive-by." It was not uncommon for one or multiple cars loaded up with armed rival gang members to drive down surrounding streets with the intent to shoot at anything or anyone that moved.

Being 16 allowed me some new privileges, such as going to parties and dances. Hispanic girls celebrated their quinceañeras, coming of age at 15 or 16, so there was no shortage of parties to attend that year. Quinceañeras are a really big deal for our community. A church ceremony precedes a big family and friend celebration that includes dinner and dancing. Since both of my parents loved to dance, I was allowed to attend these gala events as long as I went with Richard or Patty, or brought Rosa along. It didn't matter to me as long as I got to go. Richard and Carlos were at the marrying age and as their friends were getting married, we would tag along to the receptions and dances. I learned quickly that I loved to dance. I couldn't get it out of my system; I just couldn't get enough. I have memories of many of these events where we just danced all night non-stop. I wish I had that stamina today!

What was really interesting to me was that although I did not hang out with the Mexican girls from school, other than those with whom I had GAA, they would sit with me or allow me to sit with them at parties. I sensed that they were looking out for me or taking care of me. I suspect that they were probably girlfriends of Mike's friends and kept an eye out because I was his girlfriend. At school they barely took notice of me, and I didn't have many of them in my classes. They were taking home economics classes while I was taking calculus or physics. When I'd get to a dance or party, my brother or sisters would quickly go their way with their friends. One time I was with my friend Susie and we ended up at Alma Hernandez's house. There they proceeded to get me to change my clothes before we went out. They didn't dress me sleezy, like in short skirts, or put a ton of makeup on me. They just got me to change out of the clothes that I would go to school in. I didn't solicit their friendship, but they were quick to accept me. However, once we got back to school on Monday, they again would walk by me in the halls and barely make eye contact with me. Alma was the exception; she and Susie became good friends to me in my later years at high school. I believe it had to do with the fact that I hung out with Mike. They all felt that I could do better, and knowing the trouble that came from being associated with him, they seemed to keep watch to make sure I didn't get in the middle of anything dangerous. Some of them had boyfriends that belonged to rival gangs that didn't get along with the Largo. Some of them had brothers who were affiliated with rival gangs. At some of these dances we could always feel the tension rise as guys from different gangs began to arrive. It would always start out cool and calm until someone would wave their gang sign on the dance floor. Then before long, everyone was throwing out their sign. It wasn't soon after that a fight would break out and ruin the night for everyone. I still see Susie from time to time and Alma became extended family on Mike's side once we got older so I get to see her at family functions.

My relationship with Mike took a toll on me socially, academically, and emotionally. I think back now and realize how much I missed out on in high school because I was so focused and obsessed with him. I know he cared about me and he showed it in his own way. I often wonder if we would have ended up together anyway if I had stayed focused on doing well in school. I know my grades could have been better and I could have contributed more to GAA and the clubs I was associated with. My friendships slowly drifted and I eventually stopped spending time with Lynne, Gloria, Bonita, or anyone else. Susan spent a lot of time at my house and she became one of my few close friends my last year at Dominguez. Mike was my very first "boyfriend" and I truly didn't know how to manage the feelings I had for him. I didn't understand those feelings myself and was too embarrassed to talk to anyone about it. Most of my memories from senior year are sad ones. Everyone was against my seeing him because he was such a bad person. His reputation preceded him wherever he went and he was definitely feared. He was also highly sought out by members of other gangs in the area. He was obviously a dangerous person and had probably done some pretty bad things; I really shouldn't have had anything to do with him. One thing he did do is to keep all of his ventures to himself. He didn't share with me anything that went on after hours. But I have to say that he also protected me. Many times — and I mean many times — while at a party or dance, he would tell me to leave. I would argue that I wasn't ready to and he would force me to go home. Sure enough, the next day I would hear about the fights that broke out or the shootings or stabbings that took place after I left.

As I reflect on those days, I believe that part of the attraction with Mike was that he was different from all the other "boys" or men that I knew. My brothers were just like my father — mean, verbally abusive, treating women, including us, their sisters, like maids. We were subservient to them and that was the expectation. Mike was not like that. After dinner at his grandmother's house, he always helped to clean up afterward and dried the dishes every night. By this time, only he and his aunt Dee Dee were living in the house with his grandparents. He made his own bed, cleaned up after himself, and did his share of dusting and straightening up on Saturdays when his family cleaned house. At my house, my mom would be mortified if either of her boys picked up his own plate off the table and walked it to the sink, let alone make his own bed. Neither my father nor my brothers EVER picked up their dirty clothes off the bathroom floor after their showers. My mother ironed all of their clothes; it was an expectation.

I learned a lot from Mike. He was very intelligent and knew a little about a lot of things. To this day, I still enjoy watching *Jeopardy!* with him because he gets the answers right. He retains so much trivia in his head, I don't know how he does it! I already liked rock and roll; Lynne and I would ride around in her mom's Mustang listening to Credence Clearwater on the car radio, but Mike took me to my very first concerts. I was fifteen when I saw Iron Butterfly "live." He also took me to see Black Oak Arkansas and Foghat before I was 16 years old. Although he had a look of anger and bitterness on his face, I saw kindness and goodness in his heart. He was kind and protective of his grandmother. He took care of his aunt Dee Dee who had Down's Syndrome and I oftentimes found him speaking with her and making her laugh. She loved to dance so he'd put on the radio and tease her as she attempted her best "Temptation walk." I enjoyed his family life and I wanted to be a part of it. I think part of the attraction was the fact that his life was "better" and different than mine and I was in awe of their family dynamic. It wasn't until later in our relationship that I realized there was more than plenty of dysfunction in his family as well.

I worked at a local hamburger stand called Doug's Corner which was located at the bottom of the bridge that spanned from Paramount to Compton and went over the 7 Freeway, now the 710, and the river bed. Everyone stopped there to eat at some point in time. I knew Mike had been up to his antics when the local Narcs would come to Doug's Corner and ask me how Mike was doing. They would ask me if he had been with me the night before or what we'd been doing. I knew they were hoping to get me to reveal something, but since I knew nothing, there was nothing to tell. I believe this is why Mike never shared anything with me. You'd think this alone would deter me from wanting to see him. I don't know why I was so obsessed. From the undercover cops I would learn about drive-by shootings from the night before and about guns that were confiscated from the guys who got caught. When I think back, I realize that we lived in a war zone and were just lucky we didn't end up as collateral damage.

On December 5, 1970, I was in the tenth grade at Dominguez and Mike was in the ninth grade, and still at Whaley. It was later in the evening, just before dusk. I don't remember where we were coming from, but his aunt Pricilla and I were driving south on Gibson on our way home and as we came upon Whaley, we saw Mike in the front of the school covered in blood. He always wore a yellow jacket and that day all I saw was red. There was an ambulance and police cars in front of the school and as much as I wanted to, we didn't stop. We continued on home so that Pricilla could tell Mama Edralin what she had seen. I was afraid that he had been shot, and it wasn't until later that night that I learned what had happened.

Robert Valdez was from the same neighborhood as Mike and he went to Whaley that afternoon to pick up his girlfriend from school. It was the end of the school day and Mike saw him approaching. They exchanged greetings and Mike asked, "what are you doing over on this side of Compton?" and Robert said he was there to pick up his girlfriend. Mike watched as Robert went down the main hall and turned left toward the girl's gym. Mike then saw a crowd of Black students gathering in the hallway as Robert passed them. As they followed Robert, Mike ran after them. It was not a race thing; it was just that Robert did not belong at the school. Mike ran toward them as he saw them have a verbal confrontation so Mike grabbed a couple of guys and asked, "What is going on?" Mike had approached the ringleaders and they said, "We're just going to talk to him." It then escalated to physical violence. Multiple guys and girls were trying to beat up Robert. That's when Mike jumped in it but was too late. Robert had been stabbed just seconds earlier. Mike grabbed and half lifted him up and blood gushed out of the left side of his neck like a fire hose. Another one of Mike's friends held off the mob while Mike picked up Robert and half carried and half dragged him away from the mob while Robert bled profusely. Mike turned left down the hallway toward woodshop when the shop teacher yelled at him and said, "He's bleeding out, put him down!" The shop teacher applied pressure to Robert's neck, but it was too late. He had bled out. Mike jumped the fence to tell the other guys from the neighborhood who were out across the street in front of the school that Robert had been stabbed. This is when Pricilla and

I happened to drive by and see his yellow jacket crimson red. Mike talked to the police and identified the guys involved. Turns out the killer had stolen the knife that he used on Robert from a kid in Mr. Lombardi's class just that day. The police arrested the leader of the mob and the killer. When the hearings began at the court house on Eastlake, in East Los Angeles, the homicide detective would pick Mike up in the mornings from his grandmother's house to get him to the hearings. Mike's testimony helped find the perpetrators guilty of murder. This same detective later wrote a book about his life as a cop in Compton, and he shared the story about Robert Valdez in his book. Oddly enough, this incident helped Mike gain unwanted notoriety in the streets of Compton.

The day of Robert's funeral, a large number of students attended. We had been warned the day before by school administrators that we should attend school the next day to avoid detention. It didn't matter, classrooms were half full that day. Mike had to go to court for months to testify. The killer was ultimately found guilty and incarcerated. Robert's death was in the paper and read as a racial attack of a Black person on a Mexican, which was not really the case. The Brown Berets, a Chicano activist group modeled after the Black Panthers, got involved and they contacted Mike. They asked him to speak at events and talk to Chicano youth about staying away from gang life and the problems with racial tensions. He was named President of the newly formed Chicano Youth Organization for Compton. All along Mike knew it had not been a racially motivated attack. The timing of Robert's death coincided with the East L.A. riots, which had prompted the Brown Berets attention. Mike felt exploited by other peoples' platforms and political agendas. Mike had a cursory interest and participated slightly, but he had vengeance on his mind.

Just as at Whaley, along with Bonita and Lynne, I signed up for GAA at Dominguez. At the high school level, it was an intramural gym class that traveled to other high schools to compete in field hockey, basketball, softball, and volleyball. I don't remember if track and field was included in GAA, but I do remember being part of the track team as well. This class always took place in sixth period and we got to wear a one-piece red jumpsuit/shorts, which was far better than the standard white shirt and black gym shorts that everyone else had to wear. This was by far one of the classes I looked forward to each day.

When we competed against other schools, just like at Whaley, we were the only integrated team, which continued to cause problems for us. It wasn't uncommon for our teammates to be shoved as they walked past someone from another team. They would stare or sneer at us. Bonita believed it had nothing to do with race; they were unhappy because we usually came out the victors. We would be taunted by the opposing teams. "We're going to kick your ass, White girl" or "Wait 'til we get our hands on you, Beaner!" One year during field hockey season, we were at Centennial High School and after we finished competing and were getting our stuff together to get back on the bus, we became aware that a group of girls with their hockey sticks were coming into the gym to have it out with us. At some point teachers came into the gym and intervened, but I stood at the ready with my hockey stick alongside everyone else on our team. It was a very stressful time and racial tensions were prevalent. Who were we to bring an interracial team to the games? And worse yet, to go home with the championship?

We didn't have to travel to other schools to be picked on for not being Black. My gym socks were stolen by a girl who was sitting right next to me. I confronted her and all it did was make her smile. My years in Compton taught me to not show fear or to let anyone intimidate me. Even if I was scared, I could not let that fear keep me from defending myself either verbally or physically. To show a sign of weakness would set a person up for future and constant abuse. There were frequent fights between competing gangs at school, between Hispanics and Blacks. No one was safe; even the teachers were pulled out of class and beaten by students.

Then there were the Hispanic girls who wanted to beat me up because I was dating Mike. These were the little "cholas" who liked him and thought I had no business being with him. One girl in particular would bump into me in the hallway as I went to class or I would see her at dances and she'd give me a look like she was going to do something. She would walk by me and threaten to beat me up after school. So, after school I would keep my gym clothes on and walk home in them. Sure enough, she would be at the bottom of the bridge across the street from Doug's Corner waiting for me with her crew. But every time I walked by, they just glared at me and let me pass. One time I told her that if she wanted to go at it, "Let's do it. But it's between you and me, not your friends." I sensed that her friends agreed with that as well, which is why they never really bothered me. One of her friends was a big girl whom I was more afraid of than anything, but she seemed to not want to have anything to do with me. She was there because of her friend, not because she had anything against me.

This went on for a while, and sometimes Jessie or one of the other Hispanic girls from GAA would offer me a ride home from school so that I wouldn't have to deal with them. It finally came to a head at a dance that I went to with my sister Rosa. The girl was there and kept giving me the eye the entire night. I blew her off and made a point of having a good time. When it came time for us to leave, she was at the front door and as I started to pass by her, she pushed me. I told her "Don't touch me" and I again tried to walk past her. She again pushed me so I pushed her back really hard and we ended up outside the door. She grabbed my hair and tried to pull my top off. All I could think of was my brother Carlos telling me, "If anybody messes with you, just punch them in the face." So, without further thought I grabbed her by the hair with my left hand, I balled my right hand into a fist and began to punch her in the nose and face. She held on to the front of my top and didn't let go. Before I knew it, she was on the ground with me on top of her, still punching her in the face. The security guard came over and pulled me off of her. She got up crying, her hands covering her bloody nose, and she staggered away. The security guard then told me to go home. As I picked up my mother's watch that had broken off of my wrist during the fight, the security guard looked at me with a smirk on his face and said, "You've got a great right hook!" It gave Rosa and me something to laugh about all the way home.

I did well in school, but as I mentioned, I could have done a lot better. I wasn't focused on my classes or my friends. If I could do it all again, I would focus my time and energy on my academics because it certainly hurt me once I went away to college. I was not socially or academically prepared to go out into the real world. I didn't do myself any favors by focusing on a relationship. You'd think I'd get tired of all the sneaking around, hiding my relationship with Mike from everyone in my family.

In tenth grade when Susan and I joined the Baile Folklorico group at the high school, I had a chance to work with some sophomores, juniors, and seniors, which was pretty cool in my mind. We practiced at the Community Center on Willowbrook Ave. in Compton, and after practice Mike would come by and we'd spend some time talking before I went home. I made friends with the kids in the group and we began hanging out from time to time and I would go to parties with them. These were the kids who mostly spoke Spanish at school. I had a great time with them and they made me feel proud of my heritage. That summer Susan and I got our work permits and taught folkloric dance to kids at the Community Center in Paramount. It was a lot of fun and we were so proud when the kids got to participate in a Mexican Independence Day parade and perform in front of an audience. They were a big hit! I don't know why we didn't go back and teach there every summer thereafter. We had so much fun and it was so rewarding.

Hanging out with Lynne, Bonita, David Kieselburg, Steve Sugita, David White, and everyone else from Theodore Roosevelt made me aware of the possibility of going to college. This was not something that was discussed with me at home, but my sister Patty was at Caltech and I got to thinking, why not me? The school counselors, I regret not remembering them, were proactive in getting us to talk about going to college. I sat in the office filling out college applications to UCLA, UC San Diego, Long Beach State, and a few out-of-state colleges. At that time, applications were free to submit so it was painless to me. They also had me sign the right forms for scholarships and grants. I would take the forms home for parent signatures and they just signed where asked to, without question. I don't know that my father or mother knew, or cared, what they were signing.

I have very little memorabilia from my childhood, but in high school I started a scrapbook. There's not much in it, but it has given me some insight to where I was mentally and emotionally during those times. I have so many regrets from high school that it shames me to think about it. If I could, I would go back and focus on my studies to help prepare me for my college years. I struggled in college for a variety of reasons, which will have to be shared in a later chapter. I remember less of my high school years than any other years. I was on an emotional rollercoaster nearly every day that took my focus away from the things that really mattered — my classes,

Gathering in front of Becky's house on San Marcus Ave., Compton, 1972.
Becky is in the center, head turned

my friends. I became a different person that I didn't particularly like and if I could go back and change ANY part of my life, it would be my high school years. As a junior, I tried out for cheerleader and it was one of the most humiliating events of my life. I couldn't do the splits, I forgot my routine, and I even hit my hand on the top of the door jamb as I entered the gym doing a cartwheel. It was horrible! I don't know what made me think I could be one of those people.

Mike was not very loyal to me and didn't hesitate to hook up with someone at a dance or party that I didn't attend. I was much smarter than to stay with someone so untrustworthy, and we broke up all the time. But sooner or later we would get back together again. It was terribly hurtful and so stupid of me to continue to give him another chance.

It wasn't until I went off to college that I realized how unprepared I was emotionally and academically. I struggled so much and I couldn't blame anyone but myself. In life we always hope to have few regrets when we reach the end of our time here on earth. People always say, "If I could do it again, I would change this or that or do this differently." I, for one, hope that we are reincarnated and are given the opportunity to live our lives again, only wiser and smarter about the decisions we make. My dysfunctional childhood only taught me to cry when life got difficult. My father would beat us until we cried, so I learned to weep quickly when things didn't go my way. I cried when I got angry, when I got my first ticket, when my feelings were hurt. I cried when my bosses counseled me or shared areas of opportunity in my management style. Imagine that! How unprofessional of me. I lacked business maturity even though I have always been good at what I do for a living. Emotional Intelligence? Forget about it! It is finally making sense to me and I am now realizing, more than five decades later, that I did not learn appropriate coping skills. And I see this weakness in my children as well, skills that I could have and should have taught them.

Living life in Watts and then Compton during those racially turbulent years helped me develop a sixth sense that helped me prepare for or avert conflict. Through the years I've lost that sixth sense, which I regret immensely. I wonder where that toughness and heightened awareness went. Where was it when I needed to be strong and confident? I suspect that the violence in my life resulted in Post-Traumatic Stress Disorder (PTSD), which was not diagnosed in veterans until the Afghan War. About four years ago, I was watching TV when I came across a commercial questioning how well students could possibly learn if they were afraid to go to school because of the recent increase in school shootings. They talked about possible PTSD. It was not an issue when Blacks and Hispanics lived in this type of environment in the '60s, '70s, and '80s. It didn't become a social concern until White schools were the target of shootings. The Columbine shootings in Littleton, Colorado got White America talking about bullying and PTSD. Really America? Only a few decades too late!

I made an appointment once to meet with a hypnotist/therapist who was going to help me learn how to process my feelings instead of crying when confronted. I ended up canceling the appointment and to date wonder if it would have made a difference in how my life turned out.

Nature or nurture? Was I predisposed to be the person I turned out to be, or was my upbringing, the bigotry, and the violence what made me who I am today? Would I be a different person if I were White or Black and lived the same life I lived? I suspect Bonita and Lynne's stories may shed some light on this debate.

PART 3: THE BLACK GIRL'S STORY

<u>7</u>

From Gary, Indiana To Compton, California

I was born in Gary, Indiana on July 28th, 1955, to Roy and Dorothy Bradshaw. I was the third of four children born to them, each of us two to three years apart. My brother Laurence Eugene was the oldest, followed by my sister Cheryl Elaine. My younger sister, Teri Janine, came along seven years after me. She seemed OK to have around, after the newness and jealousy wore off. As the youngest, I was always being pranked by my older sister or brother so when Teri came into the picture, the target moved off me and landed on her.

We had a light blue, wood-slat house on the beautiful elm tree-lined Roosevelt Street in Gary. The tall protective elms shaded all the homes on both sides. On days of light rain, our homes remained totally dry and I was happy to be able to go outside and play without getting wet. The tall trunks of armor stood shoulder-to-shoulder while their branches shielded us from Mother Nature's rain. As a small child, there were a few times when I saw the harder rain sneak through on one side of the street. It was always magical. I know that while growing up I was very well protected by my parents. In Gary, I was not conscious about racism and being treated differently. Not until after the move to California did I learn about social injustices and big racial issues. Growing up, I was aware that my father always worked with diverse groups of people, but I never realized that he (or I) was a true minority. Early on I never separated Black and White. I grew up and got along with everyone.

Growing up in Gary was like growing up in Mayberry (from the TV show *Mayberry RFD*), where everyone knew everyone and we all had standards and morals. I thought my family was middle-class African-American with the routines of the average family — church on Sundays, hard work during the weekdays, and simple outings with family and family friends in between. Nothing too fancy, but never anything without purpose or class. When I think about Mayberry and the community — everyone was very charitable and giving. Rarely was anyone ever negative. The town drunk was a sweetie-pie and the police were kind and would open the jail to let him sleep it off. Even though Gary was a bit more modern, I saw it that way. You knew on Saturdays that everyone was manicuring their lawns and the kids were all cleaning their rooms inside. There were community protocols or norms in place that were typical of communities elsewhere. I grew up with very distinct standards that I carried into my adult life and still practice and expect of others today. When my own children were growing up, I tried to instill those same morals and standards. I tried to follow etiquette I learned as best as I could. It was a battle for the times since my daughters grew up in the '90s, but as parents we can only do the best we can.

My parents were hard-working, security-minded, responsible adults who set the bar very high for us children. I felt well taken care of and loved. I always felt free in our neighborhood and never had a reason to believe I was ever unsafe. When you walked down a street, everyone greeted you with a kindness. It was beautiful. It seemed like the perfect family neighborhood (like the Beavers from the TV show *Leave it to Beaver*) where kids played outside until the street lights came on, or until your mom summoned you from the front porch, which usually meant dinner was ready and it was time to eat. I thought that almost every other kid in America was growing up the same way. I had no reasons to think differently. Almost everyone had a dog growing up and I saw most of my neighbors in church on Sunday.

My brother was in the Boy Scouts and my older sister and I were Brownies and eventually Girl Scouts. We all went to Jack n' Jill on Saturday mornings for the etiquette and life skills they taught us. Jack n' Jill of America was an African-American organization formed during the Great Depression to bring African-American children together in a social and cultural environment where we would be nurtured to flourish as community members and leaders. After Jack n' Jill, my sisters and I took dance lessons. We were quite the social butterflies. Much later in my life, while teaching in the Compton Unified School District in the late '90s, I remember thinking that the district made a huge mistake to remove most of their vocational education classes. Among those courses were Home Economics and Life Skills. Removing those courses changed the culture of not only the school community but the community at large. When the majority of students come from single-parent homes, foster homes, or are latch-key kids, they generally spend less time with an adult who would normally teach etiquette or life skills to them. Home economics or life skills compensated for the absence of the adult or guardian in the home, and in most cases, parents depended on schools to teach these tools. Today only schools located in hot spots teach life skills such as typing and keyboarding. The school I work in now is one of them. We believe there is a great need for our youth to learn everything from tolerance and how to communicate effectively with others, to how to eat, how to get in and out of an elevator, or what side one walks up and down stairs. All of these things matter. Even though my mother taught us most all of the etiquette we needed, Jack n' Jill reinforced her teachings and helped groom us as future leaders.

I don't remember going to movies or drive-ins when we lived in Gary but I do remember the trips to Dairy Queen to get chocolate covered Dilly Bars! When I later moved to California in the '60s one of my biggest disappointments was that there was no Dairy Queen in sight.

Watching TV as a family was something we did often. On Sundays we all watched Ed Sullivan and Carol Burnette and on other days I watched *The Andy Griffith Show, Bonanza,* and my Dad's favorites, *The Rifleman* and *Gunsmoke.* (Who didn't love Miss Kitty?)

Our house had a large back yard where we would often play ball, making bases out of the trees. There was a beautiful cherry tree and a green apple tree on one side of our back yard, and a huge mulberry tree on the opposite side, with a sand box underneath it. When the mulberries fell from the tree and were mixed with the sand, it made the most flavorful mud pies I could ever eat! Of course, I never ate a whole mud-pie, or sand-pie which is what it truly was, but I did taste every one I made!

The majority of my memories of Gary are great. The few that weren't so great were a bit shocking to me but I lived through them all. My most shocking memory before leaving Gary was the first time I saw my neighbor ring their chickens' necks! I knew our neighbors raised chickens and I always saw them feeding the chickens so I just thought they were pets. That's how we treated our dog. The first time I saw a chicken's neck wrung, I was in a state of shock. And I know this because I don't even remember seeing who did it. I had dream after dream of this body with the chicken's head in one hand and the chicken's body dripping blood everywhere in the other hand. I don't see a face, or even notice the time of day ... I just see the that image. I saw that over and over in my dreams for years. I was totally grossed out and definitely never wanted to eat another chicken at first, but lucky for me, that thought didn't last long. I eventually learned how the food chain operates. I'm not sure if my parents spoke to me about this but I am glad I eventually understood why it happened. Chicken is one of my favorite meats to this day! The family's Sunday dinners, and even mine today, include a lot of chicken. I also could not find it within myself to insult my mom by not eating any food she prepared and her fried chicken was the best.

Another shocking moment for me was in the basement of the Gary house. One of my favorite cartoons was *Underdog.* I also like watching *The Roadrunner, Tom and Jerry, Casper,* and *The Flintstones.* Underdog stood out for me because he was a superhero.

"There's no need to fear, Underdog is here!" He always saved the day! I liked that and it didn't matter that he was a dog. As a superhero (my hero) he could fly through the air and save people. I watched episodes of *Underdog* and he flew down stairs, out of windows and doors and over mountains and was never injured. One day, after watching too many episodes, I thought I could ride my bike down the basement stairs. I stood at the top of the basement stairs and thought to myself that it would be so cool to fly down the basement stairs just like Underdog. I took one step forward and when that front wheel hit the first step, I saw my little life flash before my eyes. That front wheel never touched another step until my bike had flipped all the way over, head first, and ended up on the floor. I was splattered onto the basement floor looking up when my bike landed on me. I wasn't scared or hurt so much as I was shocked that it didn't work. I thought about that bike trip often after that, and fortunately for me, I never repeated it.

I was adventurous and my *Underdog* memories in the Gary house didn't end there. One Saturday I had just finished watching *Underdog* and I felt so empowered by him that I believed I could burst through walls and barriers and fly. I ran to the bathroom and snatched my towel off the rack, threw it around my shoulders and tied it under my neck. Now this time I wasn't headed down the basement steps but instead I targeted the glass door. Why I didn't learn from the basement incident was beyond me. I gathered all my strength and magic juices and yelled, "There's no need to fear, Underdog is here!" And at that moment I threw myself through the door with every intention of taking off to fly. Well, as you probably have suspected I didn't get far. As the top half of my body lay over the bottom frame of the broken glass door, my lower legs were still inside the door stuck on pieces of glass in the bottom of the frame — blood was everywhere! I remember my mother's panicked face as she tried to get my legs off the pieces of glass and over the door frame onto the porch. What a mess! Even though this mission failed, I continued to watch *Underdog,* just from a slightly different perspective. I was also glad that I had that towel around my neck. It came in handy that day.

The only other really bad or shocking memory I have from the Gary house was the day that I sat on a pair of scissors that I left on my mother's French Provincial couch in the living room. I'm not real sure why I had the scissors. I probably shouldn't have had the scissors, but I was trying to hide them between the pillows on the couch in the living room, so my mother didn't see them. When she headed my way, I stuck them between the pillows quickly and then plopped down on the couch as if I had nothing to hide. As soon as I hit the couch with force, the sharp end was forced upward and punctured the underside of my knee. I screamed because of the pain but as I looked down at all the blood on my mom's couch, I became more scared about what my mom was going to do to me! My older brother and sister took me to the bathroom. They sat me on the edge of the tub with my feet inside the tub. They put the stopper in the tub and said something about me not losing any more blood. Really? I still have that scar to this day.

Another interesting (and now funny) memory for me was when my dad bought me a bicycle that he had to put together. I had finally graduated from the tricycle I had ridden down the basement stairs and was ready for a 2-wheeler. When I took my brand new, pretty blue bike out for a first spin, I ran smack-dab into a tree in front of our house and the bike broke into two pieces! I lay on the ground between the two wheels, crying like a baby. I don't know how my dad felt about the bike literally separating into two pieces and I don't know how mine was repaired but as an adult I have never purchased a bike in a box.

I share these stories because it shows that I was well cared for and had a great upbringing. I wouldn't trade my upbringing for anything in the world. Those few things that happened to me were so minuscule in retrospect, compared to all of the great things I was part of growing up. I was never traumatized as a child and never had any situation that would be considered a crisis or negatively life-changing. All of those incidents stand out in my mind because with each incident, there was always a lesson learned, with the exception of the bike. The most important lesson I learned with most all of these incidents was to ASK FIRST. No matter the thought or the probability of the thought, if you don't have enough information, or your parents' permission, then ask first or the answer is automatically 'NO' or don't do what you're thinking about doing.

As an educator today, I have seen how the majority of my students have been reared and it doesn't compare to the way I was raised. I wish my students of today could have been raised more like me. I know that times change and people change with it but there is a plethora of things I would never change. By the time many of our students get to our middle school they have experienced domestic violence, trauma, and crisis at an unbelievable rate. A good many of my students have low or no self-esteem, they don't trust anyone, and they don't dream about a future — they live day to day. I laud my parents for providing the correct setting for me to grow up to be self-confident and inspirational, with no fear to dream.

My mother was a math teacher and my dad worked for the Boy Scouts of America. My mom was wonderful. I remember watching her go to work, teach, then come home to clean and maintain our home, sew and repair many of our clothes and cook "like it was nobody's business." She gradually taught us girls all of those skills and prepared all us kids for society, as she engaged us in Jack n' Jill, the Boy Scouts, the Girl Scouts, dance lessons, instrument lessons, and more. She was a wonderful math teacher, having graduated from Hampton Institute magna cum laude as a math major. She was also the teacher in the family, for the family. I didn't think there was anything she couldn't do. My mom was a member of the Delta Sigma Theta sorority and was one of the founders of the Deltas on the Tuskegee Institute campus when she was in graduate school there. She created a beautiful home environment and taught us all how to maintain it. Every Saturday without fail we all had household chores that had to be finished before we could step outside the house for any reason. I've moved my cleaning day to Sunday but both of my children had the same routine until they moved out of my home. She also played bridge with her girlfriends, went to many social events, played Tripoley with the family, and was quite "the lady."

My dad graduated from Iowa State University at a time when Blacks could not live on campus, so he stayed with Mrs. Bettye Tate, who housed Black students. She was a part of many of our family gatherings, becoming a lifelong friend of the family until her passing. My dad is a veteran of the Army and served on the Battleship Iowa that is now docked as a historic museum in the port of El Segundo. I know that when my dad returned from the war, he was a mail carrier, but he worked for the Boy Scouts of America while I was growing up. He loved bowling and golfing and even was one of the originators of the Parmakers Golf Club, one of the first Black golfing organizations in Indiana. My dad was a quiet man. He didn't raise his voice often — my mom was the more vocal and passionate of the two. If my dad disciplined us, it was the final straw that you never wanted to deal with! Even though he was not as present as my mother (because of his job), he was definitely the final word.

We had tons of relatives and friends of the family in Gary and Chicago. Both sets of my grandparents lived in Gary and almost all of my aunts and uncles and their families lived in either Gary or Chicago. We typically visited relatives on the weekends and came together for most holidays. My Aunt Gerry's neighborhood threw huge block parties with Martha and the Vandellas' "Dancing in the Streets" playing loud for all to hear. The neighbors lined the streets with tables of homemade foods and we children ran from table to table to sample the delights. Not too far from aunt Gerry's house was the corner store owned by Jessie Gardner on Adams and 25th, which was just yards away from "Mother's" house. That was what we called my dad's mom. Mother would give me empty pop bottles, so I would run to the corner store to get my return on them for candy or Bazooka gum. When Mother had no bottles, I admittedly used to steal penny candies from the corner store and run back to her house.

Most summers my parents put us in the station wagon to travel to various states across the country. We were that family with multiple state stickers on the back and side windows of our station wagon. In elementary school I thought that was totally cool, but by junior high school it was definitely embarrassing.

I loved the weather in Indiana and thought everywhere was like Gary with beautiful white winters, rust-colored falls, rainy green springs, and humid, heated, flowered summers. My favorite time of year was fall, when all the leaves on the trees turned from green to yellow to orange and finally rust. I'm not sure who raked our leaves together in piles, probably my brother, but I loved jumping into the leaves and getting lost below the surface. To this day I love the fall and the colorful display that nature provides. It always brings fond memories of my childhood in Gary.

I was nine when my family moved from Gary to Compton, California. I really didn't think anything negative or positive about our move at first. We settled into a nice house on Mettler Avenue in the Willowbrook area of L.A., where the neighborhood was primarily White. It was just a few blocks from the border with the City of Compton. It didn't look much different from the neighborhood I grew up in. The houses were moderate in size, like in Gary, but the trees were not as pretty and green. Instead of strong old elm trees, these new palm trees were tall and skinny and didn't provide much shade, let alone protection from

Bonita, eight years old, 1963

anything. The Gary neighborhood was all Black and it was new to me to live among so many White people, but it wasn't a problem and not of real concern. I just adapted. If this is where my parents wanted us to be, then that was just how it was. As a nine-year-old, I didn't have anything to say and I learned not to say anything. We did as we were told and had absolutely no reason not to trust what my parents did for us.

I learned my address quickly because it rhymed: "I live at 1-3-4-1-2 Mettler Avenue!" I don't remember much about the house on the outside in the front except that it looked nice, but we could run in a circle inside it. The inside was also a little dark compared to the Gary house, so it was hard for my mom to catch us when she got after us, because we would run in a circle and then dart into one of the rooms. I'm sure that she wasn't impressed with this design feature since she was never quick enough to see exactly where we went. We had a good-sized back yard with a covered patio area where I spent most of my time. Behind the patio there were lots of beautiful rose bushes planted along the fence. I loved the roses back then and am sure it is why I love roses so much today.

There was a back house to the property and the lady who lived back, Mrs. Howard, was a little strange. She was a very-small-framed Black woman with red hair, who was dressed most days in her robe. I avoided any serious interactions with her after I discovered that she liked eating raw onions like an apple. Who eats onions like that? I thought she was strange so I kept my distance but was cordial when I needed to be.

Life was good on Mettler while we were there. To my knowledge there were no break-ins or domestic disputes that would bring the police. No rumors of gang activity and no reason to believe it was any different than what I saw. We stayed in the Mettler house for about a year before moving to Compton.

I loved our Compton house. We lived on Chester Avenue, where everyone had fruit trees and flowers planted in their front yards. There were 10 houses on our block, four on our side of the street and six on the opposite side, with a mixture of White and Black families. Everyone was kind and respectful. This house was bigger than the

Mettler house. It had four bedrooms and a huge den in the back. We had a two-car garage, with a laundry room in it, and a fenced-in back yard. Our house was painted a soft yellow with a brown trim color. We had two neighborhood stores a block from us on Santa Fe, and a baseball field in Oak Park with a swing set by the dugout. I used to think the park was really big until I started high school and realized as I got bigger, the park got smaller and smaller.

When we moved to Compton, I attended Augusta A. Mayo Elementary School about five blocks from my house. School was fun for the most part. I learned to play tether ball and I was getting a little taller than a lot of my classmates, so that gave me an edge. I also learned how to play four-square and began to look forward to recess more than class. I was a good student and I loved learning things but became very interested in sports in elementary school. There were plenty of kids in my neighborhood who took to the streets to play with each other once school was over and dinner was had. We had until the street lights came on. Once they did, it was almost everyone's sign to go home. If you didn't go home then, mothers hit the front porches to summon the rest of their crew. Life in Compton was good for me. I was oblivious to negative entities in my community.

Bonita's childhood home on Chester Street, Compton

When the Watts Riots broke out in August of '65, I had no idea what was going on. I just came home from school one day, got out of the family car, and looked up to see large billows of smoke in the air behind our house. It looked peculiar, not like one house was on fire but more like a whole block was on fire ... and it was! That same evening on TV, the newsmen talked about rioting taking place in Watts, which was literally a mile from where we lived! On TV there were Black people protesting, looting, and burning cars and stores and everything in their path. They were angry, but at what? The newsmen talked about an incident that involved two brothers and their mother having a dispute with police officers and how that dispute resulted in the people of Watts rioting in protest. The TV showed cops and other uniformed police, probably State troopers, protecting buildings and ordering and pushing Black people around, but I didn't know why. I did not know how this all started but nothing had a greater impact on me than the smell of smoke from the fires, from the 200 businesses that were lost in Watts just minutes away. I overheard grown-up conversations about Blacks, Whites, cops, the National Guard, and more but I didn't know what that really meant or how serious it really was.

The rioting lasted days and the news coverage dominated our evenings. I began to question why my parents moved us here so close to all this craziness. I'd never seen people fighting the police and burning property before. This was very scary. Even though the riots were minutes away, I never witnessed them myself. The only evidence I had of this time was the daily smell of smoke and the gray skies over our community. I don't remember our family having to do anything special, or being treated any differently, or us having to act another way to continue living and doing what was normal to us. At home there weren't a lot of conversations to my knowledge about the riots and I could sense that we were somewhat more guarded when we stepped outside of the house. But with any challenge, you accept it, make adjustments, and move forward, and that's exactly what my parents did, as far as I knew. I was very young and maybe they felt it wasn't my place to know all of that.

Life for me went on very smoothly. As I continued school at Mayo Elementary I progressed well. Most all of the teachers were White and female. I really don't recall many male teachers and no teachers of color. Learning came easy to me and as I entered the 5th grade, I became a bit more outgoing. I was getting taller than most of my classmates. I came from a pretty tall family, with the exception of my mom, so as I grew taller it just seemed natural, especially at home. I had good friends to play with at recess but developed a small issue in class, according to my teacher. Mrs. Lorenzo got after me often for disturbing my classmates. I would always finish my work but clearly needed more work to do because as soon as my work was done, I would talk to those around me and keep them from finishing their work. Mrs. Lorenzo was a very tall, slender White woman with very pale skin, very red hair, and red lipstick to match. She always looked very pleasant but could be very stern when she needed to be, like with me.

That year at Mayo I spent a lot of afternoons after class, writing standards on the chalkboard in her classroom. My standards were about asking permission to talk, disturbing the class, not raising my hand, and on occasion about chewing bubble gum. The standard I remember writing most was "I will not talk without permission." No matter the topic of the standards I never wrote fewer than 100 standards at a time. You would think that having to stay after school and write standards would have been a quick lesson learned for me but it didn't seem to really change my behavior. When I stayed after school to write standards, my mom would come to my class to pick me up and I would get in trouble again either on the way home with a one-arm whipping or when I got home with a full-blown spanking.

Now, my mom was a teacher, a very good teacher, so of course she had to figure out and implement a strategy that would truly change me and she did. I was in school at a time when discipline included students receiving swats as a consequence. I never had an issue that ever sent me to the office or warranted a swat of any kind, at least not at school. I began to act up early in the school year in

Mrs. Lorenzo's class and I know Thanksgiving and Christmas had not gone by. One day my mom called me into her room after I was dressed for school. She pinned a note to my sweater and told me to ask my teacher to please read the note. Mrs. Lorenzo's name was written on the outside of the note. My mom had beautiful, textbook, cursive writing. She told me, not asked me, that I better NOT touch this note for any reason and that it better be pinned to my sweater when I got home from school.

I know that I spent a good deal of time talking about how well I was raised, the morals and standards I learned, and here I am now writing standards and getting ready to get possibly swatted! We were all very mannerly, never talked backed, and respected everything and everyone. All of this is still true but there comes a time in a child's life when they try to push buttons to see how far they can get. Kids always test their powers and this time was no different for me. I was pushing buttons and pissing my mom off. My mom had no plans for any of her children to embarrass her or our family in any way and I was heading in that direction fast. When my mom pinned that note on me, I never touched it, or even thought of opening it because I would have to deal with my her directly and if you knew Dorothy Bradshaw, you wouldn't have touched it, either. I was raised during the good ol' days and she was an ol' fashioned mom who didn't play! The note quickly changed my behavior due to my fear of the unknown. I remember a lot of conversations after that time between Mrs. Lorenzo and my mom. I'm not sure whether my mom was called to school to talk about me or whether she just decided to occasionally drop in to talk to my teacher! The note that she pinned on me became a norm and I began my 6th grade year the same way. When I got to junior high school, I eventually learned that this note said, "YOU HAVE MY PERMISSION TO DISCIPLINE MY CHILD, BONITA BRADSHAW, AS NEEDED.
DOROTHY BRADSHAW"

My siblings and I were pretty good students and when we got home from school, my mom always went over my work with me and asked tons of questions about what I learned that day. I loved and appreciated that (later in life). To this day, as an educator I constantly ask students what they learn each day. My mom told me that I should bring something home newly learned each day. It didn't matter whether I liked my teachers or not. It didn't matter whether I liked the class or the subject. I was to learn something new every day that I was in school. To this day I still get excited when I learn something new.

<u>8</u>

I Didn't See Color

Way down yonder on Gibson street,
There's a kickin' ol' school that can't be beat.
It's the home of the Warriors and we know we're tough,
So c'mon mighty Warriors and show your stuff!

That Whaley cheer has stuck in my head for five decades. I attended Whaley Junior High School in Compton on Gibson Avenue. I'm always reminded of parts of the cheer we used to sing, I'm not sure whether that last line is correct but I know it ends with "stuff." Maybe my age now has something to do with being able to remember now, but back then I know that I loved to cheer, loved to dance, and show my stuff! Coming out of Mayo and going to Whaley was a big, welcome change for me. I rarely walked to Mayo Elementary which was only five blocks from my house, and now I had friends to pick up along the way (and my mom thought I was responsible enough to walk) so it never felt like a long walk or a punishment. Whaley was about 15 blocks away and there was a bus I was supposed to ride. The bus pickup was literally three houses away, at the end of my block. I could see the bus from my house! I missed the bus often and enjoyed walking most of the time.

Since we'd moved a few years before to our neighborhood in Compton, most of the White families had by now moved out. The neighborhood was predominantly Black but still the same. The homes were beautiful, manicured, and well kept. The routines in Compton mirrored those I had grown up with in my neighborhood in Gary. Most families had working parents. No kids came out to play until their homework was done. Saturdays were for chores and errands, and Sundays were for church and family gatherings. I had friends in the broader neighborhood from elementary school but I also became friends with other kids on Chester Avenue. We played outside whenever possible but I also went up the street to play with the Sessoms and Hurd kids. Occasionally Janice Dixie and Kenny Landreaux, who lived across the street from each other one block away, would come over and join us. Then there were the friends I walked to school with, but I didn't play with since they lived farther away, like the Holcombe brothers, David and Stan. They were good friends and happened to be White living three blocks over from me. I was in the same grade as David and when I walked past his house, sometimes he would join me on my walk to school.

Whaley was huge. The halls were wider and longer than my previous schools. The buildings were bigger, which made them feel more important to me. The lunch area was three times the size of Mayo's and at recess it seemed so crowded that you couldn't always see or find your friends. Instead of playing on blacktop, Whaley had a huge grass field that took up the total width of the school in back, with beautifully manicured, green grass. Outside of P.E. and sports, my seventh and eighth grades seemed typical. I don't remember much about my teachers and my classes. My very first memorable experience as a seventh grader was horrible and embarrassing for me but hysterically funny to everyone else. Maybe that incident made me block out that whole school year? It was my first week of school as a lowly seventh-grader on the lunch grounds, and I got my lunch tray and walked out the back door of the cafeteria. As I walked across the lunch area, someone called my name. When I looked to the left to try and see who called me, I walked smack-dab into a big blue steel pole! I lost my balance, dropped my lunch, and became the laughingstock of everyone around me! Being new there didn't help me muster up any strength at all to get through that moment. I just stood there and began to cry. I put my head in my chest and dropped my arms to my sides. I was totally broken at that moment until Mr. Atkinson, whom I didn't know at that time, came and walked me away from the lunch area. He walked me to his classroom, checked to see if I was really OK, sat me down, and just kept me company. I appreciated that so much and now I had a new friend. After that time, I'd sneak away like many of the kids and go into his room at lunchtime and hang out. He used to let us come in and just chill. It was nice. It felt safe.

I have to assume that because I don't remember much about seventh and eighth grades, I did well academically (as expected) and didn't get into any trouble. In my community however, things were different. When Martin Luther King was shot, everyone around me and my family were so affected. We had done our chores, played outside, had dinner, and were in the den watching TV when the news was announced that MLK had been assassinated. Well, I definitely did not know what *assassinated* meant. I just knew that my mom went to tears and was so distressed that she went to her bedroom, with my dad following. I don't know what was said or discussed but I knew that *assassinated* wasn't anything good, and that Martin Luther King was dead. On Sunday there seemed to be an urgency to get us all up and off to church like never before. There were subsequent protests, rallies, and even riots in areas over the murder of Martin Luther King. It didn't feel like the Watts Riots, it felt more like someone of massive importance was taken from a people and these people were so heartbroken and affected that this rage came from a heart-felt place.

After Martin Luther King was murdered, Bobby Kennedy was murdered two months later. He was leaving a hotel after just having spoken about his running for the presidency and was ambushed in the kitchen area before he could get out of the hotel. Losing MLK upset both the Black and White communities although the Black community felt the greatest loss. Bobby Kennedy's assassination riled both the White and Black communities but Whites seemed to be affected more. We'd lost President John Kennedy three years before and now his brother is assassinated. The talk I heard leaned toward conspiracy and government involvement, and that these assassinations were political moves. At my age I didn't truly understand politics and how all the pieces to this assassination puzzle fit, but I was soon to learn.

1968 was not a good year for me. After the murders of King and Kennedy, one horrific moment occurred outside my home in Compton. This day reminded me of the first time I ever heard a chicken squeal while having its neck wrung. The sound was so excruciating and this was no different. I didn't live far from Lueders Park in Compton but I never would have thought that I could hear the screams of passengers onboard the helicopter soon to crash in Lueders Park. I was outside and heard pops in the air, and as I looked up to see a helicopter flying over my house, appearing out of control, I could hear the screams of people on the helicopter. It was a moment I'll never forget as I watched the helicopter lose control and spiral downward into Lueders Park. As I lost sight of the helicopter going down, I couldn't imagine anyone surviving a crash like that and no one did. I later learned that the helicopter was transporting passengers to visit the "happiest place on earth," Disneyland, and that even the pilot's granddaughter was with him at the time. I had nightmares about hearing the screams for most of my childhood afterwards.

My ninth grade at Whaley was memorable. One of the highlights was being in the ninth-grade talent show. I was a cut-up at home with my brother and sisters, always singing Motown and dancing to the hits at holiday gatherings and just because, so being in a talent show was natural to me! I sang "The Name Game" by Shirley Ellis and I thought I was doing the most! My back-ups were Terri Shaw and Sheree Johnson, two of my closest friends then. We didn't win or even get close, but I didn't really care. I loved being on stage singing my heart out!

Ninth grade was filled with wonderful friendships with Lynne, Becky, Evita, Jeanetta, Terri, and Sheree. I developed a total love for sports and cheering, and I knew I was heading to Dominguez like my older brother and sister, so I was mentally preparing for that move. I was in CSF for two years now, was a mean competitor in

GAA, was a member of the Maidens, the honors service group for Whaley girls, and was on the *Smoke Signal* newspaper staff. I was ready for the next level.

I have fond memories of Mr. Atkinson and Coach Simmons but there was one teacher I did not have a fond memory of — Mr. Lasley. Mr. Lasley had an incident previously with my older sister Cheryl. I am not sure whether it was racially motivated, but I feel I paid for her situation with him when I was in his class. I know my sister felt her conflict that led to that incident was racially motivated because of the bullying she experienced at Whaley, and he was never very friendly with me and hardly ever said a word of encouragement to me while in class. I complained at home to my mom about how Mr. Lasley treated me, which is when my sister shared the incident she had with him years prior. When I saw him decades later at a reunion, he was surprisingly more cordial than he had ever been in school. All seemed to have been forgotten so I let sleeping dogs lie.

Bonita, second from right, with her siblings, 1969

I fell in love with sports while at Whaley. I was part of the GAA with all of my friends. Coach Simmons, one of the P.E. teachers, was a wonderful inspiration to me. Although a coach, he didn't have a mean bone in his body like the coaches I saw on TV. I can still see him in his blue sweats, whistle around his neck, with his round face and big smile telling me, "Bradshaw, you can play any sports you want. You got them long legs and plenty speed girl … what do you want to do?" And initially, I truly didn't know what to do. When it came to sports, my mom and dad both bowled and my dad golfed often but Whaley didn't offer those sports. I was taught volleyball, basketball, softball, square dancing, and track in P.E. I competed in almost all of those sports and got the opportunity to travel to other schools to compete. I was relatively tall so volleyball was good for me. I excelled at jumping to block a ball or stretching out to get under a ball when I was in the back row. I wasn't very good at serving or learning to spike the ball, however. My timing didn't seem to be good at all until I competed in track.

Most kids in my neighborhood went to Oak Park, a block or so away on Santa Fe. There they played mostly basketball even though there was a big baseball diamond there. The kids brought their own basketballs to the park and if the courts were full, they would dribble and throw their balls around home plate on the baseball diamond. I can still hear them throwing their balls against the chain-link fence and calling, "Next" to play basketball. I didn't go to the park that often so I never played basketball there. During those times it was only the boys you would see playing. I learned to play basketball during P.E. but I don't think I was very good at it at first. I didn't shoot very well, but I could throw the ball far (most times too far) and I could definitely hustle down the court to play defense which was about my natural speed. Now defense was something that I liked and it was easy remembering what spot to run back to down the court. I liked basketball and took a little more interest in it over most of the other sports.

I liked softball, or at least liked to run around the bases when we played softball. I wasn't that great hitting the ball, though, and when I did manage to hit it, I hit it pretty hard but never really controlled where it went.

I was also taught how to square dance (which I thought was pretty weird) in P.E. but as long as we didn't have to do it with the boys, I was OK. It was awkward but kind of fun. It was definitely different from the dances we did at home, but when I watched episodes of

Petticoat Junction or old westerns with my dad, and saw what real square dancing was, I knew we had only scratched the surface at Whaley (thank goodness).

Now when it came to track, I knew that I would love it. I was quick with my long legs and knew I could run. Coach Simmons introduced me to the 50-yard, the 100-yard, and the 400-yard dashes. I love to sprint and must admit that I was relatively good at it. I looked forward to track and even began watching track meets on television. Coach Simmons put together a relay team and asked me to join that team. I said yes (of course) and learned that I would be running the dashes and on the relay teams. I would run one leg of that relay, which was 100 yards. I thought that was a piece of cake. My relay teammates were good friends so it made the invitation so much better. My teammates were Lynne Isbell, Rebecca Rivera, and Evita van Schravendijk. I knew my team members pretty well, Lynne and Rebecca more than Evita but I thought we were the picture-perfect relay team. All of us were really good runners! We practiced handing off the baton back and forth and we truly enjoyed the relay! I liked the 400-yard run original. One lap around the track seemed so easy but now that race was cut into fourths and I was running with my friends! When Coach asked me to run anchor for the relay, I was excited! I was told that our relay team was one of the fastest junior high school teams ever. After we ran in the local and district track meet, I always heard rumors about how good we were even after I entered high school. I don't remember our time exactly (a bit over four minutes) in the relay but no one beat our record for as long as I remained in the district.

Our team ethnicity was pretty cool, as well. Lynne was White (that typical blond hair, blue eyes), Rebecca was Hispanic (with a slender sleek build and long dark hair), I was African-American (with those long legs Coach talked about) and Evita was what I would call "other." I later learned that Evita was half Dutch and half Indonesian. She was a beautiful light brown-skinned girl who looked very exotic. In school as far as I knew, the ethnicity of the team never came up, was thought about, or was an issue. I just saw friends and not color or race. It wasn't until things went crazy in high school and I lost touch with most all of these friends that I looked back at them and how I lost them. We all made it through the Watts Riots, the murders of the Kennedys and MLK, and those incidents didn't seem to have a direct impact on my junior high school days as a whole. When I heard about war, or the college shootings, I didn't relate those national issues with racism or discrimination. I think at that point I was too young and only concerned with my immediate life and family, and the activities that surrounded us.

While at Whaley I can't truly say that I experienced a lot of racism. Even considering the situation with Mr. Lasley, I didn't think all teachers or any of my peers felt the way he did or acted racist toward me. To me, the situation with him was an isolated event. My friends were people of all colors. I liked Mr. Atkinson and I felt that he genuinely liked me and he was White. I don't believe I thought of color when I considered who would be my friend, or who I would or would not interact with. Even after the Watts Riots, I didn't believe at first that the struggle involved me because I had moved to Compton from Gary, Indiana so maybe these were preexisting problems that didn't involve me. I just didn't see color. My parents shielded us from a lot of the racism that existed outside the doors of their household. Instead of focusing on the racism in the world then, my parents focused on developing my siblings and me with strong characters and personalities that would hopefully get us through anything.

One of my lowest points at Whaley was when Lynne's boyfriend, Del Floyd, was paralyzed from an accident he had on the school track. He was high-jumping and landed wrong. While we see death and injury on TV, in the movies, or on the late news, it truly doesn't hit home until it happens to you, or close to you. Although I don't know the date, I remember the day and how everyone was in a daze walking about the campus. I used to think about that injury a lot even as an adult and mother, as I had a daughter who high-jumped.

When she made it to the Junior Olympics and traveled to Alabama (which at that time was too expensive and too far away for me to travel with her) I thought about the many things that could go wrong and I thought of that incident with Del. She made it through the meet but as she met me at the airport and was telling me about her trip, she ended by saying that she didn't want to participate in track and field anymore after that meet … and I heard her. That was her last track meet and I didn't continue to have negative thoughts about the incident that injured Del.

I didn't have a boyfriend in junior high school and didn't want one. Boys were kind of weird to me. My focus was family, church, and school, and nothing else really came into play. I am sure that was by my mother's design. There were a lot of my friends who had boyfriends, though — Lynne (Del), Becky (Mike), Jeanetta, Evita, and more. It seemed to me that most of my girlfriends who were other than Black were really interested in boys or had a boyfriend. With my Black friends Terri and Sheree, we always seemed to talk about boys (because they were weird) but were very skittish when it came to talking to boys or having a boyfriend. My mother always (indirectly) told me I was too young to have a boyfriend so that was the end of that conversation. And when I speak of her saying it indirectly, you know how mothers talk to their friends but within your earshot, so you hear it just like it was said especially for you (and it probably was!). I never thought about going behind my mother's back or challenging her word. At that time that just wasn't what I did.

There were many days when I walked home from school because I was in clubs and participated in sports that had late practices and events after school. On most days I walked home with Becky to do homework at her house since she lived right up the street from the school. There was always a wonderful aroma in her house coming from the kitchen! Her mom often had food she prepared for us or was in the process of preparing dinner and I couldn't wait to be offered something to eat! To this day Mexican food is my favorite kind of food and Becky's mom's cooking is probably why. I literally could eat it every day of my life. I love pinto beans cooked fresh or refried beans days later. I truly appreciate a handmade tortilla and never one packaged from the store! I would pick flowers on the way to Becky's house to give to her mom. She deserved so much more but flowers were all I could steal and give. Even today I love flowers and use them as a gesture of my appreciation. Learning years later that those flowers were appreciated makes me feel really good inside.

When I graduated from Whaley, that summer was good. Good because I was headed to Dominguez and there was a lot to do following in my brother's and sister's footsteps. Dominguez had a GAA and I was required to have a red one-piece gym suit that I thought was great. My mom took me to buy my gym suits and all of my school supplies. It made me feel like I was preparing for a very important time in my life. I watched my brother and sister go before me and they were popular, had good grades, and were headed to college. This made my mom super-proud and it was sometimes all we heard about, so of course I wanted to make her proud, too! When I visited Dominguez over the summer with my mom to enroll, I saw girls with what I later learned were flags. They were in front of the windows of the gym looking at their reflections in the doors as they twirled red and gold patterned flags. I thought the twirling flags were so beautiful. It felt like I was looking into a kaleidoscope. The intricate patterns of the flags' colors with the added motion mesmerized me. I was intrigued and knew at that moment that I wanted to be one of them, a flag girl. While my mom was in the office, I was able to go out near a big bell lodged atop a cement block painted red and gold in the lunch area and watch the flag girls for a bit. I later learned that the big block with the bell on it was called the Victory Bell and after every school win or accomplishment, the Student Body would ring this bell as a celebration of the school's accomplishments. I wanted to get closer to see how the girls were twirling their flags so I started walking closer. As I approached a big tiled circle on the ground in front of the pathway that led to the gym, I heard someone yell "Hey! Get off SENIOR LANE!" I was startled and stopped in my tracks immediately! I looked to the right and there were two boys on a bench with letter jackets on. I didn't know them, but I definitely took a step back as I was about to enter a pathway that was "FOR SENIORS ONLY." Not only was I about to enter Senior Lane, I was about to step on the seal which, at that time, no one stepped on. You walked around the seal and NEVER walked on it. As I looked around, I noticed my mom motioning for me from the office area to come to her, as she was ready to go … so I did.

When I got home, I talked to my sister Cheryl, who had just graduated from Dominguez and was on her way to Colorado State University. I learned from her that in order to be on any of the Pep Squads, one had to first make it on the Drill Team. This was especially true for sophomores. You had to complete one successful year on the Drill Team (without incident), keep a C average, and then and only then could you try out for the JV Cheer, Song Girls, or Flag Girls, and only juniors and seniors made up the Varsity Cheerleaders (the elite group on campus). This news was good because I thought I was pretty smart, and the more I learned about Dominguez, the more I looked forward to going there. My sister had been the Student Body President and quite popular. My brother had played in the band, run track, and was a pretty sharp student as well. I also guess he was good-looking because he always had a girlfriend. They truly raised the bar for me when it came to the expectations others had of me. Another really good part about going to Dominguez was the fact that my older brother and sister were no longer there. I knew that I had a lot to live up to but with them gone, I thought that maybe I could blaze my own trail and not follow in anyone's footsteps. When I was in school at Whaley, I was always reminded about being Cheryl's younger sister and being expected to be a great student like she was. I got that from most all of my teachers with the exception of Mr. Lasley … of course. When I got to Dominguez it was no different. I was constantly reminded about my siblings and always compared to them. It was hard getting out from under Cheryl's reign as the picture of her and the entire Student Body Cabinet was nailed on the wall of the Student Body meeting room in the main office area at Dominguez. I wanted to be like her and achieve my goals and be remembered like she was, but I never wanted to be her.

The summers were always good for our family. Either my parents put us in the family car and we traveled across the country, visiting relatives and experiencing new-found places, food, and adventures, or we went to Boy Scout Jamborees with my dad. Most times when we traveled as a family, we were on the road when my birthday came around. I didn't have a lot of parties but overall, it didn't bother me one way or the other. We had intimate celebrations for my birthday and I believe that's where I got the idea as an adult that I most enjoy intimate parties, as opposed to big celebrations, when acknowledging a birthday or an event.

Music then and now is very important in my life. I grew up listening to the Jackson Five in Gary, Indiana. "I Want You Back" was one of the most popular songs of that summer of 1969. Having been raised in Gary, our family stayed in tune with the Jackson Five throughout their journey. I danced with my brother and sisters in the den and at every family event. We may have been four but the Bradshaw Four was entertaining. My Aunt Cordie and Aunt Doris would urge us to perform at Thanksgiving or Christmas. We were the entertainment! This upbeat song that I loved was how I was living! Everything that surrounded my world was upbeat and without incident. I didn't see that this particular summer was filled with more tensions across the United States than usual. I was oblivious to the tensions of the nation and the rise of inequities in the United States and the civil activism that was closer than I knew.

My father's sister was my Aunt Bobbye and there was absolutely nothing unusual about that to me. She showed up to family events and we went to her house with regularity and no particular purpose in mind except to visit family. That's just what we did with all family.

It didn't dawn on me that when we visited her house in Compton and met Jesse Jackson or Lilian Mobley that they were anything more than friends of the family. I had no idea that Aunt Bobbye was called upon by President Lyndon B. Johnson to sit on his War on Poverty Task Force in 1964 that led to the creation of the Head Start Program across the United States. I had no idea that Aunt Bobbye fostered the rise of the Martin Luther King Jr./Drew Medical Center in Compton from the ashes of the 1965 Watts Riots. I had no idea that my Aunt Bobbye was best known for her tireless work serving a multitude of communities as Director of the Avalon-Carver Community Center serving South Central Los Angeles. I learned later that my Aunt Bobbye glued communities together when civil injustices and police brutality tore them apart. I had no idea that my Aunt Bobbye was named a Los Angeles Times Woman of the Year in 1967 when I was just leaving elementary school and headed to Whaley.

Now here I am, getting ready to leave junior high school and enter high school with a totally different mindset! I began to learn a bit more about racism and racial degradation. I began to learn more about my family and how we were affected by the injustices of the '60s. As I learned more, I began to understand how groups like the Black Panthers evolved and why college students were exercising their voices in opposition to the war in Vietnam. It made greater sense to me why people's favorite songs were the Beatles "Let It Be" and Marvin Gaye's "What's Going On?" These tunes could be heard across the nation as protesters used these as theme songs. That summer of 1970 in Compton was only a small reflection of "what was going on," compared to what was happening on a much larger scale across the United States. As Blacks used their voices to rise up and fight for equity and justice, they did not always practice Martin Luther King's non-violent ways. There were spurts of violence among gangs in Compton but more so was the violence against the White residents of Compton. Malcolm X's theme, "by any means necessary" was used as justification for violence across the nation.

I use that same theme today (changed just a bit) at the close of all my emails. It reads "education ... by any means necessary." By the end of the summer of 1970 there was an exodus of most of the White residents as I'm sure they felt that they must relocate to safer environments away from Compton.

While the majority of my junior high school days went without my seeing color, I soon felt forced to and that led to an awareness of the issues surrounding the color of one's skin.

9

All Things Change

When I began school at Dominguez, many of my White friends from Whaley were gone … no notice and no good-byes. By now I was growing and learning more about the issues of people of color. I learned from my grandfather about the Black Panthers, and the global Pan-African Movement. I better understood the plights of the nation with the Kent State and Jackson State shootings, the Hard Hat Riot, and the massive protests against the war in Vietnam. Although I was reading more and more, these issues did not directly affect me until I began my first school year at Dominguez High School. My home life was unchanged and the routines were the same, and the diversity of the people my family interacted with was unchanged as well. There were no cracks in the security and love felt within the walls of my home. We did not have family discussions about racism in the nation, or the Kent State shootings. We had discussions about whether we completed our school work and what school events we had forthcoming or what events we would miss because we didn't complete our chores or meet other expectations. You know, regular stuff. I did get better, however, at listening to the adults around me and how they felt about public issues and things going on within our family and our community. What adults said began to matter to me so I listened carefully and watched them closely because a lot can be interpreted out of what people do. Actions speak volumes.

On the first day of attending any new school the first thing you want to do is find your friends. I rode the bus to school, so all my neighborhood friends were all on the bus with me. I didn't see any of my White or Mexican friends until I got to school. As I entered each class, I saw some of my friends from Mayo and Whaley but a lot of them were missing. I saw Lynne and Becky in a couple of my classes and that made me feel at ease. I don't remember seeing Evita, but I also had Jeanetta Yanni and Steve Sugita in my class with Mrs. Griffin. Terri Shaw, Sheree Johnson, and Genevieve Gutierrez made it to Dominguez and they were good friends from my neighborhood. Becky had a boyfriend when we left Whaley and continued to be with Mike off and on, until we graduated. Lynne on the other hand was kind of by herself. I believe I had one or two classes with some of my friends and most all the girls had GAA together with me the last period of the day. I later learned that some of the kids not living in the Dominguez area ended up at Compton High or Centennial High, but I was glad to have my closest friends with me at Dominguez.

Because Becky had a boyfriend, I saw her more at a distance at lunch or walking down the halls because she was always with Mike. I saw Lynne in class but lost sight of her quite a bit during the day which I truly didn't like but I caught up with both of them at the end of the day in GAA.

During the first semester at Dominguez, we had a few incidents where students were being jumped or egged into a fight if they were White. I was initially concerned about stuff like that because Lynne was by herself most of the time. My parents had also always told me to stay out of other people's business unless it involved me directly so I tried to do that. I also learned that when you come to any school and spend quality time, it becomes your second home. So, what goes on in your second home is really your business, right? It affects you whether you want it to or not. That's how I wanted to look at it. So the more I would hear of students being jumped, the more I became concerned for Lynne. People didn't know Lynne like

I did because if they knew her, really knew her, they would leave her alone. The Lynne I knew didn't see color, she saw quality and character. Her dad was a pastor for goodness sake! When I was with her, I never felt anything but acceptance. We didn't even talk about race or conflict. I don't even remember ever having an argument or fight with Lynne, or Becky, for that matter. And even though I was becoming more conscious about my blackness and what that meant to me, it never interfered with or overrode my friendship with Lynne or Becky.

One day in class I overheard some Black girls (who I really didn't know) talk about jumping a White girl in the hallway. Dominguez had long, long hallways that never seemed to end, but every 50 feet or so, there was a break in that hallway where a person could actually not be seen because they were in between the lockers or on a path that crossed the hallways. We would use the breaks to surprise someone on occasion, not to jump someone, and now some girls were talking about jumping some White girl. At first, I didn't know who they were referring to, until they continued to describe this "White girl." The way they said "White girl" was as if she had done something to them and they needed to pay her back. They spoke about a White girl who walked straight up-and-down and talked like she knew everything. How she would walk by people and snub her nose at them or walk by them like she didn't care about them at all. They interpreted Lynne's natural posture as arrogance or cockiness and they definitely didn't like it, whether they were right or not. They had no respect that Lynne didn't get into people's business or go out of her way to get in people's faces to make friends with them.

I knew they were talking about Lynne. Lynne was an athlete and confident about who she was. When she walked down the hall, she walked tall and sure. She was always simply dressed and never brought attention to herself and was always pleasant. She would walk by you if she didn't know you but she would speak and respond if spoken to. She was not a busy-body and was always polite and kind. I knew Lynne had a few challenges with some Black girls when she started at Dominguez but I am sure that she never did anything to warrant their negative attention. I wasn't tuned into just the Black issues and the Black community, and I wasn't stupid, either, and I could see what might be coming.

On the day I heard the girls talking about Lynne, I knew that I was going to get into real trouble. I just wasn't sure what kind of trouble but I could surely feel it. I didn't know about Black this or White that, I just knew that Lynne was my friend and I didn't want to see her hurt. She'd been through enough at Whaley with Del's accident and all the other racial incidents. I also felt that as her friend I needed to protect her and there was no doubt in my mind. My mother raised me to always think first about my actions AND the consequences of them. So, I knew that I would probably have to go to the office if I got involved in a fight, and that the office would call my mother (who I NEVER wanted to see at school). My mother worked for the Compton Unified School District at the time and was well-known and well-respected. If she had to leave work to come after me, I would definitely be in trouble at school and then again after I got home! I also knew that the future for me would change at Dominguez and possibly at home, too. I had never really had a fight (unless it was with my siblings ... which was nothing) and now I might take that to a different level. The anticipation of my rushing thoughts was overwhelming. I felt anxiety and fear. I was scared but then again, I knew I had to do something and do something fast.

As I prepared to leave class, I left my books in class under my seat, just in case I needed to fight. I watched the clock and as the bell rang to end class, I followed those girls out of class. There was always such a rush of students when the bell rang that it was easy for me to stay very close to them. As I followed them down the long hallway, I realized that they saw Lynne coming toward us from a distance. They stopped when they saw her and were whispering to each other. Although I was close, I wasn't close enough to hear what was said so I became concerned. At that point I walked in front of them. Aggressively I asked them, "Who are you two looking at?"

One of the girls pointed down the hall in the direction Lynne was coming from. The other said, "We're going to teach that White girl a lesson!" What did that mean … *teach her a lesson?* She hadn't done anything to them. I got very angry at that point and I told both girls, "If either of you touches that White girl, you will surely have a problem with me and every friend that I have who isn't White!" I spoke firmly and surely didn't stutter as I looked into their eyes without blinking. They knew I meant what I said. I believe that this was the first time I had ever challenged someone and although I felt scared, there was such a sense of *right* about what I was doing that I knew I couldn't stop. I look at that moment as pivotal to my belonging at Dominguez. It was like Dominguez was my home, our home, and I was protecting home.

As Lynne approached, she could see that something was up but the girls made the decision to turn and walk away. I was relieved and thought I had remedied the problem only to find that Lynne's problems didn't all necessarily go away and she would eventually leave Dominguez. I knew when she left that it was truly in her best interest, but I always missed her and wished things had worked out differently. I was in CSF, GAA, and on the school cabinet as a junior, but I never thought that she wouldn't finish with me as a senior. Lynne didn't live far from Roosevelt Elementary School and I had an aunt that lived near the school. I don't know exactly when Lynne moved out of Compton. I just know that when my aunt moved to her second home in Compton during my junior year, it was right behind Roosevelt Elementary School close to where Lynne lived. We always passed her house on the way to and from Aunt Cordie's home. It made me sad to drive by my senior year. I missed my friend.

So eventually I lost Evita and now Lynne, and in my opinion, for no good reason but I had to adjust like my parents had always taught me to do. Fortunately, I had become very active in student life at Dominguez. I was now a Don and I truly wanted to match, if not pass, the accomplishments of my brother and sister. It was not as much of a competition as it was fulfilling the need I had to be engaged fully in my education like my mother wanted me to be. I signed up for Drill Team, the Speech Club, and the Drama Club my first year. I also played all the school sports possible. At that time, we played volleyball, field hockey, basketball, softball, and tennis, and ran track. I was an above-average athlete in junior high and it resonated right into high school. Lynne, Becky, Evita, and I had the fastest time in the 400-yard relay while at Whaley and no one broke our record even after I finished high school. As people used to say back then, we were *bad!*

The teacher for the Speech Club was Pat Schilling. Mrs. Schilling was a no-nonsense kind of teacher but all students knew that she truly loved all of us underneath her stern voice. Any teacher who would come to work on Saturdays and drive students to absolutely any school to have us compete in speech competitions was awesome. We knew she had family and at times we were confused about how much time she was truly spending with them, if she was always with us. She taught English during the school day, stayed after school with the Speech Club with us until the last bus arrived, and then spent her weekends with us, and even fed us too. Talk about dedication! I loved the Speech Club. It became a real platform for me to speak my mind about almost anything! When I first competed in the Speech Club I listened to students from different schools (primarily White schools) and the students would recite famous speeches in history. When I was in tenth grade, who I saw compete and who I competed against truly didn't matter to me. I loved the competition!

I didn't know much about Samoans before coming to Dominguez but there were quite a few at school. I thought they were so beautiful, so exotic, especially the boys. I had a secret crush on Filemu Pule most of my years in high school. Even though all the Samoans were cordial to everyone, they seemed to stick to themselves and were tremendously family-oriented. Most of the Samoan students lived in a complex called Park Village. In addition to a good number of Samoans, there were a few Asians, more Mexicans, and even more

Blacks at school during my junior year. As I became more conscious of the plight of Blacks socially and politically, it made me more aware of my surroundings and who I shared my surroundings with. My last year on the speech team I sensed a change in my intentions and I not only wanted to win for the sport, I wanted to win to represent Black people because there were so few competing in this arena with me. I felt a sense of commitment of some kind, to represent. As I continued to listen to speeches there was one speech that I knew nothing about early on, but heard often… "The Desiderata." Its popularity baffled me until one day after I asked Mrs. Schilling about it, she said, "go to the library (at school) and look it up!" So I did. I soon learned that The Desiderata was written in the 1920s and didn't originally have a title. As I read the poem, I ended up liking and learning the poem and eventually recited it at speech competitions and won quite a few trophies using it. Mrs. Schilling always told me that I had the voice of a DJ and people would always love listening to me. For the most part, she was right. My being a part of the Speech Club, learning how to speak well in public, eventually led to my being a DJ in college, and I owe all that to Mrs. Schilling.

Next to Mrs. Schilling's class was Mrs. Griffin. She was another kick-butt kind of teacher and most students loved her to death, too. She taught drama after school but you could always find kids in her room even if they didn't belong, in the morning before the bell rang, at lunch, and/or after school, too. I can't remember much about what I did with the Drama Club because most of the time I was just hanging out. I truly believe that I just wanted to be around Mrs. Griffin because of who she was. She was a pretty cool teacher who seemed like she broke the rules all the time (and kids liked that). She was out-spoken and kind of hippie-ish. The one thing that I appreciated most about her was how she taught me to understand and interpret the plays and sonnets of Shakespeare. Reading Shakespeare was one of the hardest things I was ever asked to do. Although his works are known as some of the world's finest, Old English made utterly no sense to me.

So, my sophomore year I tried out for the Drill Team at D-High. The Drill Team was run by twins named Myra and Myrna Sparks. Drill Team was an awesome experience with these sisters. The twins were as precise as could be and you had to become a mirror image of them to pass all of their tests. I was good at Drill Team but I knew my ultimate goal was to become a flag girl, so I learned to do whatever it took to get by. That meant extra days after school, standing in front of the gym doors practicing and practicing and when we got through with practice, everyone went home to practice even more.

That year I participated in the Compton Christmas Parade. Everyone was asked to take off all their jewelry and accessories and they would be locked up in the band room. All of us were checked one-by-one for uniform consistency and precision. I was scared as a first-timer but my eventual comfort was in our numbers. We were relatively large and I knew that made me feel better. We looked good in our red and gold, and we sounded as good as we looked! As we finished the parade, we were able to stay and see some of the performances of other schools. As we watched other schools go by, I learned about the Compton High Tarbabes. When you see the Tarbabes coming, you'd see them being led by a fantastic drum major, then the wonderful pep squads who performed in unison to the beat of their drums. As they came down the street toward me that day, I was not quite sure how many people I was looking at. The pep squads came down one block and turned a corner, but the band was still coming! The school attach units with the band seemed to last for another three or four blocks! I had never seen so many students represent a school. The powder blue and white was stunning but I still preferred my red and gold!! The other high school in our district was Centennial. I didn't remember much about their band or attach units, ONLY the drill team called the Centennettes. They wore red and white feathered Apache headdresses that flowed down their backs to their knees and their stark white go-go boots had metal taps that clacked in unison when they danced and marched. The Centennettes were not to be forgotten!

After my year on Drill Team, I knew the flags were for me! I remember an upperclassman who was a flag girl…I believe Ethyl was her name. I knew her best friend was Carol and she was a cheerleader. These two girls were beautiful and definitely popular for their natural beauty. I used to watch Ethyl twirl flags and imagined that was me. Near the end of my sophomore year, I signed up for flag tryouts and guess what … I made the team! I was good height at 5'10" so the 36" flags were perfect for me.

When you made the flag squad, or any squad for that matter, you had to come to school during the summer for practice and also pay to go to the premiere camp that was held at the Hibbard's All-American Clinic. We were told that the best schools learned and competed at this clinic. Of course, it was nowhere near our community and it was predominantly White. Most of us had to create fundraisers to get the money we needed to attend. Most of the families of the girls on our squad could not afford a $300, four-day camp. My first time at Hibbard's camp was mesmerizing. Of course, the most popular pep squads were the Varsity Cheerleaders. All other pep squads were secondary to them. I almost believed that flags were the least popular pep squad. The pecking order appeared to be Varsity Cheer, Varsity Song, Varsity Drill or Dance, and Varsity Flag.

Bonita, Dominguez High School yearbook photo: flag girl, 1972

When we went to camp of course we stayed overnight but I didn't necessarily mingle and hang out with other girls and other teams. I had been exposed to spending nights away from home but not this far away from my family and with people I didn't necessarily know. Other girls from other teams (mostly White girls) were more free-spirited and didn't mind hanging out in other people's rooms and sleeping over with new friends and acquaintances. I was not like that and even though I had spent plenty time at Becky's home after school at Whaley or hanging out with Lynne or Evita at school, we really didn't do sleepovers or that type of stuff. I occasionally slept over at Terri's or Sheree's house (they were Black) but still not that often.

I watched the many schools come into camp and walk away with most all of the awards at the end. I became concerned that our flag squad was not competitive enough. I felt people looked to us (the Black girls) to dance our way through our routines instead of showing precision and above-average skill-set routines. After I came home from the first camp, I reflected on what I thought people expected of us versus what I expected of not only myself, but of our team. We were Black and Mexican and all the White girls wanted us to do at camp was dance. That eventually pissed me off because in all of my dealings and friendship with Lynne, Jeanetta, and other White classmates, I had never experienced that expectation. As I approached my senior year in high school, incidents like this became the norm and far more irritating.

My junior year was exciting as a flag girl. I tried my absolute best to perfect my skill as a twirler. Our captain, Anita LeVeaux, always encouraged me to be better. She told me that I would be the next captain of the team. Her words encouraged me to try harder. That year, there were six of us: Anita, Paula Bond, Betty Stitt, Candy Bruce, Cynthia Clark, and me. We were very good but I always believed that we could be better. So, when tryouts for senior year came around, I signed up to compete for captain and Anita was right. I became captain of the flag squad my senior year. Now was my time to make a difference in how we presented ourselves hoping that other people's expectations (meaning White people for the most part) would not be to just dance for them, but perform with excellence and precision for them and others.

The flag girls my senior year included Paula Bond, who was a flag girl but was also our Basketball Belle that same year. Paula graduated with me and went on to become a Fashion Fair model, international runway model, and BET commentator. We are still friends today. Ann Bravo was a junior who was very slender and tall but not as skilled as the upperclassmen. Candace Bruce was a senior, like me, and was so light-hearted and sweet all the time. Shirley Jackson was also a senior, and surprised me when she tried out because she always seemed so serious about everything. Her mother was a teacher at Dominguez, which may explain her seriousness. Donna Armstrong was a junior and not as tall as the rest of us but she managed to work those flags to the best of her ability and made us proud.

We had a stronger team than the year before when it came to skill and ability, but as captain, I always wanted more. I wanted to create a team that was capable of competing with the absolute best. That summer before my senior year, I spent considerable time in my driveway in front of our garage at home creating what I thought would be the best and most unique routines ever! We did very little freestyle dancing and increased the number of tosses and amount of precision work into each routine. I even added a few popular cheerleader hand movements to our routine to show a contemporary side! Our footwork was captivating as we shuffled and marched to the music and twirled out flags under our knees or between our legs.

When we went to camp at the end of summer, we were ready to compete with the best. I had reached one of my goals … to be accepted for something more technical than just dancing! Our routine music included "The Horse" by Cliff Nobles & Co., "I'll Be There" by The Spinners, "Outa Space" by Billy Preston, "Café Regio" by Isaac Hayes, and "Soulful Strut" by Young/Holt Unlimited. We performed these routines in the gym and they were so well-received by our peers, we knew we were performing at another level, very differently from the other squads that preceded us. We ended up placing fourth over the dozens of schools at camp! This was confirmed for me again when Hibbards All-American Clinic reached out to me at the end of my senior year to ask me to teach and judge at their clinic! I went on to teach and judge at the Hibbards Clinic for the next four summers after high school and I even today I can still out-twirl any flag girl (or boy) with my flags today … not joking.

Over the years I often thought about whether the situation with my friend Lynne could have been handled differently but I guess not. As I learned more about the civil and political challenges of the '70s, my eyes opened wider and I understood that the way things went should not have happened any other way. Time heals all wounds and as the years progressed, I seemed to have adjusted to the changes in my life. I invested more time into my school, my second home. I also believed that many of my other friends struggled with race issues while at Dominguez, too. When I was a junior, Steve Sugita, one of a very few (or two) Asian students who was with me in elementary and junior high school, wrote this in my yearbook: "To Bonita. A young lady whom I have known from Mayo. It's been a long time to know someone and there are times when I wonder if I should have associated with you. Otherwise it's been all right. See you next year. Steven Sugita." I never knew he felt that way when we were in school at Dominguez but I am glad that he shared. I also remember what Candy Bruce wrote in my yearbook. She shared with me that she wanted her last year to be the best year. That she wanted us to pull together, let go of our prejudices, and be congenial with everyone because we were the past and the future of Dominguez's history! She couldn't have said it better.

Racial tension always seemed to be looming in the air during my senior year at Dominguez. There were a few big blowouts during that year that resulted in a "walk-out" at school. As a senior I became closer with students of my own race, but that may have been because there were so many more Blacks students remaining. Honestly, I'm not quite sure why. I never changed my feelings about my friends from elementary or junior high school and I know that I never looked down on them in any way for any reason. Within the Compton community so much changed. Gang activity increased and there were at least two occasions when drive-by shootings happened at Dominguez that were identified as gang-related. My aunt, Mary B. Henry, served three terms as President on the Compton Unified School Board and pressed fellow trustees to aggressively tackle Compton's drug and gang problems to help build up poor children's self-esteem. She was also honored by the Los Angeles Urban League, Los Angles Brotherhood Crusade, the National Council of Negro Women, and Presidents Kennedy, Johnson, and Carter. My father was close with his sister and I learned that he mirrored a great deal of her philosophies and beliefs that we as a people can make our dreams a reality for the coming generations. That we must rise above division and evil and do good for mankind. The more I learned about my family, the more I understood that they were very active in the Civil Rights movement and even though they worked with a diverse group of people in their professional careers, they were proactive in all causes that improved Black life in their community and beyond. The wiser I became, the more I was ready to stand up for what I believed was right.

I ended my senior year with a bang. I was Student Body President, Captain of the Flag Squad, Editor of the El Espejo yearbook, still in GAA, and a member of the Speech Team. Seniors were encouraged to identify the colleges and universities they applied to but I didn't have to. I scored well on the SAT and ACT tests and was named Girl's State Alternate at Dominguez which resulted in colleges and universities reaching out to me to apply. I felt humbled by the honor and received inquiries from USC, UCLA, and the California State schools. I went to my counselor's (Mrs. Roberts) office and shared that I also had interests in Hampton Institute (my mother's Alma Mater), Howard University, Fisk University, and the Pasadena and Chicago Art Centers. I was in conversation with Mrs. Roberts and remember her picking up a paper and saying to me that she was just informed that the University of Notre Dame was accepting women. She went on to look at this paper for a short while, then put it down and looked at me and said, "But it's probably not for you." I looked a bit perplexed but went on to ask why she felt that way. She stated that I would probably be "swallowed up" by the competition of men. I didn't know why Mrs. Roberts even brought up Notre Dame if she didn't think I was suitable, but she kind of got my juices going over why I wasn't a good fit. I went home that evening on the bus and waited for my mom to get home. When she got home and started dinner, I came and sat in the kitchen with her and asked her if she knew about the University of Notre Dame. She said, "Yes" and that it was in the state I was born in, about a two-hour drive south from Gary, Indiana. I told her what Mrs. Roberts had said and she told me that it didn't matter what anyone else thought if that was where I wanted to go. I told her that I didn't know much about Notre Dame and the only familiarity I had was being in the den at home when my dad watched a Notre Dame football game. I did not know at the time that it was an all-male private Catholic University. I told her it was not on my original list of colleges but that now I was curious and wanted to see what it was about.

I thought about Mrs. Roberts saying that I would probably be swallowed up by the competition of men but I competed against boys in the speech tournaments. I competed against boys when I ran for ASB office. I competed against boys academically. The only place I did not compete against boys was in sports … that was it! I was intimidated by what she said at first, but the more I thought about it, the more I was insulted by what she said. My mom was always the one I talked things out with because she was "no nonsense" yet reasonable and fair. If she told me not to worry about what others said, for the most part, I wasn't going to worry. I thought

Bonita, Dominguez High School yearbook photo: Student Body President, 1973

long and hard about what both women said to me and of course my mother's words were gold. I went back to the counseling office and asked Mrs. Roberts to assist me with completing an application to the University of Notre Dame du Lac.

As ASB President I was expected to speak at graduation. I worked on my speech with Mrs. Schilling for at least two weeks before graduation. Most of that speech now is a blur with the exception of my recitation of "Invictus" by William Ernest Henley. I had worked this poem into my speech because it was one of my father's favorites. The word *invictus* in Latin means *unconquerable* or *undefeated*. I still recite it today not only for myself but for the many students I have taught. I approach life with an unconquerable spirit or frame of mind. To be successful today is challenging and one must believe that they are undefeatable to move forward appropriately in life.

I graduated from Manuel Dominguez High School in June of 1973 and entered my first class in August of 1973 at the University of Notre Dame du Lac.

PART 4: AFTER COMPTON

10

The White Girl: Surviving
And Thriving

I am pretty certain that no one who knew only about my life in Compton would have been able to predict what I've done with my life since then. Because the college I attended was non-traditional, with no exams or grades and the only requirement being a cross-cultural experience, I really couldn't fail unless I dropped out. With no constraints on what I could learn, I was free to think creatively and independently, "outside the box," which eventually helped me in my career as a scientist. In college, I quickly discovered the field of ethology, the study of animal behavior in nature, and as it meshed so well with my lifelong love of animals, I developed my education around it. After graduating from college, I took jobs as a restaurant cashier and waitress in Orange County. After I moved to Davis in northern California, I became a recreation leader for after-school kids, a bus driver for the local senior center, and a tour guide, focusing on San Francisco, Yosemite, and the southwestern U.S.

One of the birds of Mission San Juan Capistrano in 1959. Lynne's love of animals started early

I also found opportunities to become involved in animal behavior research. I volunteered for a year as a research assistant for a behavioral study at the Primate Center on the UC Davis campus and that experience led to an actual paying job observing the behavior of rats and cats for a year in the Veterinary School. These experiences then led to success in achieving my dream of living in the bush in Africa and following animals around, just as Jane Goodall had done. For two years I lived in a one-room, mud-walled hut with no running water or electricity in Kibale Forest, Uganda, East Africa. I went to Kibale with Joe, whom I'd met in college, to study the behavior and ecology of red colobus monkeys, a species currently vulnerable to extinction from deforestation.

It was not the best time to live in Uganda but, coming from Compton, I was prepared. I was used to being around people who were different from me, and I was also no stranger to violence. Uganda's ruthless and capricious dictator, Idi Amin, had been deposed nine months earlier after a reign of terror that had lasted eight years and, according to Amnesty International, cost 500,000 lives. After he left, Uganda remained in the throes of political instability, unpredictability, and violence. In my short time there, Uganda went through two more presidents and one invasion. The few times I was in Kampala, Uganda's capital and largest city, I

Lynne's house in Kibale Forest, Uganda, 1981, with employee and mentee Margaret Kabagenyi, in front, tending the garden

heard gunshots at night, and murders were all too common. Once, coming back to Kibale through Kampala on a rare trip to neighboring Kenya for supplies, Joe and I checked into the modern, multi-story, International Hotel for the night. We thought it would be safe but the manager who checked us in was murdered that night, his blood splattered on the stairs we walked down to reach the lobby the next morning. But I was impressed by the young boys at the many roadblocks. Although they didn't seem to know the basics of firearm safety as they waved their guns around willy-nilly while they talked to us, they didn't press us for cigarettes, candy, or money as we expected; they asked only for books to read.

Amin also left Uganda an economic disaster. Basic commodities that we in the U.S. typically take for granted, such as wheat flour, rice, sugar, butter, and toilet paper, were rarely available. Coca-cola appeared in the nearby town of Fort Portal only twice in two years, both at Christmastime. Fortunately, the fertile soil on the edge of Kibale Forest provided us with plenty of beans, groundnuts, vegetables, and tropical fruits to eat, and the violence seldom penetrated into Kibale Forest because the guys with weapons were afraid to enter the dark, unfamiliar forest with its exuberant vegetation, including trees that could grow to 100 feet (30 meters) or more. I had a plan that if I was ever in any danger, I would simply disappear into the forest that I knew so well.

Most of the time I was the only person in my part of the forest, but I never felt alone. There were always insects buzzing, birds singing, and monkeys calling, and occasionally even elephants trumpeting. I enjoyed getting to know the monkeys and observing how they lived their lives in a tropical forest. Over time, I learned to identify individual monkeys by their physical characteristics, such as having a crooked or pink-tipped finger, a unique tail tip shape, or a white blaze of fur between the eyes. Each recognizable individual was christened with a name, and then the fun of discovery really began. In animal behavior research, the importance of the individual cannot be understated.

By the time I left Uganda, the Africa bug had bitten me and I felt strongly that I had to find my way back. My experience studying primate behavior and ecology in nature led to my acceptance into graduate school at UC Davis to study animal behavior, with a focus on primates. When the opportunity arose to return to East Africa for more fieldwork as part of my dissertation research, I jumped at the chance. I went to Kenya's Amboseli National Park where I spent over two years studying vervets, domestic cat-sized monkeys with light brown bodies, black feet, and black faces, that are equally at home on the ground and in the trees. This time, I lived relatively luxuriously in the warden's former house, with three bedrooms, an indoor toilet, water from a tap, and electricity for four hours almost every evening. It also had a spectacular view looking out across the plains of Amboseli to Mt. Kilimanjaro in the distance. That just made me love Africa more, and when I returned to the U.S., I kept looking for other ways to return. One of those was as safari guide. My experience as a tour guide in the U.S. helped me get hired during graduate school to lead Americans around some of the national parks of Kenya, Tanzania, Rwanda, and what was then called Zaire, now known as the Democratic Republic of Congo.

After I earned my Ph.D. in animal behavior, I applied for and was offered a job as an assistant professor of anthropology at Rutgers University. I stayed there three years and then was offered a position back at UC Davis where I have been ever since. I am now a full professor in the Department of Anthropology and a faculty member of the Animal Behavior Graduate Group. I still conduct research in East Africa, I have published lots of journal papers on animal behavior and have written an award-winning book about primate evolution, I received an award for teaching and mentoring graduate students, I have advised numerous graduate students who are successful in their own right, I have influenced at least a few undergraduates to pursue primatology as a career, and I was elected a Fellow of the California Academy of Sciences. In short, I have had a full and exceedingly lucky life since leaving Compton, with a career built around education and animal behavior. But whatever adventures and successes I have had, they were achieved in spite of Compton. Academically, Compton did very little for me at best; it mainly hindered my progress. I spent seven years between undergrad and grad school catching up.

Emotionally, Compton has been, perhaps surprisingly, a mixed bag for me. It wasn't all bad but it was pretty close. Before I was jumped at school the second time I was brimming with confidence, a school leader in sports, student government, and academics. After I was jumped, I shriveled up inside and hoped it would work on the outside, too, to minimize the chances of another attack. It baffles me how one incident was able to so fully extinguish that fearless personality. If it hadn't happened, I might have gone into government or become an investigative reporter. Instead, I found refuge in animal behavior, a field of study that almost always leads to college teaching, and that's where it took me, but teaching isn't an easy fit for me. A regular part of what I do involves talking in front of large groups of people but ever since that attack, I have felt very uncomfortable in the spotlight. I dislike having large numbers of people look at me because it feels as if I'm being surrounded and threatened, as I was during the attack. When I'm giving lectures or even just talking to a group of colleagues, in faculty meetings, for example, I feel tense even though intellectually I know the situation is entirely different from the attack that occurred at Dominguez all those many years ago. Of course, feeling on edge in front of groups prevents me from being the best lecturer I could be. I may be described as passionate about animals but I know I don't deliver lectures smoothly. A kind colleague once described my style as "refreshingly unpolished." I also tend to diminish myself in front of students rather than act as an authority. Students need to feel confident that their instructors are knowledgeable, and I do know my stuff, but I continually feel the need to shrink my presence. My professional standing among my peers has also been hindered by my reluctance to give talks at other universities. I have no problems with the attention I bring to myself through writing, it's just groups of people that make me feel wary. It's a perennial challenge for me to manage that feeling so that I can function well in my job.

Out of the blue, 33 years after that second attack, I received an email from the girl whose face expressed such delight in watching the altercation until she turned to see my bloodied face. It apparently left a lasting impression on her, too, because among other things, she brought up the fight and, although she thought it had involved my sister instead of me, she recalled feeling embarrassed about the unprovoked incident. She noted that after attending Catholic schools, she found Dominguez High School to be exciting but "louder and more crass" than she had been prepared for, but then she figuratively shrugged and finished with, "Oh well … that is all over with." For me, though, it is never "all over with." It has affected the rest of my life. To help me deal with the emotions generated by my past, I take lessons from lyrics of songs I like. Nowadays, I try to keep in mind the words in a song called "Lodestar" by the Birds of Chicago, one of my favorite bands: "You are not what you've lost; what remains should not bear the cost," but it's challenging to keep that in mind.

I don't think most of us realize how little violence it takes to scar a person who's been exposed to it. We try to deal with it the best that we can. We try not to let it scar us but it takes its toll anyway, in one way or another. Was it really good for me to learn that we all carry the self-destructive power of hatred inside us? I'm convinced that those who would deny its existence in themselves just haven't been exposed yet to a situation that brings hatred out into the open, but I know that all it takes is an event that violates in the extreme our own perception of what is fair and just. Since that Christmas morning when Ramón was shot, I have felt I must always be vigilant to keep that powerful feeling of hatred contained within myself and to do my best to contain it within those with whom I interact. I do this by very consciously trying to be fair and respectful to everyone I deal with. It's not that I wouldn't be fair and respectful had I not felt that hatred within me but I might have given fairness and respect to others less self-consciously had I remained innocent.

When I moved to northern California after college, I interviewed for a job as an after-school playground leader. I wanted the job as my way of honoring the coaches who gave so much attention to the kids in the after-school program at Roosevelt Elementary and to me. At one point the interviewer told me, "You know, Davis isn't reality." I laughed and told him, "That's okay, I've had enough reality! I could use a little fantasy." He was right. For comparison, according to the Disaster Center's Uniform Crime Reports for the State of California, in 1980, the violent crime rate in Compton was 2768 incidents per 100,000 people. Violent crimes include murder, rape, robbery, and aggravated assault. In Davis in that same year, the violent crime rate was 139 per 100,000 people. Up until recently, I felt my university town was a safe haven even on the streets late at night. Davis was a great place to help turn my deep emotional wounds from Compton into more superficial wounds. I could relax more in Davis because I didn't perceive that anyone was out to get me, and there are many civic-minded people here with good intentions. Still, when I had my own family, I was the one who made sure all the doors were locked every night and even during the day, whether we were inside the house or out.

Now I am concerned that crime is increasing as the town gets larger and more crowded, and tempers get shorter. I also suspect some of the crime is driven by the draw of the proliferating bars and restaurants that serve alcohol downtown until late at night. The fact that Davis is readily accessible by freeways makes it an easy target for out-of-towners. Gangs have even come into Davis. In a bar one night in September, 2015, a man from a Norteño-affiliated gang in Vacaville, a city 25 minutes southwest of Davis via I-80, stabbed to death 23-year-old Peter Gonzales, who had come from southern California to attend his sister's wedding. Charges against the killer's five friends who were there with him that night were later dropped while he was convicted. Like many other cities in California, we also have a growing homeless population, and the homeless have been linked by some to rising property crimes. Finally, we also have our share of mentally unstable people, one of whom, on January 10, 2019, killed poor Natalie Corona, a 22-year-old Davis police officer. She had simply responded one foggy night to a fender-bender traffic accident downtown, and he came out of the fog on his bicycle and just shot her.

I don't forget that it only took a few short years for Compton to change from a nice place in which to live to a nice place to leave. If it can happen to Compton, it can happen anywhere. Locals here would probably scoff at the idea and maybe they're right. Maybe what happened to Compton was a one-off situation. Maybe no place will ever deteriorate as far as fast as Compton did, but I am alert for warning signs.

If, once we get away from the violence and into a safer life, how do we keep our minds from going to dark places again? One trick for me is to repeat a mantra every morning that reinforces in my mind the actual reality of my life now: "I have a house that keeps me warm, dry, and safe, I have a job that I like in a town that's easy to live in, I have food whenever I want, I have no pains in my body, I have no bullies in my life, and there is someone somewhere out there who loves me." But I'm still vigilant around others after all these years and not surprised when they do bad things. I would dearly love to think the best of humans as a species, but I can't.

My heart and mind agonize over those who have experienced worse events in their young lives. As violence becomes more common in schools across the nation, we all need to learn to wrap the victims in bandages of unconditional love, our arms figuratively holding them tight until they feel reasonably safe again and are ready to be released. Be prepared; it may take years. Survivors of violence can also help themselves by surrounding themselves with people who make them feel safe, people in whom they have confidence and trust. There may not be many people like that, but that's all right, it's not necessary to have very many. Find the people who care about you and who would never intentionally hurt you.

On the positive side, although I didn't fit in then and I don't fit in now, that's not such a bad thing. Being on the social outskirts in high school spared me the pressure to conform that is so commonly felt by teenagers, such that I still don't see the benefits of conformity as an adult. Non-conformity can become problematic if expressed so I don't show it outwardly very often, in keeping with my fear of drawing attention to myself, but it also gives me the freedom to think my own thoughts. Some of these thoughts have translated into new ideas and discoveries in my work, for example.

Growing up in Compton allowed me to feel more comfortable interacting with people from different cultures and backgrounds. When I'm new to a group of people and there are people of color in the group, I tend to gravitate toward them before I interact with White people. I guess I feel they will be less judgmental. Compton also helped me develop a strong sense of justice, a desire for equitable conditions for everyone, and a sensitivity for people as individuals. Several friends of mine over the years have pointed out the irony that, after having grown up in Compton, I would choose to spend so much of my time in Africa. But the two are worlds apart, even though the people in both places have ancestors in common. The people I have interacted with in Uganda and Kenya haven't gone through the difficulties that American Blacks have gone through. Africans have almost always treated me with kindness. For one very memorable example, in Uganda, when I got in line once to buy a train ticket, the people in line ahead of me insisted I move to the front. I protested, not wanting special privileges simply because I'm White. But I misunderstood. They explained that I was clearly a guest in their country and should be treated as such. That attitude really surprised me. How we are treated makes a huge difference in how we treat others. I wish we could be that generous in the U.S.

Having experienced growing up as a minority in the U.S. despite being White has given me a perspective that I find most people can't understand. When I'm around people who don't know my past and the conversation rolls around to racial issues, whether they are people of color or White, they believe I have no real understanding of what it's like to be discriminated against on the basis of skin color. From their perspective, because I'm White, I'm in a group of privilege, shielded from the experiences of those in minority groups. When I describe my formative years of being stereotyped and subjected to racism as a result of being a minority in a minority town and how those experiences have affected me all my life, most still refuse to accept that I have legitimate standing as someone who knows what racism feels like. Perhaps it's because they just cannot imagine a place where the roles are reversed, with a white person oppressed by Blacks, a situation so opposite what we have always seen in America. The academic in me wants to understand their difficulty, to understand why we are always so quick to put others in categorical boxes. Maybe it's a way for us to maintain a sense of order for ourselves when we live in societies so large and complex that we no longer have the time to learn about everyone with whom we interact. But I'm open to other suggestions.

During the 2016 Grammys, singer Kendrick Lamar gave a striking performance, starting out as part of a chain gang, then performing next to a giant bonfire, and finally ending by standing in front of a silhouette of Africa with "Compton" in white letters written over the central part of it. That final background scene immediately resonated with me, so much so that after the Grammys, I bought a t-shirt with that same image on it. After all, I grew up in Compton and I have loved working in East Africa for 40 years. I enjoy interacting with the people there. I value hearing their perspectives on life and living, which are very often more clear-eyed and more generous that what I hear from people in the U.S. For instance, I once described to my Ugandan friends a big difference between the U.S. and Uganda — in the U.S. people have money but not much time while in Uganda, people have time but not much money. Then I asked them what they would rather have, time or money, and without even pausing, they laughed and said, "time, of course." In retrospect, it was silly of me to ask; after all, no one on their deathbed wishes they had made more money but most probably wish they had more time. I also love the 12-hour days and nights on the equator and waking up in the bush at dawn to the natural alarm clock of a chorus of birds. Something about it all just feels right deep down, as if I'm finally home. I like to think that's because it is my home, my ancestral home — all our ancestors lived in East Africa for millions of years. But now, in these days of call-out culture in the U.S., I'm hesitant to wear the t-shirt in public, afraid that someone will accuse me of cultural appropriation, which in my mind is just another way of putting people into neat little categorical boxes and demanding they conform to our own expectations. But if they actually knew *me,* they would understand why that t-shirt works for me.

These days, I'm even finding a new unwillingness to see past my skin color by people in my own profession. Lately there are primatologists who would call me "neo-colonialist" simply because

Ranger Ben Otim, wife Teddy, and their children with Lynne in Kibale Forest, Uganda, 1987. In Lynne's honor Teddy is wearing the skirt and Otim is holding the radio given to them five years earlier

I conduct research in Africa and I'm White. Being pigeonholed into a particular group because of my skin color and not my beliefs, motivations, and intentions is frustrating to me. I want to shout out (but of course don't), "No, don't dump me into one of your categories. I am an individual!" And isn't that what Martin Luther King wanted for us all, to be judged not by the color of our skin but by the content of our character? I come with a personality that has never been seen on earth before and has only a short time on earth now. Some of my personality I was born with, and some of it came from my experiences as I have gone through life. I am unique and so are you and everyone else who has been here on earth. We are all individuals. We need to get to know others as individuals before we decide who is a decent person or not. If we each do this, in my mind I imagine it trickling upstream to institutions, a direction that might then also reduce alienation and pushback from many in our society. I think this focus on the individual is one of the best perspectives I developed from living in Compton. Everyone has a unique story to tell.

The value of seeing people as individuals is exemplified by my friends Becky and Bonita. When we were growing up, personality was important, not the color of our skin. It still is. My friends are strong and have always thought for themselves. How else could Becky have stayed with Mike all those years in school when everyone made it clear that he was not good for her? How else could Bonita have stood up to her classmates to protect me? As adults, neither fits neatly into our society's categorizations of Hispanic or Black women. For instance, Becky still plays sports, she has written two children's books, and she hates to cook. I know she doesn't see herself as I do, a very successful woman. Success comes in many forms, and one of the ways in which Becky's been successful is that she's the only one of the three of us whose marriage is still going strong. Bonita knows more about wines than I do even though I work at a university and live in a community where wine is a big deal. She is a force of nature; nothing defeats her. She somehow maintains a sense of humor through the darkest of times. I relish such tidbits of knowledge about them, and I always look forward to learning more. Knowing who these women are, knowing their stories, makes my life richer, and I hope my caring makes their lives richer.

Although I vowed never to return to Compton, I broke that vow and did return 36 years later, in 2009. I returned to support my sister Jeanne who wanted her five kids to be baptized in my father's former church. I was full of fear, sure we would get shot, but my mother was just as sure we would not. She lived in Long Beach, in many respects a world away, but really only 13 miles from Compton. She still sometimes attended the church and also went for jury duty in downtown Compton, and she said she never had any problems. So, we went to church, and I was pleasantly surprised to see Kelvin Filer, with whom I attended Sunday School when we were kids. We talked after the service and I learned that, after college and law school, he returned to Compton and eventually became a judge. When the service was over, Jeanne wanted to drive to our childhood home just to see it one more time. I was full of trepidation but to my surprise, nothing terrible happened. In fact, Theodore Roosevelt Elementary School is now in better shape than it was when I moved away. It even has glass windows again. The rest of the neighborhood is also quite presentable. Seeing my childhood home and neighborhood in good condition again after so many years of self-imposed exile helped some of my fear vanish along with the sense of loss that I had felt for so long because I had always thought that I could never go back home.

As I reviewed my early life in Compton, I also revisited my relationship with my father, who passed away in 1999. My father was the person who was ultimately responsible for our being in Compton. He said he'd heard a voice one day telling him he should move to Compton to do God's work. He thought it was a calling. So, he moved his family and settled there. He did a lot of good things for the community and was recognized for his efforts with various awards over the years, including being nominated for Father of the Year. My dad taught me that people can have hidden sides to them.

He was often very impatient with his kids; I think it was because he was frustrated that his responsibilities to us kept him from doing all he wanted to do for the community. I'm very sensitive to and wary of hypocrisy as a result.

He was the one I blamed when I was a prickly teenager and hated living in Compton. For a long time, my relationship with him was shaded by the belief that I had nothing in common with him — I rejected his religion and his life's work, I thought that his belief that Blacks and Whites could get along was naïve, I felt his efforts to integrate Compton were for naught, especially as conditions in Compton continued to deteriorate, and I blamed him for putting his own family in harm's way. What kind of father would do that to his kids? Why were others so important that he would risk the safety of his own kids to help them? My opinion was cemented from the perspective of a hurt teenager and it didn't change when I grew older and was living away from home. I felt a lot of resentment toward him for putting his needs above those of his family. I thought he should never have had a family. Paradoxically, I also blamed him for helping to make me feel alone so often in this world by modeling for me how to think about what's good for all and to act accordingly, not to have an agenda of self-interest. I say paradoxically because it often seemed that his reason for moving to and staying in Compton to do good was driven by his own self-interest, not by a voice he attributed to God. Regardless, he did help the community.

Unfortunately, I have found the attitude of wanting to act in ways that are good for everyone to be fairly uncommon. Maybe it's more normal to think first about ourselves than about what is best for all, especially when there are disagreements, because most of us aren't raised by ministers. When I come up against that selfish attitude, I struggle emotionally and retreat into myself again, avoiding people until time or something good happens to ease me back out.

It was fortunate that my mother saved many newspaper articles about my father along with some of his sermons and other speeches that revealed his beliefs and hopes for the world and for Compton's citizens. It has been interesting getting to know him again. I'm now convinced that the differences I saw between us when I was younger existed because he experienced success in human relations whereas I experienced mainly failure.

As early as 1953 when my father was just starting out as a minister, he wrote, "We will seek to be different by emphasizing our similarities and accepting our differences. We will seek to form bridges of understanding and helpfulness across chasms of feeling, to cement ties of good will among all groups and all persons." Eight years later when we moved to Compton, his opportunity to literally practice what he preached had arrived. In Compton my father was active in many community groups, and the Blacks with whom he interacted to advance "understanding and helpfulness" were mainly adult professionals of similar minds. They wanted to work together with Whites for the betterment of Compton; they didn't want Whites to leave. The adults were confident that integration, not just in the sense of Blacks and Whites sharing the same neighborhood, but truly working together, could be achieved. Hadn't they shown that this was possible during the riots of 1965? If only they had been able to co-opt the teenagers to their cause, it might have worked.

My Compton experience was completely different. I was interacting with teenagers who, by nature, tend to be emotionally unpredictable. We teenagers didn't come together on our own volition; we were thrown together because we all had to attend school. There was really no incentive to get to know students from other backgrounds as individuals. We didn't care about the bigger picture that was Compton, we just cared about our own little worlds. With that sort of arrangement in place, it's no wonder there was conflict between teenagers of different backgrounds. Friendships like the one I had with Bonita were extremely rare. Friendships between Hispanics and Whites were a little more common, but by and large, students stayed among their own. This remained the pattern when gangs formed and wreaked havoc in Compton beginning in the early 1970s. Despite the hopes and best efforts of the adults, I would argue that the youths of Compton ultimately caused its deterioration and notoriety because the gangs were started by and were largely composed of teenagers. The troubles with young people that I experienced or learned about in Compton led to my rejection of my father.

I now see that I am not so different from my father, after all. Now I am struck by the similarity between the underlying message in my ninth-grade speech and my father's beliefs. I emphasized the importance of learning about others as individuals as a way to increase understanding. My father wrote that the individual is sacred and the personality of each person has supreme value, that in the Christian tradition the individual is important, not the group. I don't recall him ever deliberately trying to teach me that but we both clearly thought along the same lines, believing in the importance and value of the individual in solving interpersonal problems. After all these years, I'm happy to be able to revise my image of my father, to view his efforts as successful among those individuals with whom he did interact, and to learn I actually do have something in common with him.

Finally, I need to mention my insight about Compton and my relationship with my dog Levi. I grew up with animals. Our place was home to the usual cats and dogs but also a duck, a rabbit, mice, fish, and snakes at various times. I have always felt an affinity toward animals. Whenever we'd go on family vacations and I saw signs indicating deer crossings, I'd keep my eyes peeled for them. During one vacation I watched ground squirrels for several hours while the rest of my family did something else. But Levi was the great game changer. It was amazing how well-attuned we were to each other. Levi showed me how truly fascinating animal behavior could be, and studying animal behavior became my career. As I wrap up my assessment of how Compton influenced my life, I suddenly realize that if I had to do it all over again, I would take Compton with Levi over any other place without Levi. That's a big surprise to me. For all my life I have thought that growing up the way I did in Compton during the 1960s and early '70s was an experience I wouldn't wish on anyone. But suddenly I see it differently. Without Compton, there would have been no Levi. He was my protector and my truest companion at a crucial period in my life when I felt very unsafe. He was the one who showed me the path leading out of Compton and into the future. I owe him so much. He was with me for 13 years, a year longer than I lived in Compton, and he was the best dog in the world, for all time.

11

The Brown Girl: This Is Who She Is

Before graduating from high school, I was accepted at Cal State Long Beach and UC San Diego, both on full scholarship, but I wanted to get as far away from home as I could and I saw UCSD as my salvation. It was my salvation from the tyranny of my father and the submissiveness of my mother, not to mention my brothers and sisters. For no reason that I can consider, we never grew close. It was more likely to find us fighting verbally or physically with each other than to have a friendly conversation. So it was evident that I had to get as far away as possible.

It turned out to be more than a poor Mexican girl from Compton could handle. I had never been allowed to spend the night away from home and now I was living on campus away from the small world I knew. It was difficult to make friends. I didn't fit the mold and I felt the other students' disdain.

My roommate was a Jewish young lady from a wealthy family. My mother wrote me every week and sent me $5 for incidentals. My roommate's mother drove out and bought her a $200 comforter for her bed. I went to Tijuana and bought a $2 tie-dyed bed cover for my bed. Yeah, we didn't have much in common. It didn't take too long before she moved out and I had the dorm room to myself. The few friends I did finally make were the girl next door, Annie, who went to Tijuana with me, and her Black roommate Dee Dee. Dee Dee was great and spent a lot of time with us. However, once she started dating a young Black Muslim boy she stopped associating with Annie and me. The other 4-5 friends I made were Black and Hispanic.

I didn't do well in school. I couldn't adjust to being away from home, being treated like a leper, and the classes were so hard. It was as though I never took a math or science class in my entire life! I realized that the courses I took at Dominguez did not prepare me at all for college. And I had taken higher curriculum courses like Physics and Calculus and got A's. It just totally stressed me out.

Science was particularly way over my head. I just could not understand the concepts. Going to science lab every Wednesday was ridiculous. I didn't know what I was doing and no one offered to help. I should have considered getting a tutor, but it didn't occur to me to do that. In the end, I ended up on academic probation and was required to go to community college during the summer to make up the class that I failed. I felt like such a failure when I went home for the summer. I was devastated. Doing so poorly my first year crushed any tiny bit of confidence I was developing. I couldn't face going back. The idea terrified me. My parents never knew what happened because I ended up moving out and living with my boss from Doug's Corner for the remainder of the summer months. I was so devastated and depressed; I knew I couldn't afford to take a community college class so I let it go. I didn't go back to UC San Diego and have regretted it my entire life.

Mike and I remained close while I was away at school. When I returned after my first year, he had graduated from Dominguez and had joined the army. He went to Kentucky for basic training and came home that December (1974) before they sent him to the front lines, which at that time was Vietnam. We had decided to get married before he was deployed. I was living with Susan Jacobo and her baby girl in an apartment in Long Beach at the time, which was perfect. I had decided not to tell my family that we were married because I knew they would not be happy about it. I figured we would tell them together upon his next trip back to the United States.

We were married for two weeks and then he was gone. I didn't see him again for six months, and then not for another year and a half after that. I was lonely without him, I missed seeing him. Although he wrote me just about every day, I wanted to hear his voice. It was pretty tough going for a while, but it helped having Susan in my life. She was a great support for me and made life tolerable.

Mike lucked out and was based out of Germany through the end of his tour of duty. He had a couple of close calls where he could have been sent to Vietnam but it never happened, thank goodness.

Once Mike returned from the "war" and we were living on our own, I did take classes at Long Beach Community College and Cypress College. I always loved school and learning. I knew that someday I would earn my degree and if I could chip away at some of the required credits, it would help me later on. I would take a couple of classes here and there. I knew I couldn't afford to go to a four-year college so I wasn't in any hurry to get there.

About 15 years ago I was working with my current employer at their Santa Ana office. I had made up my mind to go back to school and earn my bachelor's degree. I didn't want it for any other reason than that I had to do this for myself. I had to prove to myself that I could do it and I deserved it.

So, I enrolled in an English class at Fullerton College just to get my feet wet; I wanted to see if I could work 10-hour days and still be able to handle a class or two. Well, on my very first paper I got an "F," which got me thinking, "What the heck am I doing here?" I had already noticed that I was the oldest in the class and the "F" didn't do anything but discourage me more. I went home and Mike told me to at least stick it out for the semester. After all, I only enrolled in one class. I ended up earning a B in the class. For the next four years I took a couple of courses each semester, right after work and on Saturdays. It wasn't easy, but I was determined to make it happen. My manager and I were pretty close and we were talking about my going back to school and she suggested we take classes together. Our employer offered scholarships to its employees who wanted to continue their education, and to be promoted to manager you had to have a degree. My boss and I applied, as well as our friend Lori, and we each received money to go back to school. We enrolled at Chapman University's accelerated program and graduated in two years. I had finally accomplished the one thing that I wanted for myself. Yes, in 2006, I walked at my graduation ceremony. I thought about it and realized that the prize was not complete unless I walked.

What does success look like for someone like me? In spite of the failures and regrets in my life, I am always happy on my birthdays. I am in my 60s now and that is quite an accomplishment since I knew I would be dead before I was 30. You don't grow up in Compton and stand up for yourself without expecting repercussions at some point

Becky's graduation, Chapman University, 2006

in time. It also doesn't add an extended life expectancy when you date a gangster, either. I went into the banking world and currently work for a credit union in Orange County. I have been an Assistant Manager for most of my time here. The short stint I had as a manager was rewarding, yet I learned that I was better and happier as an Assistant. I make good money and live a good life. I am able to travel and take my children and granddaughter with us from time to time. I have the drive and ambition to do a great job in whatever position I hold, but STILL struggle with self-confidence. I put on a strong front, but am nothing but mush inside. I enjoy what I do and am happy with my life, in spite of the issues that plague my family.

From time to time, though, I think back to my youth and get very depressed and angry. Just listening to the radio can turn me upside down. Songs from the '60s and '70s bring back very sad and emotional feelings that are hard for me to let go of. I have wondered if seeing a therapist to try to talk through my life would have made any difference as to who I am today. I've had people tell me that for someone who has so much going for her, they don't understand why I always see the glass as half empty. Like Lynne, I feel that my life turned out fine in spite of growing up in Compton. I do wonder who or what I could have been if circumstances had been different. When Bonita learned that I had not finished college, she was not surprised. That speaks volumes as to how I was perceived in high school. As a quitter, someone who couldn't make it? I would love to do it all again; it would be much different.

Lynne, Bonita, and I have a connection/friendship that has surpassed time and space. No, we were not the type of friends who were tied at the hip and only ventured into the world and activities with each other, yet our bond has been everlasting, as seen in our commitment to complete this book. Our ability to have other friendships and relationships throughout our lives only substantiates the strength of our bond. Perhaps the turbulent times we shared during our young lives keeps us connected, but I also believe that trust, respect, and love for each other had a hand in it as well.

I hope my story helps at least one person see that there is hope and possibility for those who are poor, neglected, and/or abused as children. One just has to make the decision to walk away from that life and strive to improve it. But I also want to disclose that those negative feelings never go away; you just learn to push them back into your subconscious. Will therapy help to work through the trauma and repressed memories and pain? Perhaps. There are healthy ways to build self-esteem and many resources available.

12

The Black Girl: By Any Means Necessary...

When I graduated high school, I entered The University of Notre Dame du Lac in (then) South Bend, Indiana. As a member of the second class of full four-year Notre Dame women, I graduated with my BFA (Bachelor of Fine Arts) in 1977. My four-year journey at ND is truly a future book within itself, and I am sure that one day I will write it. College was my greatest challenge when it came to experiencing racism and bias. I was in a daze my freshman year because of the constant racism I encountered. Whether I was in my dormitory, in my classes, on my way to classes, or out in South Bend, I had constant racial incidents with White people. During my first week on campus before classes began, someone put a KKK (Ku Klux Klan) club sign on a tree in the south quad near my dorm Breen Phillips. It advertised a meeting date, location, and time. I don't know whether it was a joke or not, all I remembered was reading "KKK" and it appeared bigger than life. It was that moment just like you had seen on TV or in the movies, but never thought it would happen in real life. Little did I know that this incident was only the beginning of incidents of that kind that would fill my freshman year at Notre Dame. As I pushed through that year, I had no choice but to learn to adjust (of sorts) to these occurrences. I surely wasn't going to ask to come home back to California and give up, because I believed originally that I was a fighter. I looked at how I got here, even after being told that I would probably not need to apply, and if

I got here, I was told again that I probably wouldn't make it. Well, I had already begun the fight. Adjustment for me as a freshman meant avoiding large crowds of White people who might make me a target, so I stopped going regularly to the weekend football and basketball games that year. Instead, I sold my tickets to various alumni and other students, and collected a little needed income for my services. I also learned to weed through the crowd of students and make better judgments about where I was welcomed and who was most welcoming. I found great refuge in playing bid whist, dominoes, and spades in the Cultural Arts Center where most of the Black students congregated between classes. I also felt tremendously comfortable on all of the sport teams where I felt accepted and well-respected by my peers and the coaches.

I played field hockey and basketball, and ran track while at Notre Dame. I was better in field hockey and track than I was at basketball but I had a passion for basketball that outweighed the other sports. I also helped develop the women's sports program while I was a student under the work/study program that offered me the opportunity to work for Astrid Hotvedt, the Women's Athletic Director. Today, there is an area dedicated as a tribute specifically to the 35 pioneer women (of which I am included) in the halls of the ACC (Athletic Convocation Center) for developing the women's sport programs. The more appropriate tribute would be to accept our nominations into the Monogram Club (that have been previously denied).

After working for Astrid my first two years in the women's sports program, I was given the opportunity to select from multiple locations on campus for my work/study program. I chose to work for Digger Phelps in the men's basketball office since I loved basketball so much. What an experience that was! Getting to know Richard "Digger" Phelps was unforgettable! We have stayed in touch over the years and I have the greatest respect for not only his work at ND, but for the artist he is today (that most don't know about). Whenever I go back to ND, I always try to stop by Digger's home and spend time with him. One year at one of the Black reunions, I brought

Digger a piece of my artwork (African Woman of Mine) and he gifted me with one of his impressionist pieces that I hold dear today.

Regular highlights in my life at Notre Dame included the many conversations I had with Father Theodore Hesburgh, and I tribute him for being one of the main reasons I chose to stay at Notre Dame, especially through all the racism. I met Father Hesburgh my first week at Notre Dame. The campus in the fall is one of the most stunning environments one could ever witness. Walking among the changing hues of the leaves on the trees, the beautifully arranged flower beds, the statues, the lakes, and the perfectly landscaped arrangements was like walking through an enchanted forest. As I explored the campus (before noticing that KKK sign) I approached the Grotto. The Grotto was Father Sorin's (the founder of Notre Dame) tribute to The Grotto of Our Lady of Lourdes in France that he visited. I had not seen the Grotto before now and it was mesmerizing. As I approached the Grotto, I experienced a sensation that was spiritual and deep. I lit a candle and placed it and just stood in awe of the feeling.

I'm not sure how long I stood in silence but the silence was broken when I heard this voice say, "Good day, young lady." I turned around without moving my feet and saw this salt n' pepper gentleman with a kind smile. He was sporting a collar so I assumed he was a priest. I wasn't alarmed because his voice was not offensive in any way. I remember his full dark eyebrows and eyes that were pleasantly piercing. His hands were held behind his back and his posture was relaxed. I responded with, "Hi," and this gentleman went on to ask how I happened to be here at the Grotto? I explained that I was new to campus and was trying to take it all in and see as much as I possibly could before classes began. He listened and nodded and introduced himself as "Father Ted." Before he left, he told me that it was a pleasure to have met me and that he was sure that we would meet again. I had no idea that I had just met and chatted with the President of the University of Notre Dame, Father Theodore Hesburgh. He was right, though, we would meet again.

Near the end of my freshman year many of us Blacks had shared a multitude of racially motivated incidents on campus. There had been an incident on the yearbook staff that I was a part of and a small group of us students decided to make our voices known and we held a sit-in on the steps of the administration building. I do not know who the woman was who approached us but we were approached and asked who we wanted to voice our issue with. I quickly said Father Theodore Hesburgh because I had learned that if I had a legitimate issue don't take it to the workers, take it to the management. Father Hesburgh was at the very top of the management chain for sure. When the woman disappeared into the administration building, she returned shortly and looked at me and said, "Father Hesburgh will see you." Then she quickly turned and walked inside with me right behind her.

Bonita's graduation, Notre Dame, 1976; l-r: Vera Bean (grandmother), Dorothy Bradshaw (mom), Father Theodore Hesburgh, Bonita, Roy Bradshaw (dad)

When I helped organize one of the first protests of overt and covert racism at Notre Dame on the steps, she escorted me to his office and offered me a comfortable chair so I sat down. When I looked up at Father Hesburgh, I was frozen and was thinking to myself that he looked familiar. I soon realized that he was the gentleman that I had met before school started, at the grotto. He inquired about my classes and my living situation and all things about me before asking me why I was really here (protesting) today. I felt immediately comfortable with him and didn't hesitate to answer anything I was asked. We talked and talked (and I cried) about the racial tone of the campus and the incidents I had encountered since being there. When I left his office, I felt better even though we both knew that we had not solved the issue. I also believed that he heard me and felt my pain, and I felt respected by Father Hesburgh up to the day I graduated from Notre Dame.

In my second year at ND the racial tensions grew on campus surrounding one of the candidates who was trying out for the cheerleading squad and who just happened to be Black. A group of us Black students could foresee possible biases forthcoming so we decided to document the tryouts just in case. I volunteered to tape them, of course. Joya DeFoor, whom we called 'JJ', was an excellent athlete and perfect for the position. The entire process ended up as we thought. She was treated unfairly, was thoroughly overlooked, and not selected to become a cheerleader. This was not OK and the tapes told the truth so the Black students and even some White students began a petition to either make JJ a cheerleader or redo the tryouts and invite everyone in the world so the truth would prevail. We stood behind JJ and fought for her rights. Renard Gueringer wrote an article for *The Observer,* the student newspaper, blowing the whistle on all the naysayers! The Watts Riots had taught me a lot. We weren't going to riot but we took the peaceful way (like MLK) and fought our battles through protesting, writing articles, and sharing the tapes. JJ became the first black cheerleader at Notre Dame. Because of the article in the paper and the news spreading quickly about overt and covert racism, I was approached by Father Hesburgh and asked if I wanted to talk (again) and of course I did. It was during my sophomore year there that he offered me the open-door policy with him and I definitely took advantage of being able to go to his office to speak with him when I was troubled. He was always so calm and grounded in his responses to me. He taught me that no one was perfect, not even him, and that people make mistakes because they're human and sometimes ignorant, but that people should always learn from their mistakes and then make the needed corrections, so the same mistakes are never repeated. He told me that I should be more patient with people. Slow down and think about what they did and not always react so quickly. Allow people time to make the correct decisions in their life, so my life and acceptance of them would be easier. I had wonderful conversations with Father Hesburgh during my time at Notre Dame and even when I came back to campus after I graduated. I feel honored that he was a part of my Notre Dame life.

Near the end of my freshman year, I made the decision to move from the south campus in Breen Phillips, to the north campus, so I put in a request for a single in Lyon's Hall. My closest female friend at that time was Andrea Renee Ransom. She also put in a single's request to move to Lyon's Hall. I believed that living alone would help me regiment who was around me most all the time, so I did whatever I needed to do to accomplish that. When you come in as a freshman you automatically have roommates not of your choosing. You can be put in a suite, which isn't always so sweet because it means that you have three roommates! Eke! My junior year I was granted a single! I loved my room. Lyon's Hall had an underpass and my room was on top of the underpass facing the lake behind it. I kept the room for the duration of my stay at Notre Dame and wouldn't have traded it for anywhere else.

I had White friends at ND but they were primarily my teammates from the sports teams I played on. I stay connected to a few of them today through Facebook groups and am pleased to share my family, current events, and information with them, as they do with me. There were also a few students whom I had classes with, who wanted to genuinely know me. I had art classes with John Dlugolecki, whom I still communicate with today. I am a member of the Notre Dame Alumni organization in Los Angeles and take part in a few events with them annually (like the poker tournaments at the Knights of Columbus or tailgaters for the USC games) but I am more involved as a member of the Black Alumni of Notre Dame (BAND) that includes all Black alums from all years. We share our lives, achievements, business ventures, debates, and discussions on Facebook and beyond, and are able to document, share, and follow each other through our good and bad times. We support each other and know that our experience at Notre Dame is the common bond that connects us.

While at Notre Dame from 1973 to 1977, I experienced more racism my first two years than the latter two years there and all the years combined in my life. Although I was at one of the world's finest educational institutions, I found it eventually no different than any other place where racism exists. I was the n-word in the dormitory, in the cafeteria, on my way to class, in class, out on the quad ... it truly didn't matter where I was. Somehow without anyone really truly knowing me, I was the n-word. After my first year I became very militant while at Notre Dame. I sported my Angela Davis afro and wore dashikis as often as I could. I hung out less in public student hangouts and more with my friends who were Black like me and also with my team members from basketball, field hockey, or track who NEVER disrespected me or made me feel different. I had a memorable, grateful relationship with Father Hesburgh and I credit him (and my mother) for helping me get through my struggles while at Notre Dame. Father Hesburgh also taught me to stay well informed and well taught, for without education and knowledge, you cannot and will not make good decisions. During my four years at ND, the university brought Angela Davis, Stokely Carmichael, and Julian Bond to speak with students and share their philosophies, passions, and struggles. I appreciated the opportunity to be a part of these events. No Notre Dame President since Hesburgh has been able to move the campus and be genuinely concerned for ALL students like he could. He helped make students feel that they were cared for and belonged at Notre Dame.

After Notre Dame I was overwhelmed from all I went through and I struggled to learn from the situation because I was emotionally damaged. When I left, my self-confidence was shattered. I found some relief in creating my art but I believe that the personal essay I was asked to write for a book edited by Don Wycliff and David Krashna titled *Black Domers: African-American Students at Notre Dame in Their Own Words* gave me greater healing. I began to think that completing this project, too, would give me more relief and healing, and I was right. I feel writing to be very therapeutic for me, besides the fact that I believe we truly have a good story to tell. The times, the politics, and unrest we grew up in literally changed our lives for the rest of our lives. My unrest came toward the end of my high school days straight into my college years and it was truly worth purging through my writings. I didn't initially struggle like Lynne and Becky, but our similar situations led us off into three totally different directions which I find to be most interesting in this book.

After my graduation from ND, I tried to go back as an alumna to help develop the BAND organization, and began recruiting for Notre Dame here in Los Angeles with Ben Finley until I realized that I couldn't do it anymore. I realized that the bad times at ND were

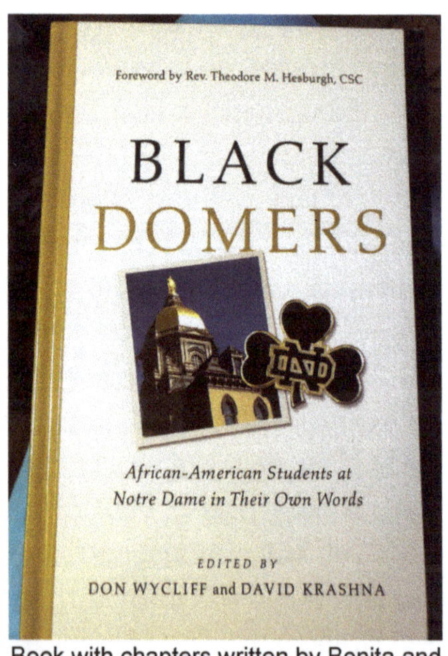

Book with chapters written by Bonita and other Black students at Notre Dame

foremost in my head and I needed a break from all of it before I could honestly come back to ND or tell some innocent young kid that Notre Dame was the perfect place for them. It took me ten years before I could rebuild my self-esteem and come back to ND and forgive the experience that shocked my world.

One could say that I was a very memorable or colorful student while at Notre Dame. I let the bad take me over after I left ND, but most of my peers didn't truly know what I was really going through. Most of my friends thought everything was A-OK. I loved sports and anything sports-oriented so I participated in any and all sport activities I could get in. Those were some of my best times at ND! I am actually in a book written by Digger Phelps called *"Digger" Phelps Tales from the Notre Dame Hardwood.* In the book he states that he believed me to be the best female athlete at Notre Dame during my four years there. What a compliment!

Digger Phelps described Bonita as the best female athlete during her time at Notre Dame

After Notre Dame I headed to Mississippi to begin my independent life and career. I had a boyfriend of two years (Bernard Warren) and we had plans to marry and settle somewhere in Mississippi. When I arrived in Greenville, Mississippi, I thought everything would be so smooth but I ran into the biggest wrinkle I wasn't expecting. I was job shopping and was somewhere just outside of Greenville when I saw a beautiful estate. It was a colonial style home that appeared to invite me in. I went to the porch and knocked on the front door and waited patiently. When no one answered in a reasonable amount of time, I knocked again. This time as soon as I removed my fist from the door, someone opened the peephole on the door and said, "Niggers go to the back!" I looked through the peephole and saw a portion of a male Black face and I said, "Excuse me?" and then heard for a second time, a little louder, "Niggers go to the back!" I thought I wasn't hearing what I was hearing. Did he just call me what I think he did? I immediately had flashbacks of ND and hearing someone behind me call me a "nigger" as I walked to class. Father Hesburgh had taught me patience and the many times this happened, it made no sense to turn around to challenge anyone because in most cases no one would be bold enough to identify themselves. So, it would just be me, pissing myself off and getting riled up for no reason because the situation could not be remedied at that moment. I stood for a moment on the porch and realized that I was in the wrong place at the wrong time and I needed to get the hell out of there by any means necessary.

I was by myself in Greenville, Mississippi, not really knowing exactly where I was or what was to come. So, I gathered myself together and walked back to my car, slowly got in the car, and drove away, never to return. This was 1977, not 1967, not 1957, or earlier. I was naive enough to think that this type of situation couldn't occur to me after the Civil Rights era. After my experiences at Notre Dame I should not have been surprised but I was. And this was a place I was considering living in, after Notre Dame? Absolutely not! I realized that I could not settle in or near a community like this so when my relationship took a dive, I took a drive right back to sunny California where it was more familiar, and I totally closed the door on relocating to the South.

I had received a job offer my senior year at Notre Dame from a company out in Ridgecrest, CA, called SCI (Systems Consultants Incorporated). They were contracted to the China Lake Naval Weapons Testing Center to design military training programs on the operation and maintenance of the A-6 Bomber. I made contact with them before leaving Mississippi and the offer was still on the table. I began my career in aerospace and designed the cartoon cells for all their training programs. I met Connie Reeder, a wonderful man who eventually asked for my hand in marriage. I loved him dearly but couldn't see myself living in Ridgecrest and settling down. Sadly, I ran from the offer and after a year I relocated back to Los Angeles and began my career as an aerospace "job-shopper" doing technical illustrations. When I look back at the marriage I had in later years, I wished I'd accepted Connie's proposal and stayed in Ridgecrest.

In L.A. I worked for Northrop Grumman, Garrett Air Research, Rockwell, Hughes Aircraft, Hughes, Microwave, and Hughes Helicopter. I stayed in aerospace a good ten years. My confidential clearance allowed me some of the best job offerings in the field. I got married in 1980, three years into this career, and ended my marriage seven years later. The only beautiful and positive results from my marriage were my daughters, Andrea Michelle, born in 1982, and Angela Mari', born in 1984. I went from sketching and illustrating to changing diapers, cooking, and cleaning so I could raise my beautiful girls. My marriage didn't outlive the seven-year itch and I was divorced in 1987, with no regrets.

In March 1991, I lived in Hawthorne, California, when the Rodney King beating took place. Communities of color were outraged. I heard chants again about getting "the White Man." What I saw was beyond belief. For the life of me, I could not fathom why the police kept beating a man who was clearly down. There were so many videos from so many angles that did nothing but confirm that there was no way that Rodney King could have fought back and there was no way that the malicious brutality was going to stop! I was surprised that on that night Rodney King did not die at the hands of the police because it surely seemed to be their goal. I felt like I was watching something out of the TV miniseries *Roots* when the Slave Massa' gotta teach his slave by over-beating him so he would finally get the message and learn a lesson! This is when I began to believe that there were real risks in being Black. The Black community's anger never seemed to settle after the beating, and it hit an all-time high when the four cops were acquitted in 1992, which sparked the

Los Angeles Riots. There were six days of rioting, 55 dead, over 11,000 arrested, and still no one was healed and racial brutality persists ... nothing again was solved or remedied. During these riots the apartment building I lived in lost its electricity in a surge and everything on my computer was lost. I lost the entire book that I was writing about my time at Notre Dame. The entire block lost power and my computer was zapped, never to be used again!

I wanted and needed a total fresh start when I left my marriage and aerospace, and had promised myself that I would choose a career that I had a passion for. I also needed to be happy for the benefit of my daughters. Art and education were the subjects that mattered most to me and I was fortunate enough to be able to combine them into a career in education as a high school graphic arts teacher. Once I became an educator, I discovered my true ultimate passion was in education, and art became a secondary entity. I acquired my Masters in Educational Administration and was entering my second career.

It was natural for me to come back to the Compton Unified School District (CUSD) to begin my teaching career. My aunt sat on the Compton Unified School Board as President and my mother had served over 20 years in Compton as a math teacher and district administrator. We loved Compton and our family was always taught to give back. I have this sense of belonging with the City of Compton and believe that the children of my community that I grew up in deserve my work more than those outside of Compton. As a Notre Dame graduate I was offered an opportunity to work at one of the Notre Dame high schools but I knew that those students did not need me as much as the Compton students, and I also needed them.

When I began working in the CUSD I learned of the 16-plus gangs that existed in Compton. I learned that I couldn't save every child like my mother had always said, who taught in Compton before me. In the first three years of my teaching, I lost five students to drive-bys, gang violence, or being in the wrong place at the wrong time. I almost stopped teaching but again I had to remind myself that I'm not a quitter, I'm a fighter, and teaching in Compton was a battle that I decided to take on. I was determined to succeed "by any means necessary." I realized that after all that I had gone through as a child and all that I accomplished as an adult, I wanted to come back to Compton and help teach and mentor as many children as I possibly could.

I was a successful teacher and administrator in Compton Unified for 18+ years. I witnessed the development and fame of many a rapper from the City of Compton, so when I hear N.W.A., Kendrick Lamar, Dr. Dre, or Easy-E, I feel a sense of pride, not disdain or fear. Yes, there were drive-bys and chaos from time to time but through it all, I learned to handle some of the worst situations possible. I learned to be spontaneous and improvise my way through almost anything. I learned to think on my feet and make something out of nothing. I learned that the leadership in Compton is plagued with systems of nepotism and cronyism, and somehow, I still believe that right will overcome all. I'm more than proud to be from Compton! When someone asks whether Compton is as bad as they say it is, I ask them, "Who is 'they'?" Because more than likely, they are the media that only seem to lean toward the stories about Compton that are solely negative. They are the naysayers who have no faith or confidence in the people of Compton. I have lived in Compton long enough to know that there is as much, if not more, positive that happens in Compton, than the negative one can read about in the paper or hear about in the news. I'm a Don for life! CPT for life!

Today, I am Director of Special Projects for Ladera Education Institute (LEI). I assisted LEI with the writing and submission of the petition to open Grace Hopper STEM Academy (GHSA) in 2013. GHSA is a gender-specific, public independent charter middle school in Inglewood, California. One of our primary goals is to solicit students from low state scoring and low economic communities to help give them a fair opportunity at educational success through any means necessary. "Any means necessary" for us means that we identify the levels of learning achieved for each and every student and teach them from their starting point before we can set the goals for their improvement. We use a very holistic approach embracing the whole child because without a socio-emotional balance no child can truly learn. I am also part of a school culture where we teach tolerance year-around. We also teach the six pillars of character that I feel we need more than ever because of the loss of life-skill classes and vocational education classes today. The school sits under the umbrella of Ladera Education Institute, a 504(c)(3) designed to meet the needs of youth educationally, medically, and socio-emotionally. I don't work to wait on an accolade; I work because I know it's needed. This profession (education) doesn't always pay what it's worth so it must be a labor of love. I will continue to work as long as the passion is in me.

I looked at the Watts Riots as a lesson about what not to do as a person of color. If I want to protest something, I would prefer not to destroy the community where I live. Today for me, there are other ways to protest that include being peaceful but in my heart of hearts I also know that sometimes there needs to be a "shock factor" to wake some people up and let them know you are serious. The Watts Riots were the first time I learned about police brutality. I also learned that "enough was enough!" This was not the first time the Watts communities of color faced police brutality! This was just the straw that broke the camel's back, the last catalyst of its kind, the shoe that no longer fit. The people of Watts had had enough! The Watts community, like many other black communities throughout the United States, had constantly dealt with mass unemployment (especially the males) and when married households had the wife working in most cases, that situation alone created dissension and despair that went deeper than Black versus Black. The economic despair affected Black relationships, Black marriages, Black families, and more. The hardship of unemployment, less pay, less opportunity, and less everything became routine. While some routines create a laziness and comfort, this is a routine that has only dug deeper into the souls of Black people like that negative itch that can't be scratched, like a fatal disease with no cure and no comfort. Although the shouts of the Watts Riots were "Get the White Man" and "Get the Police," the anger was so great and so embedded that the community lashed out at the White man first but after that, with anger growing, anyone and everyone in the way became a target! Even the Watts community became scared of the Watts community!

The Rodney King beating and the L.A. Riots had the same effect on our community and ended with the same results. Unfortunately, no one fully recovered mentally or physically from the destruction of the riots (or the *Rebellion* as many White people called it). We are not healed as a people and surely are still affected by what happened then and continues to happen today.

So here I am today. It's June 15, 2020. Three weeks after George Floyd's murder. Three months after Breonna Taylor's murder. The chants have changed but the conditions remain the same. "NO JUSTICE ... NO PEACE! NO JUSTICE ... NO PEACE!" Police brutality prevails. Massive deaths at the hands of the police have been brought to surface for all to see worldwide. BLACK LIVES MATTER has come to the forefront yet again! And while we identify that Black lives matter, we also must recognize that brown lives matter, that abused female lives matter, that LGBTQ lives matter. Here we are again, same shit, different day. And behind closed doors the n-word prevails.

I get up in the morning these days in tears. I'm angry, I'm frustrated, and I find myself at my wit's end. Since March, I've been working from home due to the COVID-19 pandemic. When I was originally assigned to remain home, I thought this would create opportune moments to get the book finished. I thought being home would be a blessing in disguise but this is not a blessing. This has become like a bad dream that I can't shake! I have had to force myself to write not just to finish this process but to give myself some type of therapy through my writing (again). While I understand the protests and the riots (even those that got out of hand and were not initiated by protesters), I am more interested in solutions. I WANT SOLUTIONS. I no longer wish to do the same things expecting a different result. I am no longer wishing to remain silent about what is going on to people of color in my city, community, or the world at large. I want solutions that are viable and can remove the systemic racist processes that lie deep within our government, corporations, communities, and beyond. I don't see this problem as a political problem because racism does not see Republicans or Democrats. While I believe in the value of my vote, voting is only one means of solving a smaller problem.

I don't want to be too comfortable in my living because when one becomes too comfortable, they don't take notice of everything that goes on around them. I prefer to stay a bit on edge so I continue to keep my eyebrows up to continue to search for the truths and solutions needed to heal our communities and save our cultures of people of color. I want to continue to teach the history of people of color because if we don't continue to do this, no one will do this for us. I will continue to build my family circle of diversity and color, and continue to grow it based on the content of people's character and respect for me and my beliefs.

When we began writing this book, I learned so much more about my friends and I hope they learned more about me. We didn't really seem to question one another or disagree often about anything, let alone our friendships. As I look at the timeline of our relationships I'm surprised at how often Lynne and Becky interpreted the same events in our lives. I also became intrigued to read about their home lives and how different they were from mine. I loved our early relationships and what we experienced in elementary, junior high, and high school, but I relish the time we spend today more. I truly love these ladies unconditionally. When I see them I feel at home. I am so comfortable in their presence I can say absolutely anything to them without remorse. I will be forever connected to them regardless of what the times might bring. We will remain friends forever. I love you both.

Afterword

Our stories reveal our personal thoughts and feelings about our experiences growing up in Compton during a very difficult time. From a more global perspective, our collective story illustrates how everyone, regardless of skin color or ethnicity or religion, must deal with trials and tribulations as part of the human condition. Some of these troubles will stem from ourselves, some from the dynamics of our families, and some from the vagaries of broader societal events. The latter source of trouble is especially pronounced now, in 2021, as we finish this book. After the turmoil of the 1960s and early '70s, it seemed things would never again get so bad in our country. Many of us who grew up during the 1960s expected positive change would occur with the passage of equitable laws following the Civil Rights movement. We thought we saw progress when we began seeing more people of color in high positions, from spokespeople in media, to elected representatives in our city, state, and federal governments, to university chancellors. We wanted to believe things were getting better for everyone in America. We cannot even attempt to believe that now. Seeing is believing. With cell phones recording so many heartless assaults on our citizens, the abuse of power by those who wield it has become clearly visible for everyone to see. COVID-19 has preferentially killed the poor and unhealthy, and since Black and Hispanic members of our society are overrepresented as victims of COVID-19, we cannot any longer deny that living conditions are worse for a greater proportion of them than White members. Right now, it feels as if we're reliving those turbulent '60s and '70s all over again. It feels as if we are soon going to lose all the gains our society made since those years. But, in fact, it's worse because people of all backgrounds are feeling it across wide swaths of the country, not just in pockets, and many thousands of people are dead and many millions are out of work because of the pandemic.

The inequality just has to stop. Kids growing up need to feel safe in their homes and communities. Without that, they cannot concentrate on their educations. Without a decent education, well-paying jobs are out of reach. People then take low-paying jobs such as those in the service sector. Those jobs keep people busy but they don't keep people healthy. A high proportion of our service workers, those we recognize now during the pandemic as "essential workers," are people of color and at greatest risk of dying from COVID-19. But kids cannot feel safe when their parents are worried about health and finances, and so the loop keeps on looping. It won't stop until we do something that will cut it. We call on those who have amassed huge fortunes and those who pass laws to rectify the inequity by all creative, lawful means possible. We leave it up to them to decide how best to do that, but we start with the common-sense suggestion that all jobs should come with a decent living wage. With resolve, it can be done. If they don't make substantive changes, the consequences for our society will be dire.

We as individuals can also collectively counter the tide of hatefulness in this time of "other-intolerance." The simple act of putting ourselves in positions where we can develop a friendship with just one other person not like ourselves is one way to begin to change our society for the better. Such friendships can exist. They are about trust and respect, which together generate appreciation for diverse perspectives. Our stories in this book prove that. We have grown and learned from each other's experiences, just by staying connected and sharing. We prove that friendship is colorblind and so is love and respect.

We hope our stories will provide some light for those who are suffering under these difficult times. In spite of the emotional and turbulent obstacles that were placed before us as we grew up in Compton, or in Bonita's case, after she left Compton, each of us survived and became successful in our own ways. We each have risen above our traumatic experiences and not let them cripple us through and through. Yes, we deal with our own internal demons, but we've learned to push them down and compartmentalize them well enough to project a semblance of a "normal" life, although present circumstances in our country threaten to derail us yet again. We hope that our collective story speaks to others whose lives are challenging, and gives them hope and the courage to rise above their current situations so that they too will find their own success in life.

Acknowledgments

Memories are precious. Like fingerprints, they are unique to each of us because we can experience the same events in different ways, as we hope this book has shown. We first want to thank our childhood teachers, friends, families, and even foes, some of whom are mentioned in our book, for helping to give us the experiences that turned into our memories, good and bad, and our families for further allowing us to pick their brains, as our memories have failed us a few times during our writing. We also thank Kathleen Curry, Harry Greene, Freeman Tinnin, and Nicole Washburn for reading the manuscript in its various stages and offering suggestions to improve the text. Harry also served as a cheerleader and sounding board from the very beginning. A special call-out goes to Angel Gray for the kind of encouragement a daughter can give her mother along the way. We are also grateful to Luisa Brenna for drawing the map of our Compton neighborhood, and to Marti Childs and Jeff March of EditPros for all their help in preparing the manuscript for publication. JT Nero, of the Birds of Chicago, very kindly gave us permission to quote lyrics from one of their songs. To paraphrase author Georgia Cates, "Music is what emotions sound like." That was never made clearer than during the pandemic when live performances all but stopped. The world felt flatter then. The words put to music are just as essential. Wise lyrics can provide guidance in life, reflect our own unexpressed feelings, and help us find common ground with others. Thanks especially to a trio of duos, the Birds of Chicago, Watkins Family Hour, and The Milk Carton Kids, whose music and livestreamed performances helped one of us make it through the dark times. Finally, we gratefully acknowledge the Chair's Research Funds from the Department of Anthropology at the University of California, Davis, for making this book's publication possible.